JAMAICAN
BY BIRTH
AMERICAN
BY CHOICE

*Third World Roots &
Character Meet First World
Opportunity & Contradiction*

OWEN EVERARD JAMES

ISBN: 1451599366
ISBN-13: 9781451599367

ABOUT THE AUTHOR

Owen Everard James is a graduate of the Mico Teachers' College (now the Mico University) in Jamaica and an honors graduate of Howard University in the United States. Mr. James also holds a diploma in Production Management from the Institute for Advanced Technical and Vocational Training in Italy. He has been a teacher, civil servant, banker and restaurateur and worked for nearly thirty years as a manufacturing executive with a Fortune 500 American multi-national corporation. He has lived and worked in the Caribbean, Canada, the United States and East and Southern Africa. He is retired and resides in Florida.

DEDICATION

The work is dedicated to my wife Icilda (Icy to all who know her), our two sons, Gordon and Gregory and our daughter (-in-law), Tracia. It is written for my amazing grand daughters Brianna Simone and Gabrielle Nicole. Certainly, their Jamaica and their America will be greatly different from my own and hopefully better; much more confusing perhaps and certainly more challenging in a number of ways, many of which I may be unable to contemplate in my own lifetime.

This work is also written in memory of my parents, Ernest and Ambrozine James, but especially in memory of my mother who always seemed to know instinctively what was best for her children. I hope that my story will also honor the memory of my brother Guilford, my role model, who died much too early. As well, I wish to honor my wife's East Indian grandmother. She never had the opportunity of schooling, yet she became a successful trader, land owner and small farmer. Against the advice and admonishment of many, she ensured that her grand daughter had the best education she could afford at a time when most East Indian families thought it pointless to send girls to school for more than a basic education.

ACKNOWLEDGEMENTS

I am obliged to acknowledge the marvelous opportunities afforded me by my country of birth as well as my country of choice: Jamaica and America. In the first case, I am especially grateful for the strength of my early and secondary education; in the second, I am forever indebted for my exposure to many of the greatest scholars, writers and books and the world of ideas, logic and reason. There are countless people I need to thank for their encouragement, generosity of time and spirit, who listened when they could have decided otherwise, offered support and guidance and helped unbelievably in sharpening ideas, arguments and points of view that were sometimes too diffuse. Many of these have asked not to be acknowledged and shall remain nameless.

My wife has been my default memory. Her support was always steadfast and sure. Our two sons have been respectfully and honestly critical as well as supportive. They often provided perspective that I may not have captured on my own. I thank my two unbelievable grand daughters who never fail to amaze me and to stimulate an easy willingness to believe that America and the world will always get better rather than worse. Their mother, Tracia, constantly astounds me with her diligence and commitment to their physical as well as mental well being. I know that they are not as bright and engaging as they are by accident. I also acknowledge the memory of my brother Guilford as a constant inspiration.

There are former professional colleagues, especially during my years in the Jeffersonville, Indiana facility that, against troubling odds, trusted me with the painful details of their hurtful experiences with bias in the workplace. These include Charles Wright, Fred Long and others; Bruce Winters, twice my boss at the facility, who exhibited unique and quite remarkable compassion and offered useful, unsolicited advice when this was most needed. I will always be grateful to Michele Coleman Mayes, former corporate Vice President of HR & Legal, who maintained surprising balance between her corporate responsibility and her willingness and boldness to ensure that fairness was never eclipsed. Her integrity and intellect are exemplary. While I do not identify the company, I must recognize the honesty and openness with which the Chairman and the President for its North America Division dealt with me regarding the issue of bias in the work place. But for their approach and involvement it is almost certain that both the company and I would have suffered significant harm on account of the willful negligence, indifference or folly of others.

I also gratefully acknowledge the dedication and diligence of my first volunteer reviewers, especially my wife and sons. Other invaluable collaborators include: Regine Racine-Bowen, a very vigorously engaging young Haitian-American; Gene and Pat Ezzell, avid readers, friends and neighbors; Dr. Edwin Jones, teachers' college classmate and university professor; Ambassador, Dr. Basil Bryan, former Consul General of Jamaica in New York, friend and follower of all things Jamaican; Robert Scarlett, primary schoolmate, outstanding cricketer and cricket historian; Clifton Cameron, great friend, entrepreneur and shrewd observer of economics and politics in the Caribbean; Shirley Carby, wise adviser on all things related to the publishing of this work; Dr. Vera Rhimes, outspoken educator and friend.

TABLE OF CONTENTS

INTRODUCTION

The collection of material for this book is as much a work in progress as is my own life. The material spans the period from my early years in Jamaica through the present. This is my story. It is not meant to be a scholarly treatise or history in any academic or formal sense. Where I think it meaningful or helpful I identify reference material used. Such reference material is never used to validate or authenticate my experience as my individual, personal experience is, after all, the heart of what I write. As such, it needs no third party validation.

The work is arranged in easily discernable and chronologically significant passages of my life: Jamaica; Canada; Kenya, East Africa; America; Zimbabwe, Southern Africa; America Reprise. As with my life, these passages ebb and flow into one another with the same ease with which the average Jamaican, depending on circumstances, reggaes from native dialect into the proverbial Queen's English. This facility, it seems, extends itself metaphorically into the ease with which most Jamaicans effortlessly accommodate and adjust their lives and relationships to the demands and peculiarities of any country they happen to adopt as home.

My life has been touched in very profound ways by my immediate and extended family as well as by many outside of this intimate group: friends, school mates, teachers, neighbors, work associates and business colleagues.

It has been shaped in great measure by much more than the circumstances of my birth. My earliest school years and my years at Teachers' College in Jamaica, my years at University in America and exposure to professional training in Italy are significant stations in my life. This is no less true of my professional life. I worked for nearly 30 years with a Fortune 500 American multi-national corporation in the Caribbean and on two continents. I traveled extensively internationally on business as well as for pleasure. While I fully recognize the deep, shallow, tangential or pervasive influence of all this I never the less take full credit and responsibility for the person I am. I have come to realize the tremendous value of seamlessly merging my formal and non-formal education. It is very clear to me that failure to accomplish this would not only have made my life much less fulfilling than it is but would make it immensely more challenging to understand the world.

I suppose there is never a better time to write than when you write. For many years I have tried to push myself to do what I am doing now but could never actually get around to acting on this sense of fleeting urgency each time it grabbed me. I cannot explain this, except to say that writing is a peculiar thing. There is a sense that the proverbial muse needs to do more than just visit. It appears she must visit at the right moment and for extended periods of time. Several recent events seem to come together at this juncture to create such a moment. The most significant of these events, perhaps not surprisingly, is the nomination and subsequent election of Barack Obama to the Office of The President of the United States along with the Republican Party's nominee for President, John McCain, selecting the governor of Alaska, Sarah Palin, to be his running mate as nominee for Vice President.

More recently, the nomination and subsequent confirmation of Sonia Sotomayor as the first Latina to join the august Supreme Court of the United States is another such event. I will explore the impact and significance of these and other related events and what they may come to mean from the perspective of my own background, exposure and experience. While these events loom large in my thinking and bring into exceedingly sharp focus how and why I see America as I do, they are like book ends to my story. As such the reader may move them in and out or around as much as he feels or may find necessary. He may even wish to abandon them altogether, although I doubt that this will further his understanding of my story. In fact, this may even impede the honest understanding of his own story if or when he should come to think of it. A string connects us all to seminal events and seminal people in our shared lifetimes.

There are some in American society who appear to have developed a very debilitating case of paranoia. They have summoned palpably irrational political conflict and contrived distractions in order to cause much public confusion. This contrivance seems to me to have its origins in an understandable but completely unacceptable fear of the *browning of America* or the diminution of the *whiteness* of America. Naturally, this is camouflaged as other things by those I call the Irrational Right. The gamut of camouflage goes from siren cries of approaching, and all but certain, communism or socialism to discrimination against white Americans and the diminishing of America because of the different, wise, inclusive and pragmatic world view of the new president. When fear among significant sections of any population becomes paranoia, frightening dangers inevitably lurk just beyond the horizon. We can only hope that the gravest of these dangers does not materialize.

It is not my intention to write a political treatise or documentary. However, no one can reasonably imagine that the events mentioned earlier are not occurrences of epochal significance in the unfolding history of America. Together, they necessarily become one of the fulcrums on which my thinking rests as I explore the more recent landscape of my life. In this regard I am very concerned about a few issues that spring directly from these events. These issues include the future of American culture as it is impacted by the inevitable and dramatic

changes and shifts in population mix, the impact and implications of the election of the first black person to the
Office of President of the United States, the installation of
the first Latina as associate justice of the Supreme Court
and how all of these events affect and are likely to affect inter-personal relationships in America. This last factor, to my mind, is of far greater significance than most
of the people I know are aware. I certainly see very little
evidence that the talk jocks or more sophisticated commentators on American life recognize this to be the case.
They certainly are not addressing this as a critical issue.

Essentially, the public institutions that for so long, legally as well as obliquely, supported discrimination and
protected bigotry in America, no longer exist. Yet, discrimination and bigotry continue to plague much of our
social intercourse in America. I do not believe that these
plagues will ever disappear from our lives completely.
The most we may reasonably expect is that they will decline to a point of insignificance. Indeed, no legislation
can reach into the very dark corners of any person's
heart. But it is crucial that we understand that the final
assault against these plagues can only be made effectively on a one-on-one basis among America's citizens. I
have very good reason to be optimistic of the outcome
at this level of social interaction in our country. Of course,
I will share the reason for my optimism with my readers.

My writing will include some personal poetry that has
been stimulated by events, the writings of others as well
as my thoughts and observations about personally critical life issues over a period of many years. I have discovered that poetry allows the expression of profound
thoughts and concepts in the briefest, most poignant
and powerful ways. Often, however, it demands much
greater effort of the reader in discerning its deepest
meanings in order to arrive at a point of understanding.
Prose is much more easily read and understood. I never
the less implore all who may read what I write to make
the necessary effort in this regard. I believe that the effort
will be worth the while as my poetry will provide a much

more intensely personal picture of how I think and why I see the world as I do.

I make no claim that my opinions or views are unique. I can reasonably claim, I believe, that as an American by choice my background, overall life experience and exposure do allow me a certain perspective that is certainly different enough to provide some readers with insights and observations to which they may not be exposed otherwise. My intention is not to attempt to convert or change anyone or even alter their points of view on the things that matter most to me. If this were to happen, however, it would be intensely gratifying. Instead, my overall objective is simply to share my view of the world and America as an American by choice with a not-so-common background, recognizing the marvelous uniqueness of this amazing country that is America.

My grand daughters need to understand this. Their generation needs to understand this. They also must understand the formative challenges America faces, as well as those they themselves will face. They should know that their personal challenges will not be unrelated to the challenges facing America. I also wish to share with them my unabashed admiration and appreciation for America's extraordinary Constitution, public institutions and relatively diverse culture as well as the extent to which these have impacted my own life and my impressions of America. It is of far greater importance to me that my perspective, points of view and observations are understood than that they be accepted. A quotation from Aristotle helps to frame my expectation: *"It is the mark of an educated mind to be able to entertain a thought without accepting it."* I can only hope to influence my grand daughters. I cannot hope, nor do I wish, to make them see America and the world exactly as I do.

If on certain issues my views or opinions appear more closely aligned with one political philosophy over another I assure you that this is not because of doctrinaire or dogmatic commitment to that philosophy. Rather, such alignment comes about because the particular philosophy is in alignment with my own and not the other way around. Those who know me well will attest that this is indeed the case and has been the case even when I lived in Jamaica where I voted strictly on this basis. I have often had passionate discussions with many of my American friends over the truly futile but relentlessly used labels of Liberal and Conservative. My own experience confirms that there are Liberals with conservative views and Conservatives with liberal views. A great deal depends on the issues at hand. In my view these labels do very little to describe political philosophy in any enlightening way. More often than not they create and sustain insidious political wedges that, over time, devalue dialogue and cause animosity.

Hopefully, in some small way I may make a personal contribution to the improvement of the level and quality of interpersonal relationships and discourse as well as diminish the rate of acceleration of the irrationality and coarseness of behavior among the disparate but equally valuable sub-groups in our culture. After all, **E Pluribus Unum** cannot be seen as empty words. The construct must be seen instead as a profound expression of hope, intent and direction.

1. IN THE BEGINNING

As I indicated in my introduction, the selected passages for relating my story ebb and flow naturally into one another. This is understandable. This realization is no where more emphatically demonstrated than in the commentary below and as well explains the immense impact of one of the seminal events mentioned.

JAMAICAN BY BIRTH AMERICAN BY CHOICE

There are serious lessons to be learned from this presidential election.

Spring forward. Fall back.

It is 6:00 a.m. on November 2, 2008 and I have just reset all the timepieces in my house to satisfy the rules of daylight saving time.
It occurs to me that America is about to reset its own national clock to a time and place in history that will change not just America but the world, forever. Some may find this frightening. Others will find it enabling. Such will be the impact of electing the first black citizen to the highest office in the land. It is an understatement to say that I feel special to be a part of this event; to be alive at this time and to actually participate in what is clearly a seminal moment for this nation as it moves itself, voluntarily, towards the goal of "a more perfect union."
It is instructive that for very many Jamaicans in this country there was always much ambivalence in deciding to become citizens until there was legal assurance that becoming a citizen of America would not mean giving up being a citizen of our country of birth. I suspect that this sentiment is true among many immigrant groups of color in this great country. And for good reason. America has always had visible difficulty assimilating people of color in a way that makes them feel truly safe

2

psychologically. There is great comfort in knowing that "home" is always there. In fact, in a manner not without paradox, this reality, more often than not, allows us to ignore or deny the existence or apparent impact of racism in our country of choice. Of even greater significance is the truth that it strengthens our belief that it is always possible to face down the beast using not just our natural sense of justice but the knowledge that as conflicted as America is about race, America, at least intellectually, has created an environment that, supported by pertinent laws, allows the reasonable seeking of redress for injuries caused by racism. In many respects America is slowly but surely coming to grips with this schizophrenia.

So what will it mean to have a president Obama?

As a Jamaican who is also a citizen of the United States, I can attest to the progressive energy of example as well as to the endless power of expectation and hope. I am 66 years old and became an American citizen in 1995. I grew up in a country whose indigenous people were Arawak and Carib Indians - sub tribes of the pre-Columbian Taino people who populated all of the Americas, including the entire Caribbean, up to the time of Columbus. They were wiped out by disease and war that accompanied the arrival of Europeans in what was more commonly known until recently as the West Indies. Jamaica became a colony of Great Britain in 1655 after brief periods of hegemony by the French and the Spanish. Like America, Jamaica endured years of slavery and indentured labor. The latter saw an influx of British outcasts, Chinese and East Indians into a part of the world quite foreign to these people and their cultures. In 1865 slavery was abolished in America. Emancipation occurred earlier in Jamaica in 1838 with the involvement of a variety of abolitionists, including former slave owners and people called slaves who knew they were not slaves. In 1962 Jamaica became an independent, sovereign nation and chose to remain a part of what is known as the British Commonwealth. Jamaican culture continues to incorporate, exemplify and live with the residues of all of these historical relationships even today. This is the perspective from which I observe the immense possibilities of this remarkable country - America.

I will always consider it the greatest of good fortunes to have had my formal education straddle two worlds: the so-called First and Third Worlds and in temporally reverse order. In the latter case one learns to get by with very little in nearly every important aspect of life. I was born in a small town in the hills of rural Jamaica. I started school at the age of four and can remember walking more than a mile to school. The entire school of perhaps a hundred students through six grades shared a single, large, open room. By any standard, but especially by the standards of today, most of us were quite poor. Many could not afford shoes and went to school bare footed up to the highest grades. In good weather classes were often held under trees in the school yard. We used slates instead of paper for writing. Our teachers used blackboards and chalk and text books were owned by the Ministry of Education and recycled for generations of students. Yet, we were all a happy lot. Then my parents relocated to the city for the promise and opportunities this offered.

My education between the age of about eight or nine through the age of twenty took place in the city. In retrospect the most powerful observation I can make about this time of my life is that the standard of education was always equivalent regardless of where I attended school. In short, the schools in poorer areas of Jamaica offered basically the same opportunities to get a decent education as those in areas that were better off. It was therefore not surprising that from my earliest years in Jamaica it was very clear to me that I could be whatever I wanted to be. There was abundant evidence of teachers, lawyers, doctors, very senior civil servants, politicians, diplomats, world class artists and athletes who not only attended similar schools as I but looked just like me. I believe there is a serious lesson to be learned here.

I worked for two years as a primary school teacher in Jamaica before coming to America to attend Howard University from 1964 through 1967. These years were as formative personally as I surmise they were for many Americans. These were the years of the Vietnam War, protests and sit-ins on and off college campuses. These were my Bob Dylan years. I also remember President Lyndon B. Johnson giving a commencement address at the University. I was also aware that Howard University was known as a "Predominantly Black College" and that in many ways it was considered not to be among the "best" colleges. The very idea of being defined as such automatically led to this conclusion.

Undoubtedly, there were then and are now similarly "Predominantly White" colleges in America of lesser light that were/are never denigrated because of the color wheel descriptor. Yet we all know that this institution, perhaps more than any other in America, gave not only this country but the Caribbean and Africa a comparatively large number of outstanding Diplomats, Doctors, Dentists, Lawyers, Politicians and Civil Servants of color. Howard University serves the world but only in America would the term "Predominantly Black College" have enduring significance and a pejorative one at that. In the Caribbean and Africa universities are recognized as such without descriptors. By and large, recognition is based solely on areas of predominant scholastic strength. I believe there is a serious lesson to be learned here.

In 1967 I returned to Jamaica immediately after graduation from Howard University and worked briefly as a civil servant before joining one of America's largest multi-national corporations with operations in Jamaica. This was the age of the infamous "ugly American." I had serious reservations about working for this company given my knowledge of its deficiency in regard to the civic responsibilities expected of business institutions in my country. The company and I came to terms on this lingering deficiency on its part and we remained partners for nearly 30 years. During this time I had assignments in the Caribbean, Canada, the U.S.A. and Africa.

In terms of my "education" versus my "schooling" I owe as much to the company as I do to Howard University and my "Third World" early education in Jamaica. I think it is Bertrand Russell, the English mathematician and philosopher, who said that his education was rudely interrupted by his schooling. I am happy to say that my education incorporated my schooling seamlessly and allows me to view the world and America in a way that may be somewhat different from the way many Americans do. It is therefore more than a coincidence that I understand perfectly the origins and definition of the thinking and philosophy of Barack Obama. It is a tribute to his background and genius that he has been able to take the majority of Americans, black and white, male and female, rich and poor, on a journey to a place in our lives and in our country where we are able to see the promise and possibilities of a better and much more universally fruitful future. There is a serious lesson to be learned here.

I retired in 2000 and decided to reside permanently in America in a place that is only an hour and a half by plane from Jamaica. In many respects Florida is also physically a lot like the country of my birth minus the high mountains and rolling hills. This is also true: Florida is becoming more and more demographically like Jamaica. On this score I do detect some elements of concern among some acquaintances here. I do not find this surprising in the least. The fact that I do not detect a sense of doom among this group is to my mind a positive countervailing force.

More particularly, in respect of an Obama presidency there is an observable (sometimes muted, sometimes voluble) sense of unease among a significant number of my white neighbors and acquaintances here. This unease is constantly fed by a massive imbalance in the media choices (and hence accessed information) made by many. Far right conservative radio is by far the most popular choice, with the Fox T.V. News network a close second. Conversely, I choose to listen to, watch and read a variety of media because I accept the fact that "my world" needs to be informed from varying points of view and not just for validation but for cultural and developmental relevance and effectiveness.

Against the will of many, Obama forces us to confront and question our positions on a wide variety of issues that we would rather not face, individually as well as collectively: race, social justice, war and its justification, personal and communal responsibility, the way we see the rest of the world. In many instances when we confront ourselves from a position of fear rather than one of open mindedness and hope we try our best to find reasons why we "should not" versus why we "should." This is the real test that very many Americans will have to face if an Obama presidency comes to pass.

As an example of the consequences of coming to behavior changing conclusions from a position of fear I recall a discussion with a very successful acquaintance. He is morbidly afraid that America will become socialist if Obama is elected president. From this position he loses sleep and loses sight of the fact that whoever becomes president serves at the will of the American people and as long as we have the right to choose our president every four years there is always the opportunity to correct any kind of injurious drift in our society. Of course, I do not discount the real possibility that the socialist fear is a default position for another historical fear – a black man in charge for real! There is certainly a lesson to be learned here.

In conclusion, I indicated to my fearful acquaintance that it would appear that, as a Jamaican by birth and an American by choice, my faith in America was much more substantial than his. I reminded him that I had lived in many countries and could have chosen to retire in any of these places but chose America without hesitation. The reason: Of all the countries in which I have lived and the many others with which I am quite familiar, none *offers greater promise of achieving a satisfactory life than America, regardless of how one may construe this. America is more than a country. America is a promise not just to Americans but to the world. This is perhaps the greatest lesson of all to be learned here.*

The foregoing presents an initial and useful picture of how and why I come to view the world and America as I do. My views are intensely personal but are clearly influenced by critical issues and events. The manner in which I recognize, accept and process this influence is what creates the lenses through which I view my world and my America. This does not mean that I, or anyone else for that matter, should dare consider my views as right or wrong. The only claim that may be rationally made is that they are unreservedly my own. It is on this basis that I share them. Naturally, there are contrary views resulting from the identical influential events which stimulated my own commentary. These contrary views no more diminish mine than mine diminish them. They all struggle in the forum of feelings and ideas but are never ever truly meaningless because they all have some value. This is why I will unapologetically and relentlessly resist the categorization of my general view of my world or of my America as liberal or conservative, left or right or any of the shades in between these often meaningless but frequently inflammatory extremes.

You may wonder how I straddle all the worlds I appear to occupy. I don't. I simply accept them and learn from them. I am at ease in them and with them. The explanation is perhaps much simpler than it appears. My heritage itself is diverse: Welsh, Irish, and African – at least. So is the heritage of my wife: Indian, Scottish and/or Irish and African. Our two sons, Gordon and Gregory, are aware of all of this, understand and appreciate their diverse heritage but do not dwell on it. We do not dwell on it but are always aware of its reality and its significance in a place like America. The vast majority of Jamaicans shares this kind of diversity and is generally very comfortable in it and with it. Very few of us trace our family tree. This would perhaps be too unwieldy an undertaking for most of us. I certainly feel no need to do so. My heritage is always with me. I can no more escape it than I can the color of my skin. Its details, while interesting, contribute no more in knowing them than in not knowing them. Yet it provides a place from which I move fearlessly to face the world in general and America in particular.

II. MY JAMAICA

Country Boy

The written accounts of the period going back to the time of slavery are always interesting and fascinating and at times even moving. Yet, these accounts will be forever distant. Naturally, more recent or current individual stories tend to have greater relevance and directional urgency. Our distance from events, even major ones, tends to rob them of some of their potency to move and excite us. We do understand their relevance and weight but basically see them as history. For this reason, I suppose, while the stories of each generation are clearly and inextricably linked to the stories of those preceding it, to some extent, the stories of each generation stand alone. This anomaly does add to my sense of urgency to tell my own story while I am still more or less in charge of not just the telling but of addressing any controversy or misunderstanding that may arise from my telling of it.

I was born in 1941 to relatively poor parents in the hills of rural Jamaica, in a tiny house on a gravel road named Wildman Street, in the bucolic little town of Christiana in the parish of Manchester, in the county of Middlesex. I believe that Wildman Street remains unpaved even today, nearly 70 years later. But for the inclusion of Jamaica in the foregoing, anyone could be forgiven for assuming I was born in England. This nominal proximity should not be ignored or seen as trifling. The fact is, the British colonial masters were not lacking in imagination. Instead, they were constantly overcome by their desire to feel and be at home thousands of miles and several weeks away from their own cold, bleak and dreary island. And so, at home in Jamaica, they were attracted to locations on the island that were as reminiscent of home as is possible in the tropics. Christiana, where I was born, is one such place. Its elevation was high enough that it was never too hot or too cold in summer or in winter. Yet, I clearly recall the fascination I had with the then inexplicable fact that my mother would leave "jell-o" outside on our window sill overnight and it would be firmly set by morning. I never knew what freezing was or what ice was until I arrived in the city of Kingston in my early youth.

The names of places should not be the only names of interest to the sensitive observer. The names of Jamaicans should be of at least as great interest. The names of the people among whom I grew up in my little town reveal not even the remotest of connection to the most overwhelmingly visible aspect of my origins – my Africanness. These names include Foreman, my mother's maiden name, Newman, Robertson, Gayle, Williams, Allen, Peart, Mullings, Rodgers, Miller, Binns, DePass, Chin, Chang, Lowe, Nam, Sam Fo. Not a single sign of a name whose origin is Yoruba, Ibo, Hana, Faluni, Guin, Mina, Ewe or Mandingo. In a perverse way, it amply demonstrates the power of *branding*. As used here, this term is precisely contextual. It signifies the extent to which the English, and other colonizers, overwhelmed and transformed the native characteristics of those they enslaved. This is so powerful yet understated a capability, that even where physical features, latent culture and language were in direct conflict with slave master given names, these names had effectively superior force, longevity and relevance in the captive societies. As in today's sophisticated world of marketing, this is the boldest of evidence that he who has the power is able to brand. He who is able to brand is able to leave a legacy which is uniquely his.

Accordingly, the continuum of color among the people with whom I passed my earliest years never made it beyond the brownest shades of white. Most of these people never left Christiana until they were adults and some married within their own families to close and not so close relatives. Whether this was by design, by pure happenstance, ignorance or indifference to their family tree, remains very difficult to explain. One result, of course, is that a number of off springs from such unions exhibited signs of mental defect.

From the perspective of someone my age, early Jamaica seems a relatively simple and straightforward place. We all knew our places in the social hierarchy, children as well as adults. Children should be seen but not heard. Adults in positions of authority, or who were thought to be for whatever reason, were automatically deserving of respect and unquestionable deference. Children trusted all adults and the word of an adult was indisputable. The word of an adult was also his bond. Crime was just about non-existent, except for what I would later come to know as praedial larceny, a concept in English law that allows conviction for stealing a farmer's produce from his field.

Shame was also a very effective tool in enforcing acceptable behavior in the community. There was an unforgettable incident involving an unmarried couple who lived in a barracks style group of houses. The man in the relationship was so upset with his girlfriend that after a very heated argument he became incensed and attacked her with a machete. He chopped her on the arm, threw away his machete, ran to a nearby saw mill and hanged himself. He was obviously not troubled by living in a common law relationship but could not endure the embarrassment and lingering stigma of viciously attacking his girlfriend. To my knowledge, his suicide was the first in the community.

Most of the families I knew were directly or indirectly involved with subsistence farming. Common crops at the time included citrus, bananas, Irish potatoes, yams, pimento, also known as allspice, and coffee. On Friday afternoons and Saturdays the market bustled with both commercial and subsistence farmers trying to earn a living selling produce. There was also a butcher's shop at the market and meat was sold fresh each "meat day". Citrus, bananas and, to a lesser extent, pimiento and coffee were export crops. This fact created a subsidiary industry involving the selection, bagging and transporting of these goods into the city of Kingston for grading and subsequent shipping abroad. I recall a neighbor of ours who was the very first person in the town to own a brand new Bedford truck. This made him an instant celebrity and confirmed him as a man of much substance. He was not a very kind or friendly person.

Many stories abound about his abusive behavior to his children, especially to his only son. As a result, all of us children called him Mr. "Chu." This was the word commonly used to get the attention of pigs. Understandably, we dared not use the name to his face or in the hearing of any adult. It is laughable that the name was clearly meant to be disrespectful. Yet, as children, even among ourselves, we could not help but preface the derogatory nickname with the respectful "Mr." He was also the first person I knew to acquire a radio. The radio was magical. How could a voice come from this wooden box on a table? It would be many years before I would come to understand how this was possible.

I remember that a number of us would steal away from home at dusk to huddle under the window closest to the radio at Mr. Chu's house to listen to the BBC broadcast of world news. Do not get the wrong impression. It was not the news that attracted us. It was the absolute incredibility that the radio functioned as it indeed was intended to. I think that at the time Jamaica had not too long started its own local radio station known by the call letters ZQI. This station was operated by the government and basically channeled the BBC at specified times of day.

Apart from listening to the neighbor's radio the most common pass times included making and playing gigs (tops), marbles, hop scotch, jump rope, jacks, see-well-lash, making and flying kites, climbing trees, playing tag which we called "chevy chase" (for reasons still unknown to me), swimming in the ponds in the neighborhood and hunting birds with slingshots. This is not an exhaustive list but is clearly enough to have kept us busy and out of trouble for a very long time. I never owned a manufactured toy until my early teens when a grand aunt who had migrated to America would send barrels of astonishing goodies home at Christmas time. All my playmates made their own toys just as my brothers and I did. Our lives were carefree and uncomplicated. We never the less had chores. Just about every family had a few animals: pigs, goats, cows or chickens. In addition, there was no yard that was without a dog. My younger brother and I shared a happy, affectionate black and white mongrel called Trixie.

Most households were self sufficient in basic ground provisions like bananas, potatoes, yams and peas or beans and vegetables. As children we all shared in the responsibility of attending to these things. Since there was no piped water supply, many families had water tanks. These tanks were filled naturally by rainfall collected by gutters attached to roofs and channeled into these tanks. In times of severe drought families would have to purchase water from the Parish Council, the local government authority. The water would be delivered by trucks like that of my neighbor, with a large metal container secured temporarily to the bed of the vehicle. In most cases the water tanks were covered by a simple zinc roof but in some cases the roof of the tank was actually a slab of concrete on which coffee beans or other things would be barbecued by the natural heat of the sun. Those who could not afford to install tanks simply collected rain water in large forty five gallons metal drums. Understandably, water was a valued commodity and was treated as such. Even when baths were taken, children would often bathe together or re-use the same bath water.

Our small house, like many at the time, had a detached kitchen and toilet as well as a storehouse for provisions and meat. Large strips of meat were cured by smoke from wood fires as food was prepared on an open, elevated, wattle-and-daub fireplace in a lean-to kitchen. This meat was hung from a wire line secured a couple feet above the fireplace for several days or even weeks at a time as a part of the curing process. This process goes back to the days of slavery when the meat from this process was called *boucan*. The word is the root of the word *buccaneer*. Pirates became known as buccaneers because they commonly cured meat in this manner. The yard was bare. Little or no grass would grow because of the constant foot traffic and sweeping of the yard with brooms made from bramble. I never wondered at the time why we swept the bare ground even though there was really nothing to sweep away. All that sweeping accomplished was to give the dusty, bare earth interesting patterns made by the rough bramble brooms. Somehow this made the yard appear clean and well kept.

I remember collecting parched coffee beans from our neighbor's barbecue and helping to pound the beans into powder with mortar and pestle. These items, then of purely utilitarian purpose, would soon lose their utility to become items of decoration when it became not only fashionable but cost effective to purchase pre-ground coffee beans in bags, tins or bottles. It may seem strange to many but I grew up drinking coffee with breakfast from as early a time in my youth as I can remember. This was common practice all around Jamaica. The influence of the British habit of drinking tea instead of coffee remains so strong, that Jamaicans, even today, will quite frequently and effortlessly ask for coffee as *coffee-tea*. This meant having coffee at tea time when the British would usually have their customary tea. Clearly, the influence of the British colonizers was as pervasive as it had at times been perverse.

Even so, I gratefully acknowledge the part played by British religious groups in supporting education in Jamaica from the earliest days following the abolition of slavery. In fact, even today in Jamaica, many of our schools are what are called church schools because they are intimately affiliated with churches. Among these are the Roman Catholic, Anglican, Methodist and Moravian. These churches are major providers of education from elementary through secondary levels.

The elementary school I first attended was connected to the Moravian Church whose history goes back to the middle of the fifteenth century in what is now the Czech Republic but was known then as Bohemia and Moravia. As far as I can recall Zorn Moravian School was the only school in the town of Christiana. Attendance was aggressively encouraged by the church, teachers and, of course, parents. There were no public mechanisms to enforce attendance but it was clear that the vast majority of parents acted on the conviction that one of the best things they could do for their children was to ensure that they learned to read and write even though many of the parents could not do so themselves. Still, when crops had to be harvested or planted children were kept out of school to help at home with these chores.

My family left the town of Christiana when I was perhaps seven or eight years old for the neighboring town of Mandeville. Like Christiana, Mandeville was a little piece of Britain away from home. Again, the name is not without significance. In many respects Mandeville was like an English village. The climate and countryside were even more favorable to those who would long for the welcome but usually relatively brief period of balmy weather in parts of the British Isles during spring and summer. The town is about two thousand feet above sea level with daytime temperatures between 70F and 75F and at nighttime between 65F and 70F; ideal by nearly any standard. The color composition of the population in Mandeville was no different from that of Christiana. In very many respects both towns were essentially the same. Mandeville, however, was a larger and more bustling place by the standards of bustle at the time.

I believe the family relocated because my father was offered a job at the Manchester Hotel. This hotel was an imposing, typical, colonial wooden structure, completely painted white with buildings and grounds immaculately maintained. It was the meeting place of the movers and shakers from all over the parish of Manchester as well as their foreign visitors, of course. We never spent a long time in Mandeville as the family moved on to the city of Kingston that seemed to promise more and greater opportunities.

City Boy

The city of Kingston was then as now the capital of Jamaica. Kingston had replaced the old Spanish capital of St. Jago de la Vega, later Spanish Town, in the late nineteenth century. Though a mere sixty miles or so from Mandeville it was so very different it may as well have been six hundred miles away instead. As active as my imagination was, nothing prepared me for the likes of the city. I do not recall the mode of transportation we used to get to Kingston. I do remember however, how busy a place the city was. There were people everywhere. Far more people than I had ever seen in one place in my young life. I now had an accurate description of what real bustle meant. In addition to the countless masses of people there were hand carts, buggies drawn by horse or donkey, buses, cars and tram cars all around.

While I had seen buses and cars before I had never seen so many in the same location and in such variety of colors and models. I certainly had never seen tram cars. These were like open train coaches with running boards, ran on iron tracks and had a flexible wand which ran from the roof of the coach to the electric power line above. I learned that this was how the tram cars were powered. The cars had bells which made easily identifiable clangs. These bells were used liberally as the trams made their way through the streets they shared with pedestrians, cars and horse drawn buggies. My parents held on to the younger among us with unusual firmness. Just as well, because I was unlikely to brave crossing any street without the assurance of their grip on my arm. To a little boy from the country new to the city, the city was overwhelming, to say the least.

Our first rented accommodation in the city was on Liverpool Street in Campbell Town. This was near both the tram lines and the bus service and not very far from downtown Kingston. A typical Chinese shop was next door. The shop occupied the ground floor of the two storey building and the family, as was common at the time, occupied the upstairs rooms. Three or four houses separated us from another Chinese shop farther down the street on the same side as the first shop. I would very soon discover how much the Chinese among us dominated the shop keeping business.

My father's first job in Kingston was at the then world famous Myrtle Bank Hotel on the edge of the city on Harbour Street, directly on the waters of Kingston Harbour. The Myrtle Bank Hotel was among the most famous playgrounds of the wildly rich and famous at the time, in spite of the fact that it took five to six days by boat to get there from America. This was early in 1950. I recall the year because it was not too long afterwards that the island was struck by one of the most devastating hurricanes. This was the infamous hurricane Charlie of August 1951. It wreaked havoc over a large area of the island but especially the central and eastern sections of the country. An excerpt from the Jamaica Daily Gleaner of August 2004 recalling the wrath of Charlie makes it clear just how destructive the hurricane was.

Hurricane Charlie revisited - August 17, 1951 published: Wednesday, August 11, 2004

By Kevin Clarke, Gleaner Writer

THE GLEANER'S headline of Friday, August 17, 1951 was 'Hurricane may hit Jamaica today'. This eerie forewarning, however, did not prepare Jamaica for the onslaught of Hurricane Charlie, which at the time was the most severe hurricane to hit the island in 70 years.

The report indicated that the storm was moving exceptionally fast and while meteorologists were hopeful that it would stay its course and keep to the south of the island, they projected that wind speeds at the centre of the storm could increase from between 18 to 20 miles per hour to 75 miles per hour.

UNLEASHING FURY

At 8:30 that night Hurricane Charlie struck, unleashing its fury with 125-mile per hour winds and rain. In its aftermath, the hurricane left 154 people dead, 25,000 victims homeless and a decimated Banana and Coconut industry with the downing of trees in three parishes while, water, telephone and telegraph services were disrupted and roads made impassable.

The hurricane leveled houses, wrecked ships at port, destroyed the Palisadoes Airport installment and the Victoria pier. A collapsed dormitory at the General Penitentiary allowed 76 convicts to escape. They, along with other unlawful entities, would later wreak havoc on Kingston's business district with rampant looting.

HARDEST HIT PARISHES

The hardest hit parishes were St. Thomas, Kingston, St. Andrew, St. Catherine and Clarendon with Port Royal being completely destroyed for the third time in its history. The Corporate Area had over 12,000 people homeless, St. Thomas 10,000 and 3,000 elsewhere in the island. In total, over £16 million worth of damage was done and it took the island over five years to fully recover from the effects.

In the ensuing days, **The Gleaner** told the many stories which were created with the coming of the hurricane. Stories of death proliferated, such as that of the father of three who in an attempt to save his youngest child lost the other two when the house he left them in collapsed, or that of the eight elderly inmates housed in the corporation infirmary who were killed when the roof of their wards caved in.

NOTEWORTHY TALES

Other noteworthy tales were gleaned as well, such as that of a group of convicts, who after saving the occupants of a tenement which had collapsed, trapping them inside, held up and robbed a grocer on the same premises. But through it all the country was trying to find some semblance of normalcy, though many citizens had taken refuge in various church halls around the island. **The Gleaner** airdropped copies of the daily paper into various towns.

The effect Hurricane Charlie has had on the psyche of Jamaicans is still with us today. People of that generation will always reiterate the fact that they survived it and to some it is regarded as the ultimate sign of resilience.

Our house itself was not spared. It lost its entire roof. I was nearly ten years old at the time but remember the experience as if it were yesterday. This was my first hurricane. Ignorance does offer some comfort, false though this may be. Although my parents attempted to get us to appreciate the potential dangers, we certainly never imagined these as they turned out to be. We now had our own radio. I remember the brand being an Ecko. I suspect that this brand has been extinct for many years now. I recall that we were all listening to the BBC broadcast of the 5th cricket test match between England and South Africa at Kensington Oval in Leeds, England. By this time the quaint ZQI had become the more impressive Radio Jamaica. The cricket broadcast was interrupted frequently for updates on Charlie.

We had already boarded up windows and vulnerable doors, secured all loose items outside in the yard and placed them safely under the house. At some point during the broadcast we were instructed to immediately seek shelter under tables and similar heavy pieces of furniture. Just then the broadcast ended abruptly as the electricity went. We could hear the wind howling and whistling outside. Before long the zinc roof was completely blown away. My older brothers and our parents made sure that all of us younger ones were safely huddled under our large, heavy dining table and a nearby bed as the rain pelted down with the force of little marbles catapulted at high speed against every object in the house.

Suddenly the wind and rain ceased. The unexpected silence though welcome was frightening. We all came out of hiding and looked up to where the roof had been. We saw a night sky full of twinkling stars. We thought the hurricane had ended. Just as we were about to celebrate our good fortune we heard the sound of a rumbling train approaching. This was followed by the renewed assault of wind and rain. We had been lulled into a false sense of safety by the passing eye of the hurricane. It was a lesson none of us would ever forget or ignore again. We all survived Charlie's wrath without injury. When morning came we were not prepared for the devastation that lay around us. Even so we had to be prevented by our parents from rushing up to nearby Hampton Street to witness an even more catastrophic consequence of Charlie. There was a headless corpse in a yard not far from our house. The head had been severed from the body by a flying sheet of zinc. The sign from the farther Chinese shop was lying in our own front yard. This did put everything in perspective for us as a family. We had been very fortunate indeed.

My younger siblings and I were farmed out to nearby friends and neighbors for sometime while the roof of our house was replaced. By this time I had started primary school just over a mile from home. The roof of my school had also been destroyed. Students were reassigned to neighboring schools for about a year while the school was being repaired. Hurricane Charlie was my marker event for the start of our life in the city.

In the years after Hurricane Charlie my family moved house a number of times but never outside of a radius of about six miles from Liverpool Street. I returned to my old primary school and life settled into comfortable routine once again. From time to time my parents would allow me to return to the country to spend some of my holidays with my Godparents and former schoolmates. There was a family who also lived on Wildman Street in Christiana with whom my parents were very good friends. My parents had six boys and two girls while all five children of the other family were girls. Both families were close enough for acquaintances to think we were blood relatives. The father of these girls worked as a driver for one of the major bus companies in Christiana. His schedule frequently included roundtrips from Christiana to Kingston. This allowed me to travel for free on the visits I made to the country.

Traveling to the country by bus was always an adventure. The bus was more often than not quite full. Most of the passengers were itinerant sellers of crops and wares who were known as *higglers*. The origin of the term appears to be a corruption of *haggler* as, by the very nature of how business was done in the local markets, haggling was a natural way of life. No one bought anything for the price asked by the seller. Even the higglers themselves would have considered this very strange behavior. This kind of trading between city and town was of great significance to both. The higglers took produce into the city and returned to the towns with stocks of the latest house wares. In this way the city dweller got his food and the people in the town were introduced to creature comfort items like down pillows and ceramic bowls and goblets.

By 1954 I was ready to move on to secondary school. I had no idea just how daunting a prospect this would be for my parents. They were not unique in this respect as the cost to attend secondary school was prohibitive for most parents like mine. I passed the admission's exam to attend one of the more prestigious secondary schools in the island. This achievement made both my parents and siblings proud and happy for me. I was too young and too far removed from the financial realities of my parents' situation to understand that while their pride and happiness were certainly genuine their faith in their ability to pay the required school fees was quite tempered. Fortunately, in 1955 the government of Jamaica initiated an experimental secondary class program in selected elementary schools. Participation in this program was free. Still, in my mind there was superlative value in attending a prestigious traditional secondary school. After all, at the time such schools offered the very best opportunity for upward social mobility in Jamaica's class conscious society.

This concern was not baseless as representation in traditional secondary schools was disproportionately in favor of the children of gentry. In fact, one study **(The Comprehensive High School In Jamaica by Audrey Eloise Lindsay)** reveals that of 84,000 children from poor families who sat the common entrance examination for entry into secondary school a mere 978 were accepted while of 4,000 from families of the upper class 1,155 were accepted.

The British may have left Jamaica an outstanding civil service but it left an extremely elitist system of education which would take generations to unravel. I am a graduate of one of the experimental secondary classes. The stated intent of this special program was specifically to assist the poorest but most deserving children in getting a secondary school education. It provided the soundest of foundations for my ongoing education and demonstrated unequivocally the potential for successful outcomes when children, regardless of social status, are given fair opportunity.

The intellectual curiosity that was kindled during my years in the experimental secondary class has remained with me and has made my years since then more interesting and satisfying than they would otherwise be. Given the very limited exposure of children from poor families to robust intellectual debate informed by the great writers and thinkers, it is with some astonishment that I look back at the fact that many of us were curious enough to seek out incremental information about personages like Socrates, Plato, Aristotle, Karl Marx, Euclid and

Pythagoras, Tennyson, Wordsworth, Shelley, Masefield, and others.

We read a great deal: the traditional set books like *Macbeth, The Tempest,* John Buchan's *The 39 Steps,* Homer's *Iliad,* Virgil's *Aeneid,* Melville's *Moby Dick,* Jonathan Swift's *Gulliver's Travels,* D. H. Lawrence's *Lady Chatterley's Lover* as well as personal selections like George Orwell's *1984* and Omar Khayyam's *Rubaiyat,* Hemingway's *A Farewell to Arms* and *The Old Man and the Sea.* Of course, we also read lighter fare like *The Hardy Boys* and *Nancy Drew* series as well as the then ubiquitous *"All-in-pictures"* and the most popular comic books. There was constant competition among a number of us to see who could read the most books in a year. We listened intently to anyone who appeared intellectually stimulating or challenging. Many trinkets of additional knowledge were gleaned from our excursions into this smorgasbord of literature and inevitable argument and debate. This experience served to encourage continued learning and eventually stimulated a deep and lasting desire to travel, write and teach.

It is documented that the students of the experimental classes out-performed the average traditional secondary school pupil. A statement published in the **Jamaica Daily Gleaner of March 4, 1960,** after the Senior Cambridge examination results were released, validates this fact. The note is as powerfully poignant in its sentiment as it is thunderously brief in its criticism of the new government which had abandoned the experimental secondary class program:

'Bravo, says E. L. Allen

Mr. Edwin Allen, former MHR, has sent the following telegram to the Mico Practicing School, the Kingston Senior School and the Central Branch School on the results of the School Certificate Examinations:

"Bravo. By your magnificent performance you have blazed trail for enlightened educational practice, delighted friends, astonished skeptics, confounded critics

*and rebuked Government for killing scheme so benefi-
cial to poor children." '*

To my knowledge, the graduates from this experimental secondary class program include a Rhodes Scholar, a
physician, engineers, entrepreneurs, business executives,
teachers, college professors and ministers of religion.

The experimental secondary class I attended was a
part of The Mico Practising School which was affiliated
with the oldest Teachers' College in the western hemi-
sphere, **The Mico Teachers' College**. There was a memorable incident affecting my entire class at The Practising
School. The incident involved a very highly regarded,
grumpy, taciturn Englishman, who was the Vice Principal
of the Teacher's College at the time. He tried his best
to teach the class Latin which we understood to be a
dead language. To his chagrin many of us treated it as
such. He was very highly regarded as a scholar for his
demonstrated mastery of multiple subjects as well as his
double baccalaureate from Oxford University. He was
nick named "Pythy" (short for Pythagoras) because of
his demonstrated and very highly regarded prowess in
mathematics. Each time he arrived in class he would
greet us in Latin: *"Salvete discipuli."* We in turn would respond: *"Salve magister."*

The class was required to stand while greeting the
teacher. For no known reason, on one particular occasion the class greeted the teacher but did not stand to
do so. Pythy stormed out of the class to the school principal's office in anger to indicate his disgust at our behavior. He indicated that he would no longer teach a rabble
such as we were. The principal disbanded the class stating that the class would not resume unless we all brought
our parents to school for a meeting on the matter. In addition, a written apology to Pythy had to be provided
by each student. We complied but were convinced
that Pythy's behavior was as stark a micro example of
excessive colonial power on display as we were likely to
see.

Graduation from the experimental secondary class at The Practising School meant that we had all sat our Senior Cambridge exams. These exams were set, monitored and marked by the University of Cambridge in England. Jamaica was still a colony and our education system was essentially British. Senior Cambridge was a complicated undertaking. As I recall, students had to pass at least five or six subjects, including English, under a mandated number of categories. We were taught Latin and Spanish, Arithmetic, Algebra and Geometry, English Language and English Literature, Health Science, Religious Knowledge, Geography and History. Regardless of how well students did on other subjects, failure to pass the English section of the exam meant that such students would not receive the Cambridge Certificate. Instead, those who passed other individual subjects at a certain level were given General Certificates of Education for each of these subjects.

In June of 2009 graduates of my experimental class met at the school in Jamaica to celebrate the 50th anniversary of our graduation. I was moved to write a poem for the occasion. The poem not only celebrates the formative value of the experimental class but forces us to reflect on the meaning of our lives.

Class of '59

Like country,
Diverse in origin and place,
From Half Way Tree,
From Providence,
From Mico Practising, we came.
On own "Quinquireme of Nineveh."
Destination known,
Compass set,
Journey began.
We our own cargo, own vessel's hands.

Effort with talent's steady mien
Greets shared high expectations.

Many, many challenges abound.
We test as we are tested,
Stumble but neither fall nor fail.
Discover our hidden corners,
Jagged and rough, blunt and smooth,
Explore our depths,
Discard our worst,
Encourage our very best.

'Salvete discipuli'.
'Salve magister'.
Upright, salutation's mantra we repeat.
Seated, insult assumed though truly unintended.
Pithy Pythy struts, acage in self made circus.
Class undone.
Parents summoned.
O me miserum.
Sugar me! Fiddle sticks! A parent's exclamation.
Salvation comes in speedy, penned, near' feigned
     regret.

The enforcer stalks from time to time,
Snails' sole afoot, ignition off
He coasts in neutral's hushed deception
To espy puberty's excess
On chancy trips from timid innocence.
Attrition's pain endured,
Culled by fourteen
Sixteen we become.
There are no losers here.
All have grown, all are given wings.

At other Gamaliels' feet we sit
Affect less dubious, intent direct.
No devices to ensnare do they enlist.
Committed to the discipline of curriculum
At moments sharing smidgens of themselves.
Yet sometimes less is more and more is less.
Discovered 'neath defensive armor's skin

Reluctant uncut gems and flowery things.
It was not a time of brash display.
Modesty ruled; an exacting king.

Virgil, dead language's host
For whom the bell tolls,
Haunts us with help
From 'mates and Pythy foe.
No resurrection guaranteed.
We accommodate time's endless trials.
All tests of scholarship we take.
Confronting twists and turns along the way,
No permanence to first accommodations,
Or learners' lodge apart and new.

New building to shared pavilion,
To first accommodations returned.
Nomads, like soldiers marking time,
In place but not in charge of their own fate.
Yet not for us anxiety or feisty wasteful tears.
Shakespeare, Hemingway, Hardy Boys, Enid Blyton,
All-in-pictures, secured in books with pedigree,
Pleads, 'Come go away with me to Scotland'.
Signs of sad decline to decadence
Defenseless on its face.

Nickname's whimsy like Pavlov's bell
Elicits sharp, engraved recall.
Common origin belies perfect appliqué:
Humpty Dumpty, Shelley Belly, Long John Silver.
Endearing, unforgettable sobriquets
Excite ever lively tongues,
Gently tone the muscles of the face,
Transport to halcyon days and risky escapades.
Slipe Road bar, old juke box, fizzy drinks, coy look-outs,
False alarms, zinc fence hazard, dry gully's promise of
*   stealthy safe retreat.*

The beginning
Pregnant with its end
Confronts us once again.
Such is the nature of beginnings
And we must start anew.
On gentle wind,
In storm, in hurricane
We float away or scatter,
Rolling stones that gather moss
O'er fifty years of pursuits and endeavors.

Somewhat diminished but not obscure,
Itself pregnant with its own beginnings,
The end approaches certain in conclusion.
Horizons, now static in our eye's embrace
No more alarm with false edge or endless distance.
Clearly feeble in its delayed dotage,
Fear fumbles with long donated teeth.
We ignore its wagging, wrinkled finger,
Assured by what we have become,
Separate as well together.

What does it mean?
This span of fifty years.
In countless words and numbers
Its sum exceeds the total of its parts
Alike the total of our years.
What do we owe?
What can we give?
How much to dearest second mother?
Surely, we can never have enough
So offer lives as gratitude, down payment on our debt.

Maniacal Ahab, nemesis Moby Dick,
Mapple's dismal pulpit, Queequeg's tattooed soul
To Melville's pages now sequestered and confined,
No longer confuse or concentrate our minds.

Doubtless, memories we mislaid,
At times wary of making friends
For fear of making enemies.
Forfeiting friendship's wondrous gifts
We are what we have become,
Not what was promised us; Our promise to ourselves.

Like evidence of lowly acorn
Writ large in mighty oak
We shout across the gap of generations
In everlasting monotone, 'forget us not,
The championless, those who can ill afford'.
For who knows what we may become?
Ending up on others' distant shores
Bearing gifts from first beginnings' bounty,
Prodigals perhaps, always asking,
Can we come home again?

To Half-Way-Tree, Mico Practising and May Pen
*   All-Age*
To Kingston Senior, Central Branch, All Saints and
*   Providence*
Where much has changed yet much the same
*   remains.*
Social wedges in septic, deep divides endure,
Sons of gentry's refuge yet opportunity's default.
Unfortunate, misled, those who had not, have not still,
Unaware the shuttered vintage years
Of Teacher Allen's hospiced revolution.
Its legacy on galleons forever seeking shore
Hearty, healthy, prolific evidence aboard.

If in beginning's womb the end endures
We can come home again.
The circle never breaks for 'tis not time's intent.
We can come home again.
Even if arrival is not destination's end
We can come home again.

Though sleep comes easy and dreams more fleeting,
"Surely, surely, slumber is more sweet than toil, the
    shore
Than labour in the deep mid-ocean, wind and wave
    and oar;
O, rest ye, brother mariners, we will not wander more".

We can come home again!

We have come home again!

We have come home again!

Moving On

I proceeded directly to the Teachers' College from the Practising School. I was an outstanding student and an exceptional athlete while at the College. I graduated as a teacher in 1962, the year of Jamaica's Independence. At the time I was among the youngest to graduate from the Teacher's College. While a somewhat impressive accomplishment it was also a distressing liability. I had much difficulty securing a position in several of the schools to which I applied for assignment. The common refrain was that, at the age of twenty, I was too young. One headmaster openly confessed his deep concern that I would have great difficulty with the older girls in the senior classes in his school.

Eventually I secured a position at the Rennock Lodge Elementary School at Rockfort, in the outskirts of Kingston. The location was in a troubled area at the foot of the Wareika Hills. It was not an attractive assignment. In fact, apart from the headmaster, I was the only male among a staff of five or six teachers. He confessed that he had been waiting for some time to find a male teacher so he could leave the school for a promotion as an Inspector of Schools. He made the position attractive by indicating that as the only male on staff I would be the de facto teacher in charge although the succeeding acting head teacher would be one of the older female members of staff. This did indeed turn out to be the case.

I spent two years at the school. They were rewarding and maturing years. A fascinating truth is that I learned more Mathematics and English teaching these subjects than I learned when they were being taught to me. The experience stood me in good stead when I subsequently left the island in 1964, on a Teacher's scholarship from the Ministry of Education, to attend Howard University in the United States of America.

America Briefly

Hello America. Goodbye America.

I sat the final exam of my final year at Howard University on a Thursday. My wife-to-be arrived in Washington D.C. on the following day. We were formally engaged on Saturday and left Washington D.C. that very day for Toronto and Montreal, Canada. Montreal was the site of Expo '67. We spent a week with an older brother, a school teacher in Montreal, and attended our first Expo. My heart was already back in Jamaica. In retrospect it had really never left. Even during my very best days on campus, Jamaica beckoned with fierce intensity. During my time in Washington I was very often homesick and recall drinking myself into a stupor with rice wine at a friend's on my very first Christmas night in Washington D.C. The temperature was 19F. It must have been 76F in Jamaica at the time. My homesickness had less to do with the discomforts of winter or the constant evidence of intolerance and discrimination around me and in the rest of the country, than with an unyielding desire to return home and make a contribution to the land of my birth. So powerful was this desire, I refused to take up the offer of a scholarship to pursue graduate work in journalism at Northwestern University in Evanston, Illinois. My wife, my fiancée at the time, frequently offers a much more romantic alternative explanation.

My Howard University years were very stimulating years. I majored in Philosophy and minored in Economics, graduating with honors in three years. There was an active association of Caribbean students and much involvement in campus activities. I always marveled at what appeared to me then to be the easy display of wealth by many students: Flashy Mustangs, Pontiac GTO's, Dodge Darts, Chevrolets, Cadillacs and stylish clothes, fraternity parties and the extravagancies of Homecoming. Only in retrospect did I realize that while these trappings may have been signs of wealth to me, they were in fact merely indications of how available and affordable such things were in America then. It was difficult for me to comprehend this, given the fact that, at the time, owning a motor car in Jamaica was quite an accomplishment and certainly a sign of success if not wealth. All things are relative. Never the less, with very rare exceptions, it was necessary for Jamaican students to have some kind of employment to be able to pay tuition and to live.

Despite the fact that I did have a full year's tuition guaranteed because of my scholarship from the Ministry of Education in Jamaica, it was still necessary to work. The most popular jobs for students were as taxi drivers, waiters, cashiers, switchboard operators and hospital orderlies. I worked briefly at the last two jobs simultaneously, the latter on week-ends only. After a couple months at both I had to settle for a single job as I sometimes fell asleep in class. I kept the switchboard job at a posh high rise apartment building in Georgetown, not far from the Capitol, on the 11:00 P.M. to 7:00 A.M. shift on Mondays, Wednesdays and Fridays. I was amazed that students attending Georgetown and George Washington Universities could afford to live here. Not a single non-white person resided in the building. I later learned that these students came from very wealthy families. I never made the time to travel much around Washington D.C. or the surrounding suburbs. Studying was my focus; returning home to Jamaica as soon as possible was my objective.

Being a graduate opened up immense opportunities for a Jamaican returning from studies abroad. Unlike today, I knew of no university graduate in Jamaica who was unemployed or had to accept menial jobs in order to earn an income. In short order I went through stints in the civil service and banking before finally settling on a management trainee position with the Seprod Group of Companies in Kingston. They were the largest producers of edible products, soaps and detergents and livestock feed in the Caribbean. This was my formal introduction to my education in industrial management. I learned to manufacture and package cooking oils and margarines, toilet soaps and laundry soaps, corn meal, animal feeds and laundry detergents. I also learned to manage staff and a unionized workforce. This was the beginning of an unending fascination with the complexities and challenges of manufacturing consumer goods.

I married in 1968 while with the Seprod Group. In 1970 I was sponsored by the company for an ILO fellowship to attend the Institute for Advanced Technical and Vocational Training in Torino, Italy. The Institute was more popularly known by its French acronym, the BIT (*Bureau Internationale du Travaille*).

My experience in Italy was very instructive. Participants in the ILO program included students from Guyana, Egypt, Cyprus and Ethiopia. The group was a little United Nations in itself. I became friends with an Italian family, the Monticones, through their daughter who visited the BIT in order to improve her English by speaking with English speaking students. The family was originally from the mountainous area surrounding Torino called Pie Monte. I was taken to visit the grand parents one weekend. Pie Monte was as quaint a place as I had ever seen. Streets of cobblestone, little houses that reminded me of the ginger bread house in the fairytales of my youth, very old people who appeared to be dressed too warmly, hunched and walking with canes and small children who found me a curiosity, much to the embarrassment of my friends.

The children followed me around for several blocks and a few of them finally became courageous enough to touch me on the arm in the manner one might wipe water away. My friends explained their curiosity; they had never before seen a black person. Their great grand parents had during the Second World War. My friends found the incident embarrassing. I found it interesting and perfectly understandable and said so. A year later the Monticones accepted my invitation to visit me and my family in Jamaica. Interestingly, they had never seen the sea before and found the color and temperature of the water at the Negril Beach incredible. The father, Lorenzo Monticone, certain that none of his friends would believe that the sand on the beach was white, took home a small bottle filled with the evidence. Their behavior exhibited curiosity no different from that of the children in Pie Monte.

One of the highlights of the program at the BIT was a visit to my class by Haile Selassie, Emperor of Ethiopia. Once known as Abyssinia, Ethiopia is the oldest state in sub-Saharan Africa. The emperor had visited Jamaica earlier in 1966. As a Jamaican, I was well aware of his stature as the accepted representative of God on earth among the Jamaican Rastafari brethren. For a man of diminutive stature, I still recall how magnificent he looked and how regal was his bearing. I completed the fellowship obtaining a Diploma in Production Management and returned home to become the Production Manager for the Seprod operation. A year or so later I was promoted to Plant Manager. After five eventful years with the Seprod Group I struck out on my own with a small group of like minded friends to start my own business manufacturing and marketing confectionery. This venture did not work out as I had hoped and after just over a year I sold all the equipment, paid off creditors and re-entered the job market.

Over several weeks, I endured some three or four intense interviews with a Canadian expatriate senior management consultant before being told that he represented a very large American multi-national company. It turned out that he was once the local Managing Director for this company had retired and decided to reside permanently in Jamaica. I had hastily left America only to fall back into the extended arms of America in Jamaica. In my opinion, the behavior of the consultant mirrored the one sided view of American international policy at the time: know as much as possible about the other party but reveal as little as possible about yourself. It is a fact that American corporations abroad are an integral part of America's information network overseas. It was the case, and continues to be the case, that these companies provide very extensive and useful data to America's embassies in the countries in which they operate. The interests of these corporations are the interests of America. And so, in many ways I was, after a fashion and not without some reluctance, in America once again.

The company was impressive in terms of its management structure, control systems, performance standards and linkages to other subsidiaries and its corporate offices in New York. It treated its expatriate management extremely well by prevailing local standards. I was pleasantly surprised to see that the subsidiary's General Manager was a Jamaican who had started his career with the company many years earlier as a local salesman. He had only recently returned from assignment abroad as part of his preparation to become the first Jamaican General Manager of the local subsidiary. It is standard practice for any native who was potential General Manager material to be moved out of the local subsidiary before he could become the General Manager in his home country.

There were very significant gaps between the treatment and compensation of expatriate and native management employees. While initially there was no

41

Jamaican in positions equivalent to any position held by an expatriate there are reasonable ways in which to judge relative compensation and benefits never the less. These were the days when native employees seldom complained. To be fair, the company's compensation policy had two distinct tracks: one for expatriates the other for locals. In the latter case locals were compensated strictly within the compensation patterns which prevailed locally. The differential was so great between the two however, that it made the expatriate track appear grossly unfair. Like the information network referred to earlier, this also was reflective of the broader economic relationship between America and Jamaica; between a First World country and a Third World country. These problematic imbalances in relationship continue to play themselves out today in multiple ways in a number of Third World countries.

I was the first Jamaican to replace an expatriate plant manager in the local subsidiary. Before the expatriate departed, the company needed to convince itself that a local replacement was up to snuff. I was required to spend a month between the corporate offices in New York and the company's largest manufacturing facility in New Jersey. Before joining the company I had worked for the largest regional manufacturer of consumer goods as plant manager. It was quite a useful coincidence that I had manufactured products for my new employer under contract while with my old company. On account of this I detected that the company had far less concern about my knowledge of manufacturing operations than it had about my willingness and ability "to fit in". For me this was a most revealing discovery since never before did I ever have to give special consideration to whether I made other people comfortable or uncomfortable in any private or professional setting.

I recall being taken to lunch at a very upscale restaurant in Manhattan by a manufacturing Vice President. I sensed that he was clearly observing my table manners. The irony was that, as far as I was concerned, his table manners were indeed very questionable, based on my familiarity with typical English table manners. This is an experience I always recall with much hilarity. I had come full circle and was now ready to return to Jamaica as an acceptable replacement for my expatriate boss.

It is my experience that American multi-national companies are reluctant to replace their senior expatriate managers in local subsidiaries with natives. The question of equivalence of qualifications is never the entire reason for this. An overriding concern of head office is always the question of trust and whether the native will *fit in*. This latter concern is as critical as any other. It is also the one requirement that offers the company the greatest flexibility to hire or not hire native candidates or to dump existing native employees. The definition of the term is as difficult to nail down as jelly because in the final analysis it is absolutely subjective. There is some irony here, because no one appears too concerned whether the expatriate may or may not fit into the local culture or with the native subsidiary population. On occasion this neglect has been known to cause serious problems.

The matter of *trust* is not too dissimilar to that of *fitting in*. The concern here is whether the native is likely to make things difficult for the company in his native country should disagreements arise between the native and the company. Natives hired at senior levels in the subsidiary, more often than not, are very well connected locally. Such connections may be used for good or ill. In Third World countries the ill side of the equation can be very disruptive as my own experience as an expatriate myself will show.

Jamaica, like any third world country at the time, was quite deferential to its multi-national guests. The major bauxite companies operating in Jamaica tilted the scale heavily in this direction, for example. Vast deposits of bauxite ore, the key ingredient in producing aluminum, were discovered in Jamaica in 1952. The subsequent mining and conversion of bauxite into aluminum quickly made the island a world class player in the supply of the mineral. The industry accounted for over 50% of the country's foreign exchange earnings as well as the employment of a critically significant portion of the island's workforce. One result of the deference shown to multinationals was that although my company's business footprint in the island was relatively small, its influence was not. It was very clear that the local subsidiary, in addition to sharing the halo of the bauxite companies, was able to leverage the international stature of the parent company to good advantage.

We had easy access to the government, to the press, to banks and, naturally, to the American embassy as well as to the embassies of other countries. There was never a problem obtaining work permits, for example, and we were always able to learn earlier than most when there was going to be a devaluation of the local currency or a change in the rules governing the issuing of import licenses. The ability to access these types of information offered critical advantages that many larger local companies never enjoyed. These types of contacts created a valuable, reliable network for gathering critical business, economic and political data and allowed the local subsidiary to make a good impression with head office.

We had two or three business reviews with corporate personnel each year. These reviews were intensely focused events covering every operating function of the company. They required a degree of thoroughness in preparation that always amazed my local business contemporaries; especially since reviews included the company grounds, offices and plant complex. Housekeeping was of critical importance to our corporate visitors. The demands of these reviews over time probably exceed the rigors of working for an MBA degree.

There were sometimes unusually surprising occurrences during some of these reviews. On one occasion a young corporate VP expressed disgust that we took as much as fifteen days to get products from Jamaica to Trinidad. The more he talked about what he saw as an indefensible failing the more amazed local management became. He asked how many miles separated Trinidad from Jamaica. He was told Trinidad was about fifteen hundred miles away and that we made four stops in between. "Then explain," he demanded with visible disgust, "why I can ship products in a few days from New Jersey to California which is twice the distance?" He was unaware that Jamaica and Trinidad were separated by fifteen hundred miles of the Caribbean Sea. This demonstrated a surprising degree of ignorance that I found incredible. Comic relief it certainly was not.

Locally, the reputation of the company as an exceptionally well run business added great value to the personal management portfolio of native executives. This fact sometimes created retention and salary scale problems for the local subsidiary. To my mind this problem is a better problem to have than its alternative. It once became necessary for me to use this leverage when the company kept delaying a planned promotion based on the departure of the expatriate manufacturing director.

When the time line for the director's departure was not met I was quite concerned. It would not have been unusual for this time line to be extended indefinitely given the known preference to have expatriates occupy positions at this level. As a precaution against this very possibility I had requested and received written confirmation of the time line. It was one of the conditions to which the company had to agree before I in turn agreed to accept their job offer. I was very much aware that similar commitments had been made by word of mouth to previous native executives but were never honored.

Very early in my career I came to realize that when faced with this type of problem there are really only three responsible options. One option is to be stoic and simply accept that there is nothing you can do but accept the problem and live with it. Another is to take positive action to address the problem, confident in the expectation that you will prevail. The final option is to leave the company. I call this options process the

'Jamaica Rule' or the 'J' rule. This rule would come to my rescue a number of times as I advanced in the company.

As a native executive of such a high profile company I was fairly well known in local business circles. All that was necessary was for me to drop the word that I was on the job market. In short order the word got back to the company. The general manager met with me. He never mentioned what triggered this meeting but the timing could not have been a coincidence. His hands were tied, he said. It was not his decision but New York's. However, in good faith, New York had authorized an interim salary adjustment and confirmed that the expatriate would definitely leave within three months. In my entire time with the company this adjustment was the largest percentage adjustment I ever received. True to its word, the company transferred the expatriate as promised. Shortly after I took the position the company reorganized its Caribbean operations as the Caribbean Group. The new organization was run out of Jamaica. Jamaica was now responsible for operations throughout the English speaking Caribbean. This included Trinidad, Guyana, Barbados and Dominica. I was now the first native Regional Manufacturing Manager. The 'J' rule had proved its worth.

During this period the local subsidiary was changing fairly rapidly. The positions of Marketing Manager and Financial Controller were soon taken over by Jamaicans working under an English General Manager. The former Jamaican General Manager had been transferred to head office and would shortly be promoted to the position of Vice President. In the eyes of the entire Jamaican management team this was not just good for the former GM but enhanced the image of the company locally. His advancement also made us contemplate possibilities we never would have contemplated before.

Even as the company was changing, significant changes were also occurring in Jamaica as well as throughout the rest of the Caribbean.

The Times They Are A-Changin'

It is perhaps useful to have a brief overview of some significant cultural and political shifts in Jamaica with 1962, when Independence was achieved, as the vantage point from which to observe these changes as pre- and post-Independence. I will limit my observations to the period between 1954, the beginning of my teenage years, and 1978 when I left Jamaica for Canada with my family. While referenced events in many ways undoubtedly reflect specific knowledge gained from my presence and schooling in Jamaica, I am totally responsible for the observations I make about these events. Like many who have written about this period, I obviously lived through these years as well. Despite this commonality, however, I may view them somewhat differently.

Prior to independence in 1962, social life in Jamaica mirrored that of our British rulers. Color and class were critically aligned and significant factors. Their impact on the daily lives of Jamaicans was very clear to me. Imagine a color chart with colors going from white at the top through modulated shades of white darkening to black at the base. The closer to white the color the higher one was in the class hierarchy. Since the vast majority of Jamaicans was black their color secured their place in the huge underclass in Jamaican society. Even as a teenager this fact was plainly visible to me. As indicated earlier, like many Jamaicans, I carry some of the genes of the traditional upper class. While this may have been helpful to some extent, it was certainly not enough to make my family a part of the upper class even in a peripheral way. Shades mattered.

My parents rented the house in which we lived. No one in my family owned a car. My father worked as a bar captain in any hotel in which he found employment. My mother worked at home as a seamstress. I would sometimes have to take my father supper while he was on the job and remember that I could not enter the hotel in which he worked through the front entrance. I do not recall seeing a black guest in any of the hotels in which my father worked during my teenage years. Banks, for example, perhaps the most visibly imposing of all private institutions then, were particularly typical of how the color scale worked. It would be years before I would see people who looked like me managing any of these institutions.

It is interesting to observe how the transition occurred. At first, all managers were white or as close to white as possible and, as in the general society, position in hierarchy reflected the country's color scale described earlier. By the late 50's and early 60's the color scale began to disintegrate at an accelerating pace. The sequence and gradation of its decline are interesting. The Chinese led the advance, followed by the Indians. The darker skinned Jamaicans of visibly African descent were generally the last. Naturally, there were exceptions but these do not invalidate the general truth of my observation.

At the same time the civil service, the police, the army, the nursing and teaching professions reflected the country's population mix much more equitably. Even so, the very top positions in both the police force and the army were held by persons with the least visible pigmentation. Politics by this time was beginning to respond to the obvious needs of the Jamaican masses. In this case it must be understood that Jamaica, prior to Independence, was a Crown Colony under the rule of the British, represented on the ground by a British Governor General with executive powers.

While labor unions were the womb of the indigenous political movement these unions were essentially run by upper class Jamaicans. It is no accident that these unions gave birth to Jamaica's two major political parties, The People's National Party (PNP) and The Jamaica Labor Party (JLP), or that the first Chief Minister and first Prime Minister had direct links with these unions. In this cauldron of social and political change, Jamaicans like me realized that the changes we were witnessing were pregnant with the promise of a better life for an increasing number of us. It was also very clear to us that education was the critical key to capitalizing on this promise.

Each of my parents had come to their marriage with two children from earlier relationships. This was not unusual in Jamaica then and not too unusual today. The marriage produced four additional children. I am the fifth of these eight children. I never understood the complexity of this family amalgam until I was almost out of my teens. The reason is that nothing in the behavior of my parents, my siblings or the people around me as much as hinted at it. My parents, especially my mother, were deeply committed to making sure all of us received an education. This would not be easy. Elementary schooling was free but schooling beyond this level was costly. We all completed elementary school but only my eldest brother, the brother who followed him, myself, the younger of two sisters and youngest brother were able to proceed beyond the elementary level with our schooling.

My eldest and youngest brothers completed technical school, the one locally, the other in America. The brother who followed the eldest brother was the first to attend university and graduated from McGill University in Canada, eventually becoming a school principal in Montreal. My younger sister graduated nursing school in England. Looking back, it is almost unimaginable that my parents managed to help so many of us obtain this much education given their meager incomes. It is a living testament to their commitment and faith as well as to the beneficial effects of the changes that were taking place in Jamaica. My family's progress is representative of the progress of hundreds of families throughout Jamaica during this period.

When the new flag of Jamaica was hoisted and the Union Jack of Britain was removed from flag poles in 1962, a new era had truly begun. Independence would bring about significant changes in the country at both the national and personal levels. The national motto of Jamaica, **"Out of Many One people"**, reflects the multi-racial origins of its population. In large measure, it also explains very powerfully why Jamaica does not have hyphenated Jamaicans. No Jamaican of African, Chinese, Indian, Syrian or Israeli origin ever identifies himself by his heritage followed by a hyphen and the name of our country. We all consider ourselves, regardless of our heritage, simply Jamaicans. This fact creates a substantial cultural bridge we all cross routinely without fear or concern that our heritage will be defiled, diminished or lost.

This does not mean that there is not a number of Jamaicans of each cultural group that may be identified over generations as purposely marrying within their cultural group and class. Indeed, there have been a few brief episodes of backlash against these groups in the not so recent past. In my opinion, such backlash resulted less from revulsion at intentional cultural isolationism than from what some among the masses saw as economic exploitation. This sentiment arises from the fact that Jamaicans of Chinese, Indian and Middle Eastern origins, for example, have traditionally controlled much of the retail trade in Jamaica to an extent that is quite disproportionate to their numbers.

Generally speaking then, it is fair to say that the impact of race and class in Jamaica has gradually diminished to a point where it is of significantly less concern to the vast majority of Jamaicans. It is now clear that the race and class issue has been largely replaced by the all but intractable issue of the *Haves and Have-nots*. This change in Jamaican society is not restricted to Jamaica but is visible throughout the Caribbean where, in some respects, the mix of cultures is not as diverse as it is in Jamaica. Not surprisingly, this offers much greater opportunity for polarization. Such polarization is visible in Guyana and Trinidad where the populations are composed of two significantly large groups, the one of Indian heritage and the other of African heritage. By and large these two predominant groups have not cohabited or inter-married to the extent that such groups do in Jamaica.

We cannot discuss the post Independence period without reference to the nature of politics after Independence. In this regard I will go directly to what is perhaps the most controversial period in recent Jamaican history. The JLP under the leadership of first, Sir Alexander Bustamante, then Sir Donald Sangster, Hugh Shearer, Edward Seaga and currently Bruce Golding, is basically a political party that is more closely aligned in philosophy and outlook with the Republican Party in America. The PNP whose leaders were Norman Manley, his son Michael Manley and more recently Percival Paterson and Portia Simpson, not surprisingly, is more closely aligned with the philosophy and outlook of the Democratic Party in America. These alignments appear to be more Machiavellian in nature than anything else. From time to time local conditions in Jamaica make these alignments ones of pure convenience more than of basic philosophy or outlook. Third World politicians constantly walk a tightrope in their relationships with First World countries, especially the United States. As one American politician is famous for pointing out, in the final analysis, *all politics is local.*

In Jamaican politics no political leader wants to be in America's bad books. Yet, this is exactly where Jamaica Prime Minister Michael Manley found himself during the early 1970's. I will ignore the years preceding the Michael Manley years because these years were, by and large, what I choose to call the vanilla years in Jamaican politics. Not that they were not important years but the truth is they did not, in any profoundly meaningful way, depart from the prevailing orthodoxy of newly independent countries which survived and later escaped from the British colonial system to claim independence.

Michael Manley is generally felt to be the most charismatic and flamboyant Jamaican politician of all. His mother was British and his father, the first Chief Minister of Jamaica, was of Irish and African descent, a Rhodes Scholar and internationally respected barrister in his own right. The younger Manley was a journalist, trade unionist, an intellectual, author of several books and, of course, Prime Minister of Jamaica. Both father and son completed their tertiary education in England. The younger Manley became Prime Minister in 1972.

It was immediately apparent that his intention was to take the country in a new and decidedly different direction. His thinking was essentially driven by his concerns over the gross social inequities that were pervasive in Jamaica at the time. By any measure he would have to be called a visionary. He is without a doubt one of the most remarkable figures in the post colonial period of Jamaica and the rest of the English speaking Caribbean. His influence continues to be felt today because of the outstanding role he played in the social, legislative and political life of the Caribbean and his advocacy of a New International Economic Order (NIEO). He was an unparalleled defender of the sovereignty of ex-colonial countries, was highly respected by such bodies as the Commonwealth of Nations, the Non-Aligned Movement and the African, Caribbean and Pacific Countries (ACPC). He was always in the vanguard of world statesmen who applied international pressure to dismantle apartheid and minority rule in southern Africa. Up to the time of his death in 1997, he was the Vice President of Socialist International.

His most transformative legacy is in the social and legislative reforms he implemented in Jamaica. These include a National Minimum Wage, Maternity Leave with Pay, the introduction of a Bauxite Levy, a National Literacy Program and the Status of Children Act which ended discrimination against children born out of wedlock. ("The Michael Manley Foundation": www.michael-manley.org). I recall very clearly, words from one of his most popular campaign songs in the Jamaican vernacular, *"No bastard no deh again, everyone lawful"* (translated freely: *there is no such thing as an illegitimate child*). This last piece of legislation changed the way people saw one another in Jamaica forever. I call it a piece of forever legislation. It was absolutely transformative in its impact. Jamaicans would never henceforth see any among us as less than another.

The bauxite levy, though purely economic in intent and effect, was almost as critical in consequence. It triggered serious backlash from the bauxite companies. Coupled with Manley's nationalism engendered push to have qualified Jamaicans participate in the management of these foreign companies, the levy was a bitter pill. In addition, Manley attempted to create a bauxite cartel like the oil cartel in the form of the International Bauxite Association or IBA.

It is noteworthy that of six or so local bauxite companies, five were American and one was Canadian. This exception made little or no difference in the extent to which pressure was applied by America against the Manley government. It did not help that Manley was seen as too friendly with Cuba's Fidel Castro and Tanzania's Julius Nyerere. Manley also preached the gospel of what he called *Democratic Socialism*. This added fuel to the fire of the ire America felt about his government. He was seen as a firebrand and communist in disguise on the verge of destabilizing the entire Caribbean region. This was much too intolerable a situation on America's doorstep for America to be willing to tolerate. It is a somewhat open secret, supported in principle by the *CIA Diary of Philip Agee*, that the CIA attempted to destabilize and sabotage the Manley government. It is the widely held view that Manley's defeat at the polls in 1980 was partly due to the involvement of the CIA on the ground in Jamaica, in support of the opposition JLP under the leadership of Edward Seaga, a Jamaican of Lebanese descent and a graduate of Harvard University.

Overall, it is fair to say that Manley is certainly among the most outstanding figures of the post-colonial era in the Caribbean. He is certainly among the most highly regarded internationally. The social reforms which Manley implemented were a watershed in the area of social mobility in Jamaica. I certainly feel that the Manley years presented immense opportunities for qualified Jamaicans to advance their economic lot. At the same time it presented severe challenges for the business community. Businesses now had to adjust to an awakened, awkward nationalism that, like the proverbial genie, once set free can never be returned to its bottle easily. I believe that my employment by the local subsidiary of one of the largest American multi-national companies reflected a truly directional change in how these companies, as well as large local companies, would see their human resources strategies going forward.

It is unforgettable that Manley, in response to the business community's deep concern and apprehension about his policies, told voluble, complaining business people that if they were as fearful as they seemed to be there were five flights a day to Miami so they did not have to remain in Jamaica; they were free to leave on any one of these flights. This triggered a firestorm of protest and certainly set in motion an exodus among the entrepreneurial class that would have long-lasting, unfavorable impact on the local economy and Jamaican society at large. Nothing Manley did to attempt to mitigate the effect of his intemperate words could lessen their impact. The law of unintended consequences is very unforgiving.

Never the less, no observant commentator can deny that Manley awakened in the average Jamaican an unshakable and profound belief that *his time had come* and that he had every right to expect equal opportunity at upward mobility in Jamaican society. In a sense, the exodus that was taking place, while initially quite disruptive in its effect, was in fact creating a wide array of opportunities for many Jamaicans. These Jamaicans would otherwise have had to wait much longer to move up the social and economic ladder. Society and culture, like nature, appear to abhor a vacuum. There is no doubt that a vacuum was being created by the rapid decline in the elite and entrepreneurial classes. This vacuum had to be filled. And it was.

Not unexpectedly, this process was somewhat dislocating at first. After all, regardless of what the newly upwardly mobile class of Jamaicans may have thought, education or knowledge on its own, while necessary, is seldom sufficient under circumstances such as the ones in question. Experience does matter. It would therefore be some time before this new class of Jamaicans would arrive at a place where not just they would be comfortable but where those in the population whom they served would cease making endless, unflattering comparisons between the level of competence of the "old guard" and the new. In my mind this was a trade off. Sometimes one learns to be a good, strong swimmer by being thrown into the deep end of the pool before being taught to swim formally.

By the mid 60's my parents had bought their own house. In 1967 my fiancée and I made the customary deposit on our own house which was promised to us in time for our wedding in June of 1968. This promise was never kept. After our wedding we moved into rented accommodations not far from my parents' house in one of the new, mass produced, middle class neighborhoods called Harbour View. This location was on the eastern side of Kingston Harbour no more than a quarter of a mile from the sea. Housing was becoming an issue of much significance as many started to move into the middle class. Entire subdivisions were being built and sold out in months. The period was the beginning of an extended real estate boom that would contribute significantly to a very large number of middle class Jamaicans moving into the once highly exclusive upper class. Our own house was handed over to us almost a year later than promised. By this time we were both in more senior positions in our companies.

We started our family in 1969 with the birth of our first son, Gordon (named for one of Jamaica's national heroes, George William Gordon).

My Father

My father, who had retired, ran a wholesale liquor business with my eldest brother who, by the late 60's, had started his own businesses. The wholesale liquor business was doing well. Late one Saturday afternoon as my wife and I were having dinner the telephone rang. The liquor store had been held up and my father had been shot. This incident traumatized our entire family. The senselessness of the crime was incomprehensible. He was rushed to the University of the West Indies Hospital where, to our chagrin, he had to lay on a gurney for several hours while hospital staff attempted to find an X-Ray technician. The attending Emergency Room physician confirmed that he could do nothing until he had X-Rays available.

Eventually, the technician was located playing dominoes in the university cafeteria when he should have been on the job. This was as shocking an experience of malfeasance as I have ever witnessed. I wrote a very strongly critical letter of complaint to the hospital but never had a response. My father survived two surgeries over the period of a week but the damage had been done and he succumbed a couple days afterwards. I was in despair. I could not get it out of my mind that but for the criminal negligence of a technician my father may have survived.

For over a year I was haunted by the incomprehensibility of the entire episode leading to my father's death.

It left me not merely wondering about the fragility of life but its purpose and the inexplicably horrid behavior of those upon whom the public had every right to depend. I soon started to recognize the significance of what had happened not only to my father but to me and my family. As survivors of this traumatic event, something in our own persons had also been murdered. My father's murder was indeed the early harbinger of a scourge of criminal activity that, in a few years, would begin to engulf the very fabric of Jamaican society. The gunman was never apprehended and the crime remains unsolved.

The loss of my father was made more distressing by the fact that I was only just beginning to have what I consider a balanced relationship with him. Up to the time of my marriage, my father appeared to be merely passively participatory in the lives of his children. His presence always loomed large on our horizon but only because he was the ultimate disciplinary threat. I cannot recall my father playing with me, hugging me or kissing me. There was always fearful respect but little if any intimacy in our relationship. Because of this I vowed that my relationship with my own children would be diametrically different. To my great joy I have managed to fulfill this vow.

Still, the presence of my wife and the arrival of our children appeared to change the troubling, glacial aspect of my father's personality. In fact, to my wife he was a demonstrably loving and actively caring person whom she easily called Dad. She loved him dearly and never fails to caution that I may be overly judgmental in my view of my father. In her opinion, in all probability my mother did discuss their children's plans and accomplishments with him privately. He chose not to vocalize his own sentiments to his children. He visited often and baby sat at the slightest opportunity. All in all, he seemed to love spending time with us and played with his grandchildren the way I wished he had played with me as a child. I was just beginning to see a much more attractive side to my father when he was violently taken from us.

The change in my father's behavior stimulated lengthy and frequent discussions with many acquaintances, friends and relatives. These discussions revealed that my father was not at all unique in his parental distance. In fact, it appears that my father's parenting style was typical of men of his generation: fathers worked to satisfy the family's economic needs, applied a heavy hand in the disciplining of the children but by and large remained on the periphery of the family's life. This realization not only allows me to add value to the contribution of my father to our family but enables me to forgive him for what I initially saw as a gross failing on his part as a father. I very much regret that he never lived long enough for me to discuss this very emotional issue with him.

A Burning Question

For the very first time I began to question my commitment to my country. Neither my wife nor I could shake a sense of foreboding and doom as we witnessed an ever increasing spate of criminal activity, including wanton rape and murder. People were now afraid and the police appeared incapable of controlling the situation. There certainly was no sign that the authorities could reverse the now visible trend. It was time to consider alternatives to remaining in a country to which I had returned in the stupor of patriotic fever and with the highest of expectations.

By this time both my wife and I had been promoted to senior management positions in our companies. Our combined incomes allowed us to purchase a new house in an upper class neighborhood overlooking the city of Kingston and Kingston harbor. In a manner of speaking, we had finally arrived. At night, when the view was most impressive, the city lay like an expansive, shimmering crescent of sparkling diamonds below us, belying the downward spiral in the quality of life in a community in which we had come to take and expect such great comfort. The fact that we were able to keep our old house which was now rented, added to our sense of optimism about our future in Jamaica. Accordingly, in spite of our growing unease with conditions in Jamaica we both thought things would eventually get better. We were convinced we could not live as well or as comfortably anywhere else. Even as departing friends said goodbye and pleaded with us to seriously consider leaving, we put up a brave front, convinced that, as my mother often said, *"This too shall pass."*

One very good friend in particular, marveled at the fact that while we were busy improving on our new house he was in the process of selling off his businesses and liquidating all his other assets in preparation for his own departure to Florida. He warned about what he saw as the inevitable impending disaster of the collapse of the national economy and the rapid rise of communism. He was not a fan of Michael Manley and he had credible contacts in the opposition party who were privy to sensitive and confidential government data which led him to the conclusions to which he had come. While I understood his decision to emigrate I could not support it. Frankly, I thought at the time that leaving was for the faint hearted and those whose commitment to our country was always questionable in the first place.

If the earlier five flights a day to Miami comment by Michael Manley triggered an exodus, exploding crime against ordinary citizens and an economy now under immense strain from rising oil prices only accelerated it. We witnessed the speedy departure of many more friends and acquaintances to Vancouver, Toronto, New York, Atlanta and Miami. Many of them left without warning and it appeared they were cautious to the point of near paranoia. Even those closest to them only came to know of their departure after the fact. This degree of caution was understandable in some ways. The scourge of gun crimes had become so frightening that in 1974 the Manley government created a Gun Court which granted special powers to the judiciary to try gun crimes *in camera* and without a jury. Then, in 1976, in anticipation of general elections and a further rise in gun violence, a national State of Emergency was declared.

To most Jamaicans this was cause for great alarm. But crime was not the only issue. In an attempt to staunch the flow of foreign exchange out of the country the government had implemented the strictest controls, limiting the amount of hard currency emigrants could take with them to $50.00 U.S. each. The penalties for violating these new, burdensome foreign exchange regulations were frightening, to say the least. Penalties included the confiscation of all the funds in question, fines of multiple times the confiscated amounts and the real possibility of time in prison. But Jamaicans are nothing if not ingenious.

Currency was being removed in all sorts of unbelievable ways: in hollowed out furniture, in car tires, in the linings of suitcases, in casts protecting false fractures, in the linings of clothing, between the pages of books and inside baked and canned goods. Funds that could not be removed in these ways were spent on valuable Jamaican goods like hand made mahogany furniture which would be shipped as personal effects but would quickly be sold at destinations abroad. It must be said however, that one of the strongest motivators for this rapidly accelerating exodus was the fear of parents for the safety of their children and the fear of husbands for the safety of their wives.

Eventually our discomfort with the deteriorating situation reached a critical point and we felt it no longer made sense to continue to swim against the tide. It was time to seriously contemplate our own departure. It became clear to me that everyone had his own threshold for departure and some of us had a much higher threshold than others. I indicated my concern to my company and alerted head office management in New York of my intention to leave Jamaica. The initial response from head office was to dangle the possibility that I could very well be the next General Manager for the subsidiary were I to remain in Jamaica. When I respectfully rejected this possibility I was subsequently offered an opportunity in the U.S. operations.

My reservations about living in America had not subsided and I politely suggested to the company that I would very much appreciate an opportunity in Canada instead. To its credit and my surprise the company offered me a position in our Canadian company in Toronto. So it was that in 1978 my family and I took up residence in Canada.

Essentially, we were starting our lives over without funds in a new country. There are those who view leaving Jamaica as the easier of the two options of staying or leaving. I do not think this to be the case. In many instances those who leave do give up very much, especially in terms of life style and personal relationships, both of which are of almost transcendental value to Jamaicans as a rule. Fortunately, the painfulness of this loss is often mitigated by the fact that in very many instances, when Jamaicans migrate to Canada or America, they usually have relatives or very good friends already living in the areas to which they go. This is not at all unusual among immigrant populations. Very often, however, while this may address the aspect of personal relationships it seldom addresses lifestyle issues. We have friends who left Jamaica as substantial, firmly entrenched members of upper class Jamaican society but fell to the very floor of the social hierarchy in North America. They had given up everything that guaranteed their comfortable life style on departing Jamaica. It would have been an easier choice for them to have remained.

When Jamaicans emigrate their concern is usually less about where they are going than about what they are leaving behind. In my own case this dilemma is best revealed in the two poems below: **The Land** and **Soldiers of Fortune**.

The Land

It rises in a thousand bosoms
'Tis a buxom full-chested land
Where palm trees set the rhythm
And the mindset calls the tune
Where the ordinary folk,
Sometimes the folk upon the hill,

Still talk of brer 'Nancy and brer Tukuma.
It is heartland
Where streams and rivers
Tumble through the countryside
In disjointed games of hide and seek
To pound and trickle from ledges
Then sally to the sea.
It is an old land
Of ways as old as morning's foggy fingers
That smother the plains
And clutch at the crutch of the hills.
The fog is tailored for the countryside
But the landscape changes
To pulse tomorrow's heartbeat
New tunes set to familiar rhythm
New breath drawn of familiar air.
Can we lose the old ways without losing?
The land! It lives for us despite ourselves.

Soldiers of Fortune

We are soldiers of fortune we
Who tramp a foreign soil
After mind and means pedigree
Ends commensurate with our toil.
Countless trips ensure a curious end
Pride and conscience are eclipsed
All save ourselves we comprehend.

Speak, do, desire, and feign love
For our ever shrinking world
The caged pristine turtle dove.
A scholarly lie, cheerless, cold.
Damnable, in the end we plead
With them and the many me
For pity's sake let me bleed.

Riding rough shod and naked
Over pedigree pointed years

We see them empty and vapid
Unworthy the salt of late tears
Crowned evidence full grey hair.
From unmanned to unmachined
We waited much too long to care.

Now in an instant the heart is dense
From living and loving and remembering
From wishing and grieving lost innocence
From delayed release from base brass ring.
Excusing we sell on the bleak black market
Enlightened we camouflage our ignorance
Adrift on the sophisticate's magic carpet.

Our new world whispers in our ear
'To live for me is to meet all tests
On an island world where all is near'.
All lands America's chastened forests
Wherein she plows forsooth to reap
Emasculating the intention of our dreams.
Beguiled, in the end we all must weep.

Deep the furrows in our world we see
Yet brittle and shallow our concern arise
Like seasonal allergies from which we flee
To dare dilute the dialogue to surmise
More often wonder why screams form
Fail to escape their cave of painful birth
Or grow in volume to move or to alarm.

Shall I invert Claude McKay
Uncertain of my own direction?
Shall I return before the end of day
When returning is resurrection?
Still I sold where I should not market
Scavenger at my now paltry carcass
Bewildered, falsified, odor temperate.

Harassed by self examination
I wonder at the price of gold
Will there ever be celebration
When for a pittance I am sold?
Yet my birthright remains secure
Though freely I put myself in bondage
Fair exchange is surely sad folklore.

There is no fortune in being soldiers
Fighting battles for others' fools gold
Across fields of burrows and corridors
Where we are bought and others sold
No fruit to reap from bogus harvest
Mirages in the desert of our dreams
In which we gather seeking rest.

There is a price above the vulgar gold.
Regardless history's uncertain hand
That reaches out to caution being bold,
A fearless rebellion stalks the land
And puppet masters lose control
As puppets sunder strings to stand
Upright, loose, free to flee or to patrol.

III. CANADA

Welcome To Canada

Welcome to Canada. This is the cheery greeting with which visitors and returning residents are welcomed on arrival in Canada. I always find this refreshingly friendly and comforting. It is as close as an immigration officer can come, I imagine, to giving one a hug.

Canada, like Jamaica, is a member of the British Commonwealth. This fact means that Jamaica and Canada share a common relationship with our former British colonial masters. It also means that many of our public institutions are, if not identical, almost so. In this regard the parliamentary and judiciary systems, the framework of schools and universities and the place of religion in society provide points of reference which engender a sense of comfort in immigrants from other Commonwealth countries. Of even greater significance is our common language. So my arrival in Canada, while somewhat disconcerting because of my penury, was far from uncomfortable. In any event I had three brothers already residing there. Two were in Toronto and the other was in Montreal. By this time the only members of my family remaining in Jamaica were my eldest sister and brother and my mother.

It is fascinating to contemplate why so many Jamaicans reside abroad. While the exodus on account of crime and economic concerns does tell a story, it can only be a part of a larger tale. My father, for example, made excursions to Cuba, Guyana and England in search of a better life but eventually concluded that Jamaica was where he ought to be. Many Jamaicans explored likewise and concluded similarly. Yet there is no doubt that an equally large number has concluded otherwise and has spent most of their lives, if not their entire adult lives, living abroad. I sometimes wonder whether the voyage from Africa to the Americas and the Caribbean during slavery left a genetic marker in our gene pool predisposing us to a desire to facilitate a Diaspora. It seems we are constantly escaping from a middle passage during which up to 30% of our forefathers perished. In a sense, Jamaica has degenerated into a sort of static middle passage from which many constantly attempt to flee. The following verse reflects the angst and confusion of abandoning a troubled ship but wishing it safe harbor.

My Country 'Tis for Thee

Could it be we are out of time?
Is triage permanent territory
Hostile to rhythm and rhyme?
Promise and hope now paltry
Fail to stem patricidal crime.
Sadness yields to the mourning
Insistent reality demands.
There is no trace of morning
As resolute, lonely evening stands
In the shambles of our declining.

Born fi dead not just sons and daughters
But the very soul of nineteen sixty two.
Lament the tale but confront our fathers.
Not so many but yet a remarkable few,
Complicit in the crafting of disasters.
It used to be the abyss loomed
Only now and maybe with regret
There is no abyss just the doomed.
Impostors, leaders made erect
Disheveled intentions never groomed.

In the fever of our shared pain,
Arrest the slippery vagabond courage,
Charge its ramparts with disdain,
Counter politics' poisoned porridge,
Map new routes, bypass numbing fear.
See gentle Taino, mystic Rasta man
Numerous patinas in between,
Spanish, English, Chinese, Indian.
To the vacuous merely Halloween
Not the helix of unique caravan.

What are the lessons learned?
Are there no more safe spaces?
The constituency of the concerned
Search for light in deep, dark places.
Ash remains where fires once burned.
History, always reliably unforgiving
Promises the future only just deserts.
The future, eternally unrevealing,
Indifferent even if signaling alerts,
Makes faith and hope demeaning.

Can a nation really, truly die?
Or does it survive in Diasporas
Constantly reflecting, wondering why
Its vanishing point like bold fedoras
Hints at the hidden as much what's awry?
Blinded by what in hope we are expecting,
We fail to see much remains the same
And grope and shuffle in the gloaming,
Our memory the patriot's white cane
Voices fade to fearful handy whispering.

Surely we contribute to our own demise.
Offsetting numerous great achievements
Savage garrison wars no longer need disguise
Their evil growing in boundless increments
Ensuring the powerful's birthright to reprise
Is there no cure for that which ails?

No secret escape paths we may secure?
All paths strewn with ten penny nails
For a crucifixion we must yet endure
When blind Justice drops us on her scales.

Despite the steep unending price
In the coin of hapless bondage paid
The long freed slaves must sacrifice
To lords and masters of a new raid.
No ransom, even innocence, will suffice.
All are hostaged, not a one is spared
A bruising on the field of rife confusion
Where advice solicited or not is feared.
So strong are hope and reason in reunion
Against destruction's agents unprepared.

My country 'tis for thee I mourn.
Though your landscape surely will endure
Your people the violent cannot suborn
With fearful silence and dreams impure
Leaving children diminished and forlorn.
Once refuge of the courteous and kind
No longer virtuous and in steep decline
Erstwhile exemplar of unity to mankind
E pluribus unum abandoned, lies supine
Like favorite fruit's clinging remnant rind.

I recall from long ago and in different note,
Some troubled poet in deep distress
And seeming endless pain, this prickly quote:
"Ah, what can ail thee, wretched wight,
Alone and palely loitering;
The sedge is wither'd from the lake,
And no birds sing."
His private pain and plaintive woeful cry
Bear sharp relevance to present place and time.
But nothing dulls the pain, no one answers why.

I remain grateful that my company was very considerate of my financial circumstances and agreed to provide a significant advance in order to facilitate my settling in on arrival in Toronto. One of my brothers loaned me a car so I could get around without difficulty. We rented a town house, registered our two sons in school and set about putting our lives back together again.

I worked as a production engineer in the subsidiary's Industrial Engineering Division. In the group were a Filipino and a French Canadian. I added some Caribbean color. The VP of Manufacturing to whom the Division reported was an Australian whom I shall call Proctor. We had met before at regional meetings when I was the Regional Manufacturing Manager for the Caribbean Group in Jamaica. He was very accommodating and invited me and my family to his home for a barbeque and to have our families meet. It was a very helpful gesture as my wife and I did learn a lot about life in Toronto from a perspective somewhat different from that of my brothers who lived there. Proctor and I were destined to work together again under much less accommodating circumstances many years later.

After a few months my wife felt that our domestic situation had become routine enough to allow her to seek employment. She attempted to parlay her Jamaica experience with the telephone company into an advantage and applied for a position with the Canadian equivalent of her old company in Jamaica. Simultaneously she sent applications to a number of other companies whose operations appeared compatible with her knowledge and experience. Three months went by without any positive responses. Just when she was about to despair she had an invitation to a job interview with the new Canadian Lottery Corporation. This company was being set up by an American corporation on behalf of the Ontario Lottery Commission. My wife's professional forte is customer service and training. She was a perfect fit for the position in question. In less than six months we were now both employed, our children were enrolled in school, our lives were beginning to return to normal and hope was again ascendant. We commenced planning to purchase a house and our own car.

In Jamaica, apart from the purchase of large items like a motor vehicle or real estate, we never considered using credit. In fact, the idea of credit was quite foreign to the average Jamaican at the time. We grew up seeing purchasing by cash as the only method for purchasing things. As a result, all the items we had purchased since arriving in Toronto were purchased with cash. As soon as I attempted to purchase our first car I realized that this was not a wise thing to have done.

When I had decided on the car I wanted and the dealer ran a credit check I was told that there was a problem. I could not be sold the vehicle because I had no record of credit in Canada. I proudly explained why this was the case, thinking that my explanation would have made a favorable impression. After all, I was debt free, both my wife and I were employed and neither of us had a criminal record. It was perverse in the extreme to realize that in order to obtain credit I had to have had credit. In order to address this incredible problem my wife and I had to make extraordinary efforts to credit certain household items prematurely. We credited a television set, beds, a dining table and other items to ensure our credit worthiness with the motor car dealership. This was a truly remarkable experience of immense value, with lasting implications for my understanding of how the typical economy works in the so-called First World.

Having addressed my pseudo-credit problem, we eventually purchased a car and later a family house in Scarborough. We filed immigration documents for my wife's mother who is hearing impaired and had lived with us in Jamaica since our marriage. She became a landed Canadian immigrant shortly thereafter.

Canada is a remarkable country, especially in respect of the elderly and the young. Our surprise bordered on shock when we learned that we were eligible for "milk money" for our children. The health care system was also astonishing as were the remarkable cleanliness of the city and the presence of innumerable public parks and bike trails. It was patently obvious that the country cared about the welfare of its citizens. Sure, taxes were noticeably higher than was expected but in return the public received services in number and quality that made it a very fair exchange.

Our first winter in Toronto was instructive and formative. No matter how plentiful the snow on the ground overnight, by the time we were ready to drive to work in the morning the streets were all clear of snow and traffic moved with little inconvenience. The winters were long, very cold but bearable because of how both the residents and municipalities dealt with winter. It was not a wrathful imposition of nature but one regular, passing aspect of it. There were things to do and places to see in winter all over the city and province. The children treated winter as a kind of adventure. I recall their first encounter with snow. They dressed appropriately for it, skated on it, ate it, frolicked in it, demanded we take photographs of them in it and play with them in it. Their behavior told us that at five and nine they had very quickly and painlessly made the necessary transition from Jamaica to Canada.

I was somewhat ambivalent about the fun aspects of Canadian winter, mostly because of its duration. Winter in Toronto lasts roughly six to seven months and longer in other neighboring places. Inevitably, I would remember the weather in Jamaica with yearning the longer winter lasted in Toronto. I recall remarking to my wife quite excitedly one early morning in May, that I could hear the twitter of birds outside our bedroom windows and see tiny buds on the naked trees in our yard, even as the strong morning sunlight shimmered on the residue of the previous night's snowfall. My wife reminded me that this was not unusual at that time of year in Toronto and confessed that she had never heard me exult similarly about the birds and trees when we lived in Jamaica. This was quite a revelation of the stark truth that you seldom appreciate what you have until you lose it. After all, nearly every day in Jamaica is like a spring day in Toronto. This is so common a reality that Jamaicans generally take it for granted.

The First Energy War

Shortly after I joined the Canadian subsidiary the oil cartel implemented the infamous and destabilizing oil embargo. This had an immediate and disruptive effect on the entire company as well as North America at large. The effect of the embargo was not all bad. In the case of the company specifically, we became much more technically innovative and more committed to effective worldwide communication, especially of our response to the impact of the embargo. Energy conservation became a universal mantra and incentives were developed and publicized throughout the company to ensure profit protection, operating integrity and future growth in spite of, and perhaps as much because of, the oil embargo. Employees were encouraged to car pool, overtime in the plants was curtailed significantly and travel on company business was planned and coordinated to a level of detail unseen before.

I remember that the lights in my office were controlled to respond automatically to my presence in the room. When I left the space the lights went out. When I returned to the space the lights came on. It was an impressive demonstration of purpose and will. All around us innovative work was being done in a most impressive cross functional manner on ways to be more energy efficient. The ingenuity of my company and North America in general made a deep and lasting impression.

Ironically, it is the lasting impact of the purposefully innovative, combined corporate, provincial and national response to the oil embargo which makes me feel almost indifferent to the ongoing plight of the continent as it faces, once again, a self induced energy crisis. The continent chose indulgence over long term conservation. It chose short term convenience over the temporary inconvenience of discomfort and sacrifice. Small, energy efficient cars came into vogue, individual citizens as well as corporations and states actively conserved.

The oil cartel undoubtedly realized the potential long term catastrophe this state of affairs portended for their own abilities to gouge consumers and did what any self respecting monopoly would do: it played a game of yo-yo with oil prices. We played along with them in this game and ended up where we are today. Small wonder many pooh-pooh the scientifically verifiable potential for environmental disaster due to our profligacy with energy. It is noteworthy that Brazil, certainly a Third World country at the time, understood the game and responded quite differently. Because of the tough decisions made in response to the energy crisis, Brazil is now energy self sufficient and invulnerable to the price manipulations of the oil cartel.

Personnel Dilemmas & the Passing of a Brother

Proctor, the VP of Manufacturing, was being transferred to New England to be in charge of a new medical supplies related business the company had acquired. He had to be replaced. After a few months the company announced that the VP of Manufacturing in the Philippines subsidiary was being transferred to the Canadian operations. His profile was circulated and it revealed that he had been in the Philippines for seventeen years. He was American and had married a native woman. The minute I saw his profile I concluded that the company would have great difficulty relocating him.

After seventeen years in a place like the Philippines he had gone native. He had acquired all the trappings of wealth that any Third World country would afford a smart, white expatriate. He had a palatial residence in Manila, maids, gardeners, security guards, a chauffeur and, of course, a company car. He even had become a friend of Ferdinand Marcos with whom he played golf. When company big wigs visited he was able to get them onto Marcos' yacht. The company saw this relationship as invaluable. Naively the company never understood that it would never be possible to relocate this executive. The company could not afford it. Neither could the expatriate executive.

The Philippine VP eventually arrived in Toronto on what was a normal introductory, routine tour of the operations. I remarked to my colleagues that it was interesting that he never brought his wife. They did not see this as a problem. This was understandable as most of them were not married plus none had been as exposed to the rules and etiquette of international transfers as I was. He remained for about two weeks and returned to the Philippines, supposedly to tie up loose ends for his move to Canada. He returned again after about a month, again without his wife. I was now certain that he had no intention whatever of moving to Canada. What was surprising to me was that Proctor had left for his new assignment and he officially took over Proctor's vacated position. He never looked for a house but remained in the Royal York Hotel not far from the offices and plant. And his wife never arrived.

After about three months he met with all of his managers and staff to confirm what I had surmised all along. Rather than allowing us to learn of his decision second hand he wanted us to know from him directly that he would not be staying in Canada and, in fact, would be leaving the company altogether. We learned that he returned to the Philippines, took up an equivalent job with the largest native owned competitor to the company in the Philippines.

In late 1980 I was invited to our corporate offices in New York to discuss the possibility of taking a position in East Africa. After a number of interesting, eye-opening interviews I accepted the position of Technical Director for the company's operations in East Africa. Although it was the company's intention that I leave for Kenya by year-end, issues with obtaining my work permit delayed my departure. Regrettably, in December I learned that my older brother in Montreal was seriously ill. He had kept his illness a secret for an entire year, forbidding his wife to tell any of us about it. He was afflicted with Lymphoma and by this time the doctors had indicated that, but for a miracle, they did not expect that he would survive. My two brothers who lived in Toronto as I did, accompanied me to Montreal every week-end to visit with him. In spite of what the doctors had indicated I could not bring myself to believe that he would die. He was often visibly weak but otherwise appeared healthy.

It was very difficult to come to grips with his condition because my brother had been an outstanding athlete who had represented Jamaica internationally. I asked him to allow me to accompany him into the doctor's office on one of his visits. By this time I had done some research into the disease and its possible treatments. *Interferon* was then a new and potentially effective intervention drug and I wondered if it had been included in his treatment regime. I was informed that it had been, as a last resort. The doctors felt that the evidence did not yet exist to justify its routine use in the case of my brother's illness. I was despondent. I had hoped that this might have provided one last chance of slowing down, if not reversing, the infection's assault. My brother, Guilford, died in January of 1981. He was only a few months away from his 48th birthday. This was my second experience with death at close range. The second time was even more devastating. It is terrible when a parent dies. The death of a relatively young sibling is horrifying. My work permit issues were resolved in late January and my family and I left for Nairobi, Kenya.

I am aware of very few regrets in my life. The passing of my brother gave rise to two of these: I never realized until after his death that my brother, in fact, had been my role model all along; his untimely death robbed me of the chance to tell him so. I considered my brother's death a second alarm alerting me to the need to come to grips with the fleeting opportunity of life and the harsh finality of death. I continue to search for questions as much as I search for answers.

Searching

We worry at our idiosyncrasies
As well as those of others
At what our bodies look like
What we wish they could be.
In vain we would be some other.

Why dare wish the impossible
So diminish ourselves
To be less than we are, we were, could be?
We move away from what we are
Though beyond is the increment to seek.

Beyond ourselves we find
That being we don't actively look for
The one who finds uncertainty certain
Ignorance a frightful, great calamity
Knowledge but incomplete escape.

Does imagination fail us
Or do we shrink from what we see?
The strange, the mysterious, the unexpected?
Where do we turn for peace and comfort?
Not to ourselves but to some imagined other.

All possible worlds may in fact exist
In parallel with one another
Leaking from time to time
One into the other
And our presence does not matter.

Could this explain vain or real imaginings?
Ghosts and goblins? Genius?
Hopes and dreams? The mysterious?
Knowing that we do not know?
Awareness of some other?

The questions come and do not leave.
There is no single, simple answer
As we stumble in our maze of doubt
Worthless map in trembling hands
Deficient eyes seeing only shadows.

Are we lost in a place we've found
Or have we found a lost place?
Still the questions do not leave
Still the answers do not come.
Are they perhaps one and the same?

Questions and answers, answers and questions: they are the devices we use in our attempts to make sense of the inexplicable. Regardless of whether we ask or answer we are always in transition between confusion and understanding.

Transition

Mind again in spate
A chaste thought
A halting step.
Already today is done
Perhaps tomorrow.
Cremate me in life
Catharsis. Peace.

Life is not hope or love
Days or nights
Or a situation.
Greater than the sum of its parts
Much more than a mystery.
Life and death
Is there a difference?

In life I know nothing of death
In death I know nothing of life
Yet think of both in one.
Perchance both are one.
Hold me in both
As you would in one
And judge me.

I grow old
Not fat or thin, short or tall
Just old.
I know nothing
Not this place or that thing
Not you
And you do not know me.

The days are spent
The years
I am old and nothing
Still I am
And should not need to voice my being
Should not need.
Should not need.

Would a sojourn in Africa help put my life and life in general into meaningful perspective?

IV. KENYA, AFRICA EAST

Back to Africa

When I moved to the city as a boy in Jamaica, there was already a movement called the *Back to Africa Movement*. The movement was the early 1900's brain-child of the Hon. Marcus Josiah Garvey, Jamaica's first National Hero. The movement encourages all Black people everywhere to think of Africa as their natural home and to strive to return there as the ultimate escape from, and bulwark against, racism and discrimination. The idea is central to the philosophy of the indigenous Rastafarian movement. Naturally, when many of my Jamaican friends heard that I was going to Africa, it was cause for much excitement and an avalanche of questions.

In a sense many of my friends considered my assignment to Africa as a return to the homeland and not a simple work assignment. In other words, I was suddenly, and not without some divine intent, the embodiment and representative of the Diaspora returning to its roots. My wife and I did not share this delusion. The truth is that many Jamaicans had already been to Africa as physicians, nurses, engineers and lawyers and for the simplest of reasons – to help where they could. In fact, a Jamaican barrister, Dudley Thompson, himself a Rhodes Scholar and Queen's Counsel, was among the outstanding team of lawyers, mainly English and Indian, who represented Jomo Kenyatta (subsequently Kenya's first

President) during his trial by the British as an accused Mau Mau activist in 1952.

On our arrival in Kenya one of the very first persons to whom we were introduced was a Jamaican pediatrician, Colin Forbes. Colin was among the most highly respected physicians in Nairobi and was the doctor of choice for all the expatriates' children. Colin's story is interesting. He came to Kenya with his Canadian wife after graduating from McGill University's medical school in Canada, fell deeply in love with Kenya and Africa and simply remained. For three months every year he devoted his time at no charge in neighboring African countries to treat sick children. There was also a number of other Jamaicans there, all of whom came to Kenya from England. None of these Jamaicans had arrived in Kenya as supporters of the *Back to Africa Movement*. They were all making their own way on the merits of whatever skills they brought to the continent.

In an ignorant, quirky sort of way, my company was unintentionally playing into a similarly questionable view of the significance of the psychology of my returning to my African roots. At one stage during my interviews at our corporate offices in New York, I was told that one of the reasons I was considered among the most favorable candidates for the assignment in East Africa was because the company thought that as a black person from the Caribbean the natives would find me more easily acceptable culturally. In other words, I could mend my fractured heritage to the company's advantage.

The General Manager in Kenya was Guyanese of Portuguese descent. His complexion was high on the color scale mentioned earlier. There is no doubt that his place in the color-class hierarchy in Guyana was quite influential in his having been the General Manager there prior to being moved to East Africa. There was no doubt as well that he was a smart man. There was serious doubt, however, that he was the most qualified for the position he occupied were we to remove the color continuum aspect of qualification. The plant manager of the Guyana subsidiary was lower on the color scale but had a college education, read voraciously and appeared much more qualified but for his disadvantage in the one critical respect of color. The same observation could be made of the marketing manager who was also of Portuguese descent. Once again shade mattered. It was evident to me that the plant manager understood his disadvantage and was permanently and visibly angered by it. As a result he was seen by all, even those in far removed head office, as a misfit.

I was told that the Kenya General Manager treated the native workforce with very little to no respect. In Kenya in the 1980's this had the potential to cause the company great difficulty, especially in regard to the plant operations where there was a unionized workforce. The company felt there was a real possibility that industrial action would eventually be taken to shut down the factory. Frankly, the company thought that, as a black Jamaican, I would be able to right the ship in terms of how the native workforce would likely view me and, by transference, the company. As I would soon learn, this was a terribly flawed assumption.

As is customary, the company arranged for the packaging, storage and subsequent shipping of our personal and household effects and paid for a property management company to oversee the maintenance and leasing of our house in Toronto. My mother-in-law accompanied us to Kenya at the company's expense as a dependent of mine. It would take three months for our household effects to arrive in Nairobi. In the interim we were housed in the New Stanley Hotel, the old hangout of many famous writers, including Ernest Hemingway who was still lionized there, as impressive pieces of memorabilia in the hotel bar witnessed. The hotel was too close to the street, making it difficult to sleep at night, so we relocated to the Intercontinental Hotel. I started my assignment while my wife arranged for our two sons to be enrolled in the American International School. It was not long until the company's worst concerns about the industrial relations climate in the subsidiary were confirmed.

Owing to the time it took for the company to obtain my work permit, the person I succeeded on the job had left the subsidiary several weeks earlier. As a result the GM met directly with the native Plant Manager each morning to review plant performance and problems. I sat in on this meeting for a couple days, basically as an observer. The gross disrespect shown by the GM in these meetings was appalling. During one discussion he told the Plant Manager in no uncertain terms, and with profanities for emphasis, that he was worthless and that no Kenyan, not even his great grandchildren would be able to learn to operate anything let alone a complicated factory. I was embarrassed. More accurately, the GM's behavior was offensive to me. One can only imagine what it must have meant to the native Plant Manager.

This type of undignified, crass, disrespectful behavior was totally at odds with the stated policies of the company. Every manager in the company should have been aware of this. I decided that I would not allow the Plant Manager to endure another such insult and raised the issue of his behavior with the General Manager. His response did not surprise me. His view was that I did not know *these people* and that the manner in which he dealt with them was the only way to get things done. I refuted this weak, self serving defense and referred him to the company's policies. Moreover, it was obvious that his reprehensible behavior was itself self defeating. It did not bring about the results he claimed to be seeking. I indicated that if he were not prepared to change his behavior in keeping with the company's policies I would cease allowing the Plant Manager to meet with him. If he insisted in continuing his meeting practice I was prepared to inform head office that it was impossible to work with him. Instead, I would meet with him directly, as necessary, to review operations. Not surprisingly, he quickly agreed to this new arrangement. Clearly, he was not prepared to change his behavior. Neither was I willing to tolerate it.

In the meantime my wife had started to look for a house for our family. We soon discovered that this was not a simple proposition. A few years earlier, Kenya's infamous Ugandan neighbor, Idi Amin, had forced the majority of the Asian population of Uganda as well as masses of native Ugandans to flee Uganda. Kenya, and Nairobi in particular, became the place of choice for refuge for a large number of these displaced Asians. One of the consequences of this influx of Asians into Nairobi was that houses for rent were remarkably scarce even before the time we arrived. Available housing, such as it was, was far below the standard we would consider acceptable. Even worse, the cost of what was available was prohibitive given what the company had indicated as my housing allowance.

We were now faced with a dilemma made worse by the fact that, by North American standards, even the GM of the subsidiary lived in what we considered substandard accommodations. One expatriate manager, in order to find accommodations within his allowance, lived more than twenty miles from the subsidiary. Even so, he was obliged to store some of his household effects in an outbuilding. It also meant that his daily commute was over forty miles and nearly three hours. Needless to say, the operating cost for his company vehicle was astonishingly exorbitant. My wife and I were in agreement on a cardinal rule: on no account would we, as expatriates, live in a manner below the standard we had enjoyed in Jamaica. The challenge would now be on two fronts: the first, to find acceptable accommodation; the second, to get the company to adjust our housing allowance in keeping with conditions no one had anticipated.

Meanwhile, to say I was busy at the plant is an understatement. Among the major operational issues were housekeeping, standard operating procedures, equipment utilization and efficiencies, maintenance, training of personnel and succession planning. Excessively long hours at the office became the rule rather than the exception. This meant, unfortunately, that my wife had very little help from me in house hunting or much else for that matter. This state of affairs, it must be admitted, is not unusual during the first several months after moving to a new assignment, especially in a location like Africa.

I recall the first visit of my corporate boss, the VP of Manufacturing for Africa and India. His visit lasted nearly a week, partly because he too was new at his job and had not been to Africa before. On our first tour of the plant and site he compiled a list of over a hundred items that was in need of urgent attention: from painting, to replacing missing windows and machine guards, to improving sanitation in the cafeteria. Like Africa generally, this presented quite a challenge. I prioritized the list and created a timeline for addressing the items on this basis. The timeline stretched over several months. Housekeeping and maintenance are equal opportunity failings in nearly all Third World countries but more so, in my estimation, in Africa. This is dramatized vividly by observing how even wealthy natives treat their very expensive cars, many of which are traditionally Mercedes Benz models. Damaged or malfunctioning vehicles are seldom repaired and are driven until they cannot function at all.

At home in the Intercontinental Hotel, my wife was pulling out her hair trying to find a house. In a few weeks our furniture would be arriving and there was no indication that we would find satisfactory accommodations. I communicated my concern to the local GM. He understood the situation and was generally sympathetic. I hinted that in all likelihood my housing allowance would prove to be inadequate and would have to be increased significantly. He expressed deep reservations about this possibility. I in turn indicated that I would not move out of the hotel until satisfactory accommodations were found. At this point I was beginning to refer to my "J" rule in my own mind. Accordingly, my wife and I decided on the process by which we would address the entire housing issue. She would see at least three to five houses a day; list them along with their critical positive and negative attributes and the cost of rental. I agreed with my wife that I would try to get home in daylight so I could visit the houses with the highest potential, even if these were only remotely likely to be acceptable.

In order to avoid controversy, we created a list of the factors which would qualify a house as satisfactory or adequate. The list is repeated here for emphasis and to demonstrate the fact that no unreasonable or outrageous demands were being made of the company. The list, not surprisingly, was influenced by our knowledge of what was actually available.

Satisfactory housing should:

- be reasonably secure
- be located at a reasonable distance from the plant, say no more than 9 to 12 miles
- accommodate eight rooms of Canadian size furniture and other personal belongings which the company, at its own expense, was shipping to Nairobi
- be comparable, within reason, to accommodation provided expatriate executives of similar companies and status
- have at least one four piece bathroom and one powder room
- have a telephone or allow easy access to one
- be clean, well maintained and adequately supplied with water
- have a reliably functioning sewage system

On this basis, we documented twenty-seven of about forty houses that we saw. We determined that four of the number qualified as satisfactory. The average rental being asked would require that my housing allowance be doubled to about $1,200.00 U.S. per month. If my recollection is correct, the exchange rate at the time was around eight Kenya Shillings to one USD. The initial allowance had seemed more than adequate at the time my compensation package had been agreed. After all, my house in Toronto would be rented at the time for about the equivalent of $600.00 U.S. per month. In less than a month our container of household effects would be arriving at the port in Mombasa for shipment over land to Nairobi. I alerted head office to the urgency of the situation. Coincidentally, just before the arrival of the container the subsidiary management would be attending a business review in Harare, Zimbabwe, at which the corporate VP for Africa and India would be present. Time was set aside for a sidebar review of the entire housing issue with the local GM, the VP and me. It was March of 1981. Zimbabwe, formerly Rhodesia, had secured its Independence the previous year.

On arrival at the airport in Harare, formerly Salisbury, I was surprised to see that the immigration documents still said Salisbury and Rhodesia. Worse, there were questions on the entry forms that, in my estimation, hinted at the apartheid practices of just a year earlier. One such question asked that I list my race. There were two white expatriates traveling with me. They quickly suspected that I may be annoyed by the question and were concerned that I might let my annoyance be known. They suggested that I not make an issue of the matter. I did not. I simply indicated *Human* in response to the question of my race. To the credit of the white Zimbabwean immigration official he appeared to ignore my testy, documented response.

The business review took place in the renowned, world class Meikles Hotel. We also had suites at the hotel. It is an impressive hotel with service to match. On the final day of the three day revue we had our sidebar housing summit. All the documentation I had prepared was in the hands of all parties. It should be noted that the corporate VP was the former Jamaican GM who had been promoted to head office from the Jamaican subsidiary. This added an interesting twist to the meeting. I was asked which of the listed properties I would consider renting. I indicated the one in a new, Canadian style subdivision that would cost twice as much as my agreed allowance. The local GM was asked if he had seen the property. He had. He was asked if he would live in the house I had chosen and if it were better than his own current accommodations. He responded in the affirmative on both counts. My choice was approved and my allowance adjusted accordingly. Now the inevitable internecine struggle would begin at the subsidiary.

Sure enough, the other expatriates, an Englishman and an American, on learning of the outcome, were quite upset and suggested that the favorable outcome was influenced by the fact that the VP was Jamaican like me. I absolutely understood their discontent even though their contention was without merit. Unlike them I acted against what I saw as an unacceptable situation. I had applied my "J" rule, confident in the outcome I sought because I was convinced my contention was justified. I consoled them by predicting that, in due course, their own allowances would be adjusted. I knew that there was no justification or benefit for the company to allow such an anomaly to continue indefinitely. Whatever mitigating influence my consoling advice may have had was short lived. On hearing of the discontent among the group, the VP was overheard to say that those who had accepted their poor accommodations without complaint should be prepared to live with them. For nearly six months the atmosphere in the office and between the affected wives and my wife, was troubling. It all righted itself after my prediction came through and everyone had his allowance adjusted. It was very gratifying to have all parties thank me for forcing such a welcome change in their circumstances.

While living in the hotel awaiting the arrival of our household effects, my wife had made friends with a couple of expatriate wives. The husbands worked for the Good Year Tire Company. Not surprisingly, the husbands met and became friends as well. These connections were very useful as they helped to keep us all aware of what may prove helpful or harmful in the policies being discussed or implemented by local government authorities. We also were able to compare our individual company policies, especially those affecting expatriate compensation and benefits.

Our personal and household effects arrived and we moved into our new house in Rhunda Estates in the northern suburbs of the city of Nairobi. The house was on about five acres with a fenced off stream and tree house at the far end of the property. The location overlooked a large tea plantation. The house itself was new, very modern and attractive. Unlike the vast majority of houses we had seen, this house accommodated Canadian size appliances. It was not long before we had settled in, hired a maid and gardener and had the company provide the ubiquitous twenty four hour security guard service. In short order we arranged to get two dogs for the boys. One was a Corgi-Terrier mix and the other was a thoroughbred German Shepherd whose documented pedigree went back directly to Germany.

In an attempt to ingratiate myself into the local culture I had gone out of my way to invite a number of native managers to my house for dinner and parties and to include specific managers in invitations to business lunches with suppliers and government officials. No one reciprocated. I thought this unusual and sought advice from the native sales manager, a Kikuyu. The Kikuyu tribe is the largest tribe in Kenya and is the tribe of the first president of Kenya, Jomo Kenyatta. It was not accidental that members of this tribe occupied most of the very influential positions in government, the civil service and business. Except for senior expatriate managers and my Indian purchasing manager all other managers in the company were Kikuyu.

I asked the sales manager to be brutally honest with me. "Why have I been unable to feel as if I am accepted by natives in the company?" I asked. He explained that when they heard of me and saw my photograph they were delighted and felt that finally someone who looked like a Kenyan was going to be a senior manager in the company. However, after my arrival they realized that I was no more than a "massive confusion" because in every important respect I was no different from the white expatriate, a *muzungu*, in Swahili, the most commonly spoken language. I did not, after all, really look like them; I did not sound like them; I was not treated like them by the company and I certainly lived like a white expatriate. Interestingly, the word *muzungu* is also the word meaning *foreigner*. This is not a confusion. The explanation is that, historically, all foreigners or expatriates were white. Although I was not white, as an expatriate, the word applied to me equally. This peculiarity would be witnessed again elsewhere in Africa.

I was a little confused by this explanation and pressed him further to explain the difference between me, a black expatriate, and a white expatriate. He explained by relating a parable: If I were to ask for the hand of his sister in marriage and he took me to his village to introduce me to his parents they would have the greatest of difficulty accepting me for their daughter. A white foreigner, though problematic himself, would be much more acceptable. I asked for further clarification. He explained that in Kenya the natives clearly understood the white man. They did not understand someone like me. This experience, like nothing else could, made it clear that my color held no advantage for either the company or me.

Truthfully, it would be no more acceptable for a non-Kikuyu Kenyan male, say a Luo, to find ready acceptance, as an experience I relate later will reveal. The fact is, I was more of a stranger and foreigner than any white man could be. I still wished to know what I could do to "fit in." His response surprised me. "There is nothing you can do," was his reply. "You simply have to wait for acceptance. You will know when it comes if, for example, you are invited to attend a wedding or funeral in the village." Both events did occur over the next several months.

The wedding invitation was first. A Jamaican young man living in England met and fell in love with a Kikuyu girl while both were at university in Birmingham. The girl's father was in England as a diplomat. When the diplomat and family returned to Kenya the Jamaican followed his sweetheart to Kenya where they became engaged. He adopted us as his surrogate family in Kenya and introduced us to his fiancée and her family. In this way we played an intimate role in his wedding. We hosted his Jamaican English family during their stay in Kenya for the wedding. There were two ceremonies: the first was native traditional; the second was typical colonial British.

The second invitation was to the burial of the mother of the Plant Manager. The village was more than two hours from Nairobi. My wife and I arrived at the village just after mid day. It was impossible not to observe the many children running around in noisy play. There was no sign of grieving among the adults either. This was unexpected and quite unusual behavior under the circumstances. After the usual introductions and respectful exchange of greetings, I asked the Plant Manager to explain. He revealed that the period of mourning was over and that this portion of the ceremonies was more celebratory. The fact is that his father had several wives. Polygamy is in fact permitted in Kenya. The passing of one of these wives meant the passing of one of several mothers. The children had lost one mother but several remained. In the eyes of each child in such polygamous families, each mother is effectively the mother of every child. To be honest, I had always thought of polygamy as an outrageously terrible cultural aberration. My exposure to the realities of the custom was an eye opener.

It is apparent that polygamy, as practiced in Kenya, appeared to satisfy a number of very critical needs in village society. One of the most important of these is economic. There were animals to tend, crops to plant and reap, children to raise and every likelihood that the man of the household would be away frequently working in the city to supplement any other sources of income which were more often than not insufficient. As families grow and domestic chores multiply, it is not unusual for the first or senior wife to propose the need for a second wife. She usually helps to choose the woman. The process is open, participatory, respectful and honest.

The first or senior wife is always given the unreserved respect of junior wives. It is therefore not surprising that these polygamous relationships survive without turbulence or discord and are effective units in which to raise children and secure the harmonious survival of the village as a critical social unit. In these respects polygamy certainly outperforms the all too common hypocritical and discordant monogamous marriage contract imposed by a foreign religion and former colonial masters who typically inveighed against the practice while indulging in parallel behavior, simultaneously and unashamedly. Often this indulgence would produce, as they would say, bastard children at every turn.

The Kenyan subsidiary was also obliquely responsible for operations in Nigeria. In particular, I was responsible for shipping bulk product to Lagos for finishing by the plant there. We constantly experienced great difficulty clearing our shipments from the docks in Lagos. I very soon learned that Nigeria was a very difficult place in which to do business. Perhaps the most intractable reason was widespread, ubiquitous corruption. My company has a stated, inviolate and universally applicable policy of not using any but the legally recognized means to transact business. One consequence of this policy is that our goods would sit on the Lagos docks for weeks after they should have been cleared. This had a couple of damaging effects: it forced the carrying of unusually excessive levels of inventory and it often caused costly stock outs. Neither condition was helpful to the business, especially in a place like Nigeria.

Head office, while not ignorant of the environment in Nigeria, was all but insensitive to the explanations given for our problems there. It was very difficult to understand what their real intentions were regarding what should be done to operate efficiently and profitably in Nigeria. Local management in Nigeria constantly demanded that I do more to get them product and head office constantly harassed the Kenya subsidiary for failing to respond adequately to the demands of the Nigerian operations.

On one occasion I had a frantic call from the plant manager in Nigeria. He had been to the customs to clear a shipment of product from Kenya. He could clearly see the boldly labeled forty five gallon stainless steel drums on pallets on the dock but was being told incessantly that they were not there. The revelation was as laughable as it was daunting. I wondered why he was calling me to relate this tale of woe. I certainly was in no position to do anything but listen. I told him I would discuss the matter with head office and get back in touch. Head office offered no solution or advice. It was obvious that their only interest was to get the goods cleared.

The responsibility for doing so was unquestionably mine. I returned my Nigerian colleague's telephone call and basically parroted the non-direction, non-advice providing position of head office. The responsibility for clearing the goods was unquestionably his. There was no hesitation on his part as he commenced telling me of the only way in which he could get the goods off the docks. I stopped him in his tracks. I did not wish to know neither should I see any reference to how he resolved his problem on any invoice for my approval. The matter was resolved through a broker who simply billed us for services rendered. In Africa, action by third parties is sometimes the only solution to intractable commercial problems.

My time was not totally consumed by work and trying to fit in. It would have been a shame to live in a place like Kenya and not go on safari or enjoy the many fine restaurants around Nairobi. It was true then, and may still be true, that Kenya had the most fantastic game parks and lodges in Africa as well as some very fine places to dine. I still have swizzle sticks from the Tamarind Restaurant, a favorite of ours and many corporate visitors. It was at the Tamarind that I learned to drink *Dawa*. This is the Kiswahili word for medicine but is in fact used as the name for a wonderful drink made with citrus Vodka, honey and lime juice, poured over crushed ice in a chilled glass whose rim is turned in a container with table salt. It is an amazing drink. It was possible to have several of these drinks without the after effects one would have from drinking as many glasses of just about any other alcoholic mix with which I am familiar.

We made a point of going on safari at least every three or four months. Sometimes our safaris were made to coincide with visits by friends from abroad or visiting executives from head office. Our favorite game parks and lodges include Tree Tops Lodge, where the princess Elizabeth became Queen Elizabeth II on the death of her father, King George VI, in 1952; the Masai Mara, where an unimaginable variety of big game such as elephants, lions, water buffalos, rhinos and giraffes could be seen; Tsavo, the largest national game park, noted for its elephants and lions and its convenient proximity to Mombasa, an historical, multi-cultural island-city on the Indian Ocean; Kilimanjaro, the tallest mountain in Africa, where the snow capped peak with its usual halo of white cloud can be viewed and enjoyed from lodges at the base of the mountain, in space shared with roaming elephants.

Remarkably, the accommodations at all of these game parks and lodges were as good as one would expect in some of the best hotels. The service is certainly generally superior. I still have photographs taken on these safaris. Two in particular were so well taken that the photo lab in Nairobi conveniently lost the negatives. One photograph is of two mature lions crossing a pathway in front of a car in a game park while a pride lay listlessly nearby. The other is of a reticulated giraffe perfectly framed between the horizon and a brooding Kenya skyline. Many of my local friends who should know, felt that the lab had stolen the negatives to use them to produce post cards.

Our older son had a particularly defining experience of his own. His class at The American International School worked on a school project that involved a visit to Masai

Land. The Masai are a nomadic people who travel dozens of miles on foot each day with their cattle. They survive mainly by drinking fresh cow's milk mixed with cow's blood which they collect by piercing one of their cows with a hollow arrow and collecting the blood in a gourd. During his field trip his class was offered a drink of blood and milk by the Masai. We were very impressed to learn that our son accepted the Masai's proffered drink without hesitation. This was a mark of cultural maturity that has had lasting impact on his life. In fact, when he recounted the experience in an essay as part of the requirement for acceptance into Dartmouth College many years later, it was perhaps a decisive factor in his admission.

This experience along with others brought into bold relief the part culture and isolation can play in how we see others and how others see us. Although Nairobi is essentially a modern city it was not unusual to see the impressively tall, slender Masai driving their cattle through the busy streets of downtown Nairobi even at peak hour. The natives on the streets or in their cars never appeared to be bothered by this. I initially found the juxtaposed realities bothersome, especially when I was stuck in traffic myself waiting for the Masai and their cattle to cross six lanes of a very busy highway.

This insensitivity was more than compensated for the first time I witnessed a solitary, unbelievably regal Masai warrior in full regalia step off the curb into traffic on Kenyatta Avenue without as much as a glance in either direction. All traffic came to a halt to allow him passage. No one blew a horn as he crossed six lanes of traffic, apparently oblivious to any danger that onlookers may have imagined. He truly strode his world like the colossus he is. The impression was indelible. It is noteworthy that neither the Masai's chosen isolation nor his country's modernization has managed to diminish the sheer stature of Masai culture.

Similarly, I recall meeting a white American expatriate at a cocktail party once. I never saw him again for several weeks but the very next time I did see him I was a little puzzled by his unusually effervescent behavior. I was down town Nairobi on a very busy street when I heard someone shouting to me from the opposite sidewalk. I did not recognize the voice and had difficulty seeing the person; but not for long. He was the sole white person in a sea of black faces. Before I could complete my gestures of recognition he was on my side of the street and had grabbed me in a firm embrace. I was a little surprised. We chatted for a while and each detailed how he was settling in to life in Nairobi. He admitted that he was just getting used to not having many Americans around him and often felt terribly home sick. I told him I understood completely. We exchanged telephone numbers, embraced again and said goodbye.

I realized that had we been on a busy street in New York City it would have been an extremely remote possibility that he would have been as insistent about greeting me. I can only imagine how isolated he felt in Nairobi. I gathered that for the first time in his life he was a minority. I understood perfectly. I too had had the feeling.

Expatriate Blues

Even as my life in Kenya was appearing to settle into effective, balanced routine, some dark, discomforting clouds were gathering. On September 6, 1981, *The Nation* newspaper published in its Special Features section an elaborate polemic titled *"Expatriates in Kenya earning big salaries."* It was written by one Blamuel Njururi. Among other things, the article stated that, in addition to exacerbating the foreign exchange problems of the country, *"Many people also believe that expatriates are delaying the Kenyanisation programme."* My own experience with the company in Jamaica gave the article a relevance and meaning that I understood instinctively.

On the morning of September 14 I arrived at the office just before seven o'clock. Within minutes I was receiving call after call from business associates in the city asking whether I had seen the morning paper. Strangely, no one explained why I should be concerned about not seeing the paper. When my secretary arrived and asked the same question it occurred to me that something may very well be amiss. I asked her to bring me my daily copy of the paper as soon as it arrived. The revelation was shocking. One of the secondary headlines on the front page screamed: *"Mystery over expat's permit."* The seven column inches of the story ran over to the back page where a flattering photograph of me interrupted the additional ten column inches.

The article claimed that I was in the country illegally. It contended that my work permit was invalid since I was the Technical *Director* of the company but was not a de facto member of the company's board of directors. I was very concerned that were my wife to see the paper before I was able to speak with her she might assume the worst: that the authorities had already detained me. This was a distinct possibility in Kenya. It was not a prospect I wished to contemplate. I hastily left the office for home after instructing my secretary to have the General Manager call me at home the minute he arrived. Because of the time difference, it was pointless to call head office in New York. When I arrived at home I discovered, happily, that my wife had not yet seen the newspaper. As soon as she was up I showed her the alarming article, explained what had happened and indicated what I believed the company and I would need to do to diffuse what was clearly a potentially disastrous situation.

It was obvious that someone in the company had complained to the immigration authorities about my position in the company. I had my own suspicions but never voiced them. My suspicions could not be proven and certainly would not help in resolving the matter. The General Manager called and we agreed that I would remain at home until our local lawyers and head office were contacted and some discussion was had with the local immigration authorities. In relatively short order the matter was resolved and life fell back into its comfortable routine. However, the impact of the incident itself would outlive its occurrence and have very serious implications for the company and me.

A few months later, one of the three most senior executives in the company who was in line to become the next chairman arrived on a visit. After the usual day touring the facility and having a cursory business review, the local executives and wives accompanied him to dinner. Surprisingly, it was an unusually somber affair. He was seated beside me and directly opposite my wife near the end of our long table. During an exchange with my wife he confessed that he had just about sacrificed everything of value in his life for a position in the company he was now certain he would not get. He was, in fact, on a farewell tour of the subsidiaries as he would retire early after returning to America. His wife had divorced him, his children had no relationship with him and he doubted he had any trustworthy friends. As tears rolled down his cheeks he cautioned my wife never to allow me to make such indefensible sacrifices in working for the company. It was a sad but instructive tale. There was not a chance I would ever make that mistake.

The vast majority of residents in our neighborhood of perhaps thirty homes was expatriate, many of whom were diplomats, employees of the United Nations and its affiliate organizations and folks like me. There was just a single non-expatriate couple in the community. The couple was an older English man and a very successful Kikuyu woman who had one of the largest real estate companies in Nairobi. We became friends and visited each other frequently.

On one of their early visits they expressed wistful surprise at the size of our appliances. We were obliged to provide a lesson on life style in North America. They were fascinated and asked to have first option to purchase our appliances when the time came for us to leave Kenya. They also would love to have my wife's little 500cc Honda run-about. Another neighbor, a German, invited us to dinner along with a South African friend of his. It was the strangest of coincidences that this South African had lived and worked in Jamaica for the government run Jamaica Omnibus Service Company (J.O.S) in the 70's. There is a strange irony here because in the 70's South Africans were banned from Jamaica on account of the government's strong opposition to the practice of apartheid by the Government of South Africa. He had come to Jamaica via the United Kingdom and, to be charitable, it is possible that the J.O.S authorities were unaware of his status as a South African. In any event, the workers at the company discovered his unfavorable status, alerted their union and forced the government to expel him.

Needless to say, we and the South African had much to talk about. He regaled us with tales of his hob knobbing with the elites in Jamaica, some of whom we knew as acquaintances or knew of by virtue of their high profile status in Jamaica's social hierarchy at the time. They were all white or light skinned Jamaicans. This did not surprise us in the least. On the basis of his own personal experiences with some of these people, he assumed that just about every Jamaican smoked ganja or marijuana. In his mind, of course, we fell into this category. He had made a terribly embarrassing mistake. After my wife attempted to explain with civility that, in fact, she had never ever even seen a marijuana plant, let alone smoked marijuana and that none of our friends did either, he kept insisting that this could not be true. We were left with no choice at this point but to attack his ridiculous assumptions mercilessly while pointing out the shortcomings of some of the Jamaicans with whom he had been friends in Jamaica. In spite of the obvious discomfort caused by the squabble we survived dinner without any further insults. Neither of us regretted the fact that we never saw the South African again. However, the incident called to mind a related experience of mine in Jamaica.

A security guard came rushing into my office early one morning. The urgency of the situation was obvious. He insisted that I accompany him to the rear of the compound because something horrible was happening. On arriving at the location he gestured animatedly at an unusual clump of bushes that was growing very healthily as if cared for by someone. I had no idea what it was and expressed mild disgust that he had taken me away from my office on this account. He then explained that the clump of bushes was marijuana. How he knew this, was something I wanted to know. I asked for an explanation and he expressed surprise at my apparent ignorance.

He then grabbed a handful of leaves, crushed them in his hands and held the mush of leaves to my nostrils. The odor was repulsive. I realized that I had in fact smelled this odor before at parties and at sporting events at the national stadium, for example, but was never curious enough to enquire of its source. For the first time I recognized what ganja or marijuana looked like and could now identify its distinctive scent. I also realized the dilemma this presented.

A new Jamaica law made it an offense to have marijuana growing on your property. Essentially, this meant that the owner or overseer of property on which marijuana was found was liable and subject to prosecution. As an agent of my company with direct responsibility for all company property, I was at serious personal risk under the circumstances. I had the security guard burn the micro-plantation of marijuana. On investigation I learned that no one had intentionally planted the crop. The plants grew from hardy, residual seeds left in discarded spliffs that indulgent employees had thrown from windows in the factory. It was an instructive if hazardous episode in my experience managing the company's operations in Jamaica.

Resident Ambassadors

Kenya and Jamaica had always enjoyed very warm relations. These relations were advanced by the work the two countries did together on *Habitat for Humanity*. In 1981 Kenya hosted an international conference for *Habitat for Humanity*. The government of Jamaica was represented by its representative to the U.N., the Minister of Housing, the Hon. Bruce Golding, who is currently the Prime Minister of Jamaica, and an entourage of civil servants and advisors. Most of the group stayed in the Intercontinental Hotel where we had spent three months awaiting the arrival of our personal and household effects. As soon as the staff at the hotel learned that the Jamaicans were there, they directed them to get in touch with us. Over night we became resident ambassadors for Jamaica. We held a party at home for the group and had them meet nearly all the Jamaicans who were in Nairobi as well as our many Kenyan friends. It was a wonderful gathering which further cemented the Kenya-Jamaica relationship on a very meaningful citizen to citizen level.

Some months afterwards the then Prime Minister of Jamaica, the Hon. Edward Seaga, came on an official visit. We never held a party for him but we were invited to visit with him at the hotel along with a very small group of resident Jamaicans. Again, our old hotel was the venue. On arriving for the meeting we realized that the Prime

Minister had been given the very suite we had occupied when we stayed at the hotel. We also discovered at the meeting that our pediatrician friend, Colin, was a distant relative of the Prime Minister.

We thoroughly enjoyed being able to host visiting Jamaicans regardless of their particular status. Being an expatriate often offers this type of opportunity.

A Coup in August

Like most of Africa, Kenya remains a culture of tribes. Before leaving for home leave in June of 1982, I had to hire an engineer for the factory. Several qualified candidates responded to our advertisement in the local newspaper. Among the respondents were an Asian and a Luo, all the others were Kikuyu. I had the Plant Manager and Purchasing Manager, who was himself Asian, participate in the interview of the final four candidates. When I asked for their recommendation on which I should hire, the responses were strictly tribal. The Asian thought very highly of the Asian candidate and the Kikuyu Plant Manager highly recommended one of the Kikuyu candidates. I was convinced that the Luo candidate was the most suitable for the position and had to now convince both managers of this. Both finally admitted that their main concern was that given the hierarchy of tribes and with so many Kikuyu in the company and factory, it would be very disruptive to hire a Luo. Both also agreed that hiring the Asian was preferable to hiring the Luo.

The respect and deference shown the Asian population in Nairobi was legendary. It would appear that when the British left the country, although the Kikuyus were in charge of the government, the Asians filled the vacuum left in the lucrative and very influential commercial sector. The Asians were the new power brokers even though they were visibly absent from the traditional halls of power.

I referred both managers to the company's policy regarding hiring. Under this policy I could not and would not take their cultural preferences into account. The Luo was the most qualified candidate and was hired. I had developed an orientation program for him which was to be completed in my absence. Upon my return it was obvious that there were problems and the Luo engineer soon confirmed my suspicions. He was being ignored, or, more accurately, ostracized, by everyone, including the Plant Manager. This was intolerable, of course. I read the riot act to the Plant Manager and others who would be required to work with the new hire. The problems disappeared as long as I was around. It would have been shortsighted and foolish to give in to cultural prejudice and I continued to provide unstinting support for the new engineer.

I left for Jamaica on four weeks of home leave. My family remained in Jamaica so that our two boys could witness and participate in the celebrations commemorating Jamaica's twentieth year of Independence in early August. Barbadian friends of ours had, like us, gone home to Barbados on vacation. The husband, who was the financial controller of the Hilton Hotel, remained behind in Nairobi. We shared the mixed blessings of being on our own for a while without spouses or children. Almost every evening we would have dinner together and indulge our low grade, temporary addiction to alcohol. After all when the cat is away the mouse will play.

On the evening of July 31st, a Saturday, we had dinner together at the New Stanley Hotel where we were both popular with the staff, waiters and night club disc jockey. In fact, we used to supply the DJ with Caribbean music which was loved by a majority of the hotel's guests as well as the locals who frequented the hotel's nightclub. We left the hotel just after midnight. At around 2:00AM on Sunday morning the 1st of August, my telephone rang. It was the Purchasing Manager asking me if I were aware that there was a coup in progress. In my sleepy daze I asked where this was happening. I detected a chuckle in his voice as he told me that the coup was in Kenya and that the rebels had taken over the offices of the Cable and Wireless Company and the radio stations. He advised that I not leave the house on any account as this could be very dangerous. I hurriedly turned on the radio. All that was being broadcast was uninterrupted martial music. I could not get back to sleep and remained awake for the remainder of the night.

The main army barracks was no more than ten miles or so to the south east of my verandah as the crow flies. I could hear the boom and feel the vibrations from the discharge of artillery shells. Also discernable was the staccato sound of helicopters going to and fro not too far from my neighborhood. I immediately telephoned my Barbadian friend to alert him of the coup and then set about calling all my neighbors, many of whom were with embassies and may have had more information about what was happening. We all agreed that at daylight we would meet in the cul-de-sac in front of my house. Suddenly, I realized that, unknown to my Barbadian friend and me, we had witnessed the staging of the coup. I could now recall that on our way from the New Stanley we did see a number of men in plain clothes carrying automatic weapons and standing no more than twenty or so feet apart on the pavement between the hotel and the Cable and Wireless offices.

Unfortunately, two corporate employees had arrived in Nairobi on the Saturday for meetings at the office on Monday. They had checked into the Intercontinental Hotel. Their safety was now a matter of much concern to me. I tried to reach the hotel to check on them but the phone no longer worked. At our neighborhood meeting the consensus was that things were not as bad as they seemed and that everything would be just fine in a few hours. It is helpful to understand that Daniel Arap Moi, the President, had been Vice President to Jomo Kenyatta and became President upon the death of Kenyatta in

1978. It is generally felt that as a member of perhaps the smallest tribe, the Kalenjin, it was most unlikely that Moi could ever become president but for the circumstance of being selected as Vice President by Kenyatta. There is some consensus that Kenyatta made Moi Vice President because, as a Kalenjin, he could never pose a threat to Kenyatta's rule. It is also felt that the Kikuyu orchestrated the coup attempt with great timing as Moi and his army detachment were away from the city on a visit to Eldoret in western Kenya. It would be three days before he could return to Nairobi.

With a sense of invulnerability and the folly only a *muzungu* could summon under the existing circumstances, I drove into the city to see to the safety of my corporate guests. This easily qualifies as the most stupid thing I have ever done in my life. At least I was smart enough to take my passport with me. I was stopped twice on my way to the hotel and was shown an unusual amount of deference as soon as it was discovered that I was a foreigner. I located my guests and advised them not to attempt to leave the hotel for any reason until I was in touch with them again. On my return home I was again stopped by soldiers. This time the interrogation was much more aggressive and intense. I was told in no uncertain terms that I should go home and not return to the city. The suburbs were by and large very quiet, except for a residential area called Parklands that was totally populated by Asians.

The Asians never integrated themselves into Kenyan society in any but the most tangential way. Neither did they camouflage their disdain for the native population. Many stories are told of the viciousness of the attacks against their property and persons. Their places of business were attacked mercilessly, their neighborhood plundered and, as a sign of deepest hate by marauders, many of their wives and daughters were raped in view of husbands and parents. It is said that in one case a father shot his daughter dead after she had been raped by a native. It was surreal to walk around Nairobi in the days after the coup attempt. There were instances where a native owned store stood between two Asian owned stores and the Asian stores were gutted while the native store was left untouched.

Moi and his army detachment returned to the city after three days and put down the coup. The record of exactly what occurred and how many people were killed in the process remains quite unclear. Never the less, a number of influential Kikuyus, including some members of parliament, was arrested and placed under house arrest for a number of years.

For several days after the coup I was unable to communicate with my family in Jamaica. I was sure that, like the rest of the world, the occurrence would have been broadcast in Jamaica. My family was therefore aware of the situation. Most worrisome was that my wife would be worried sick not hearing from me. After more than a week I was able to get a message to our subsidiary in Zambia. I requested the transmission of a message to the Jamaica subsidiary indicating that I was safe and provided contact numbers for my family in Jamaica. It was several more days before I was able to call Jamaica from my office successfully. I instructed my wife not to return to Nairobi until I confirmed it was safe to do so. It was another fortnight before I felt comfortable to do this.

For us, Kenya would never be the same. There was always a sense of uncertainty in our minds about the future stability of the country as well as the security of certain groups within its population. An example of the latter concern is exemplified by a copy of a letter I received on September 9. The letter was sent by a group of employees to J. G. Kereini, chief secretary of Cabinet Affairs in the government. It was copied to the General Manager and the Secretary General of the Kenya Chemical Workers' Union. The letter is reproduced here with names of the company and employees redacted.

To: Mr. J. G. Kereini, Secretary of Cabinet Affairs

"We .... workers have unquestionable trust and confidence in our beloved President, His Excellency Daniel T. Arap Moi, his Vice President and Minister of Home Affairs, the Honorable Mwai Kibaki, the Government and the ruling Party KANU. We were however dismayed on 2-8-82 to hear two of our Asian employees utter words in front of other employees which could possibly shatter the peace and stability of our good Government.

The words in question were uttered by .... with .... to the effect that our Vice President and Minister of Home Affairs was involved in the August coup bid. Since Asians in this company have started behaving as though they are the bosses of the Africans (sic) employees who are much abused and disrespected, by copy of this letter we are requesting our Government to look into this matter and see whether Asians are also running our Government to the effect that they can be making such allegations even in public."

Even though the Asians did little to ensure their own acceptance by native Kenyans I did not believe that they deserved to become the butt of potential persecution on the slightest of pretexts.

Work Permit Woes

My work permit was for two years initially and was to expire in January. The company applied for an extension for another two years. After not hearing from the authorities local native contacts were pressed into service to facilitate a response. There was cause for concern as year-end was approaching. This meant that everybody, including the authorities, would be very busy. It would be easy to run out of time. Just before year-end the response came. It was jarring in its tone and unusually direct in its denial of the company's application. Among the things it stated was that the company had failed to live up to its obligation and commitment to train and promote natives into upper management positions. It was unequivocal in its position that under absolutely no circumstance would a renewal be granted for my work permit. Neither would the authorities even consider any future work permit application to fill my position. The company was in a quandary and to some extent so was I.

I would not be allowed to remain in Kenya for a day longer than the date of expiration of my work permit. This meant that my family and I would have to be out of Kenya no later than the first week of January, 1983. Hurriedly, arrangements were made to terminate the lease for our house, settle all outstanding local bills, dispose of household effects we did not plan to take with us and have packers prepare, pack and store our personal and household effects for shipping to the United States. Once again we moved into the Intercontinental Hotel in downtown Nairobi.

The company did not have time to formulate the typical plan for my transfer to another subsidiary or another country. As a result, an ad hoc arrangement was made for me to be relocated temporarily to the company's multi-plant site in Jeffersonville, Indiana. On learning this, my white American expatriate colleagues voiced their concern. They were very alarmed at the prospects for my professional survival in a place like Jeffersonville. It was Middle America where racism and discrimination were facts of life. In fairness to me and my wife whom they knew very well, they did say that they knew that we were the type of people who conceivably could get along with reasonable people anywhere. Their fear was that racist and discriminatory behavior had no basis in reason. I thanked them for their concern about my welfare and indicated that I was not ignorant of America and the issues regarding race. After all I did attend university in America and I was working for an American company. I anticipated no real problems in Indiana.

We enjoyed the usual going-away parties that were held in our honor and the children said goodbye to their friends. We then left Kenya for Indiana and Middle America.

V. BACK TO AMERICA

In the Heartland

Our flight from Nairobi was non-stop direct to Kennedy Airport in New York. On arrival at Kennedy we learned that we had missed our connecting flight to Louisville, Kentucky and would be transferred to La Guardia Airport by helicopter for another connection. None of us had flown on a helicopter before. It was a harrowing experience; one my wife vowed never ever to repeat at any cost. We flew into Louisville through very severe thunder storms along the way.

Louisville is on the west side of the Ohio River which separates Kentucky from southern Indiana. We were advised to live in Kentucky instead of Indiana as the plant site was just across the river from the city of Louisville and housing was, by all accounts, much more attractive on the Kentucky side of the river. We were told we would easily notice the plant from almost anywhere in the city because of its world famous clock which was said to be the second largest clock in the world, outdone only by another similar clock at our largest plant site in Newark, New Jersey. We were provided temporary accommodations in a set of town houses just outside the city along with a rental car. Although our move was precipitous we were accustomed to moving and were not particularly put out by this. We would make the best of a difficult situation and do our best to re-establish comfortable routine once again.

The wives of a number of managers at the subsidiary were very helpful and took turns providing advice to my wife regarding better places in which to look for houses and schools for the children. The wife of the Human Resources Manager even chauffeured her around sometimes. We had more than ample time to find a house but very little time to decide on schools for our sons. It would take three months for our personal and household effects to arrive in Louisville.

As usual, I started work promptly. My initial assignment was as an industrial engineer in the Industrial Engineering Department. The Department comprised a young manager, an accounting and an engineering supervisor and about six or eight engineers. The plan was that I would be at the site no longer than eighteen to twenty four months, by which time I would be transferred to another international assignment. There were about eight plants at the site along with administration offices and a maintenance department. The site was once a prison and one of the original dungeons remained with a frayed but intact noose left hanging on a gallows. Depending on a visitor's point of view this was either fascinating or repulsive.

It took some time for me to find my way around without assistance. A wide variety of products was made at the site and I wondered how intimately familiar I would become with all the operations during my time there. Eighteen to twenty four months was not a very long time at such a large facility even though I was already familiar with the majority of the manufacturing processes from my previous assignments in Jamaica, Canada and Kenya.

After work one evening I collected my wife and proceeded to the dealership from which I would purchase a car. The dealership was on the other side of town on the Kentucky side of the river. I was not yet comfortable with my navigation skills and, as my wife feared, we missed a turn and lost our way. We found ourselves in an area on the other side of the river in Indiana. Because of stories we had heard we became a little concerned when we failed to correct our mistake and dusk set in. Finally, we came upon an old gas station with one much rusted gas pump and no attendant in sight. We never the less agreed that there was no point in continuing to drive around with virtually little or no chance that we would improve our situation.

We pulled into the station and honked our horn. An elderly man came hobbling from the door of the little cabin that sat just off to one side of the old rusted pump station. He was wearing cover-alls and a felt hat that had clearly seen many years of use. He was unable to provide good directions but just as we were about to despair a light truck pulled into the pump behind us. The driver overheard our discussion and indicated that if we would wait until he filled up he would take us to the road leading to the dealership. We thanked him and waited. Sure enough, he did exactly as promised.

This was an eye opening experience for us as we were told that this was not the kind of behavior we should expect in a place like Indiana or Kentucky. We would never again take the word of others on what we should expect of people we did not know and who did not know us. Interestingly, on a trip to New York some time later our expectations were dashed under very similar circumstances based on what we were told to expect of people in New York. The reality, we discovered, was the opposite. In our minds the North had lost the civility battle to the South.

In the meantime the children were enrolled in school; the younger in elementary school and the older in middle school. We would later discover the totally unplanned for benefits of our sons being four years apart. This meant that they would never be together at any level of schooling the way the American school system was organized. This fact would be especially beneficial when the time came for college.

In due course we found a house to rent in a neighborhood which had the most highly rated High School in the state of Kentucky. The school had won school of the year on two consecutive occasions recently. We had learned enough about Kentucky to understand that the average school in the state was among the worst in the entire country. Finding the best schools for our sons was not merely essential but crucial. It was not at all a coincidence that the best schools were in basically white neighborhoods. As a result we ended up living in such a neighborhood. While not ignorant about the standard of education in Kentucky we were oblivious to the idea of busing.

When my wife went to register our sons at school, she was surprised that she was required to indicate the race of our children. This was confusing if for no other reason than that, as Jamaicans, we never considered the idea of race as worthy of itemized reference, especially on official documents. My wife's response to the query was that it was impossible to tell since we were of compound heritage; partly Welsh, Irish, Indian and African. She confessed that she would have no idea which part of her heritage to credit over another. She suggested that *West Indian* or *Other* be used. Since neither of these classifications was on the form in question our children were listed as Black. She was told that based on our address our children would not have to be bused. Her response was that this would not be necessary anyway as she was prepared to take them to school herself. We later came to understand the issue of busing as a means to enforce desegregation in schools. We thought this a very strange and surely inadequate way to address the problem of inequity in the quality of education provided by public schools.

Our container arrived and we moved into our rented house in a subdivision in Brownsboro, a white neighborhood fifteen minutes from the schools our children attended and about thirty minutes from downtown Louisville. The plant site across the Ohio River was only thirty minutes away.

As far as we could tell, we were the only non-white family in the subdivision. The children's dogs had accom-

panied us to America along with the two large dog houses which were built for them in Kenya. While the smaller
dog caused no concern the same could not be said of
the larger dog. The small land space available at the new
house versus the very large acreage that had been available in Kenya, meant that we had to restrict the freedom
of the dogs significantly. Both dogs had lived outside and
had free run of the entire area of our yard in Kenya. Their
new situation presented quite a challenge. We decided
to install a runner in the back yard for the larger dog. This
worked for a while until one day when he broke the runner to greet a well groomed poodle and its owner that
were walking on the street by our house. Because of his
size the owner of the poodle was terrified and expected
the worst. However, our German Shepherd simply wished
to make friends. We realized that we had a real problem
on our hands and decided to treat the German Shepherd
to obedience training. We hoped that this would reduce
the stress on both the dog and ourselves. This turned out
not to be the case. Regrettably, to the great dismay of
our children, we ended up giving the Shepherd away to
a farmer and her family.

Our two boys quickly became friends with two schoolmates of similar ages, an older girl and younger boy.
Both lived across the street from us. As a result we developed a relationship with their parents and eventually car
pooled to take the children to school. One relationship
led to another and we soon met several of our neighbors. By the time we had come to meet most of them
they already knew all about us; our nationality, where we
came from to Louisville, the company for which I worked
and the sports in which I had an interest. We joked that
although we had left Africa, we had not left the African
drums behind. In fact, the drums appeared to work more
effectively in Kentucky. The boys and I would ride our
bicycles around the neighborhood in the evenings. We
saw many more of our neighbors who would more often than not greet us with a friendly wave. We had once
again settled into comfortable routine.

As was our custom each time we relocated, as soon as we settled into our new accommodations we would invite a selected number of people from the subsidiary along with their spouses to dinner at our home. We always thought this to be a very gracious way in which to show our gratitude and appreciation for all the assistance we are usually given on our arrival in a new place. About eight invitations were hand written and delivered by me at the office nearly a month before the event. Among those invited were my boss and the site director. Everyone but the director responded before the requested date. Up to a few days before the event I still had not heard from him. I called his secretary to remind him of the invitation and to get confirmation as to whether he would or would not attend. He returned my call the next day to apologize for not responding as requested and to say that, regrettably, his wife had made a prior commitment and they would be unable to attend. However, he said, he hoped that he would be able to make up for this missed opportunity in the not too distant future.

On the evening of the dinner all of our other invited guests arrived. Everyone enjoyed the dinner and our time together and many of the wives in attendance promised to reciprocate. One person, in particular, was most insistent when my wife indicated that this was not at all necessary. She was a very likeable, attractive woman who used to be a stand-in for Doris Day when she and her husband lived in California. The compliments on the food and our house were endless and quite flattering. We were happy that we had not abandoned our tradition and looked forward to enjoying our stay in Kentucky and Indiana.

Our first winter was uneventfully mild. Our winter reference was Toronto where nine inches of snow on the ground were child's play for municipalities and conditions in which children would revel. We were amazed that an inch of snow on the ground in Louisville shut the city down, closed schools and left roadways deserted and advertized as dangerous. Employees who braved the elements to get to work were celebrated as heroes. My assumption about winter weather conditions in Kentucky and Indiana was that they would not be much different from Toronto except in duration.

Before I knew it a year had gone by. I was reminded of this fact by a request from my division's manager to provide my own assessment of how I had performed against assigned performance objectives. This was not difficult or even challenging. After all the role of the industrial engineering function was mainly an assessing, advisory and facilitating one. In large measure much of my effectiveness would depend on how the clients I served viewed my contribution to their success against their own objectives. The reviews of both my manager and my clients were all favorable. My manager was perhaps five years or more my junior and was from up state New York where he had grown up on a farm. I could sense some degree of discomfort on his part as we reviewed my performance. In the end he confessed that he felt uncomfortable reviewing my work on two counts: first, from what he knew of my background my current assignment could not possibly offer any challenges; second, given my experience and qualifications it was his view that it made more sense for our roles to be reversed. He wished to know what I was told by head office about my position at the site in Indiana. I indicated that my situation was that I should be at the site for eighteen to twenty four months before being assigned once again to the international division of the business. From his expression I suspected that there was a problem and voiced my concern. He suggested that I speak with the site director and the folks in head office.

In a disturbing coincidence, a black American supervisor approached me in the cafeteria the very next day to enquire how things were going. I had seen him before but we had not spoken. I responded that things were going well. He confirmed that I was Jamaican and came to the site from Africa. He then inquired how long I would be at the site. Upon hearing my response he said he was happy that I would not be there too long. I did not know what to make of this and asked, half in jest, whether he did not like me. He did like me, he said, but he was very concerned that I might have been there for too long a time. This, he continued, would not be a good thing for someone like me. I was surprised and asked why. His response was alarming. His feeling was that if I remained too long I would be buried there. I was sure he never meant this literally and explained that I was not ignorant of the issues at which his concern hinted. I indicated my conviction that if one were knowledgeable and diligent one would always get ahead. He smiled, wished me well and departed.

This chance meeting left me feeling very uncomfortable. Put together with the veiled concerns of my manager, the entire picture stirred a sense of urgency to approach the site director immediately. I called his office and made an appointment to see him the very next afternoon after work in his office. Our meeting was quite revealing. As far as he was concerned my presence at the site was a matter of convenience. Head Office had simply directed him to accommodate me for a few months. He basically knew nothing about me and had no idea as to whether or not any plans existed for me at his site or anywhere else. I was shocked that no one had provided him with my personnel files or even a summary of my profile. I was incredulous and told him so. I would prepare a résumé overnight for his review the next day. I left his office more confused than ever. To my credit, confusion never takes hold of my mind for long. Mentally I had already started to prepare my résumé. On arriving at home I alerted my wife to the recent disturbing events and we set about preparing my résumé. There was no time to waste.

I presented my newly minted résumé to the site director the very next morning as planned. He promised to review it and to meet with me that afternoon. I informed my manager about the steps I had taken. He then issued a note of caution which surprised me. He advised that I be very careful in my discussions with the site director as his impression of me was suspect. He then revealed that the director had called him about the invitation to dinner at my house which I had issued many months earlier. He was very concerned that I had invited him and wanted to know what it was I wanted or intended to achieve by, in his view, currying favor. I was not only disappointed, I was hurt. Never before had I encountered this type of suspiciousness and distrust. I realized that my expectations were once again injecting themselves into my assumptions about people and their motives.

The knowledge I now had was jarring indeed and made me feel that things could worsen beyond my ability to control them. I was a member of the Louisville Squash Club and could not wait to get on the courts to take out my frustration on four walls and a little rubber ball. I was now fully aware of the battle my wife and I would have to fight. The sheer burden of what I anticipated made me weep.

That afternoon, as promised, the director and I met in his office at the end of the workday. He had obviously reviewed my résumé but was reviewing it once again item by item in my presence. At the end he confessed that he was impressed and had no idea that I not only had been with the company as long as I had but that I had worked in so many places and positions. He then asked me what I thought I could do at the site. Partly out of frustration and some degree of hubris I told him I could at least manage one of the plants at the site and at most do his job. His response was offensive. "Yes", he said, "I believe you could but no one will ever allow you to do that." I felt as if I had fallen out of the sky into a stout patch of rose bushes which broke my fall saving me. I had been so happy to be alive that I had failed to notice the thorns which had punctured my flesh. In an instant I understood what my black American well-wisher was attempting to tell me in the cafeteria: I could be buried there. My 'J' rule immediately came into focus. The battle was joined.

Complementary Indifference

    My next step was to get in touch with my former boss, the VP of Manufacturing for Africa and India, at head office in New York. Not surprisingly, he was traveling and I would not speak with him for nearly a week. He played the innocent. He had little to do with how my situation was handled, he said, as it was all arranged by his boss. I told him I found this incredible and demanded to know exactly what plans existed for my career post Kenya. He could not say as he knew of none. In the same breath he wanted me to know that this did not necessarily mean that no plan existed. He no longer deserved my respect and I told him so. It was at this point that I recalled a fleeting discussion I had with his boss just before departing Kenya.

    He was in a foul mood during our last business review and commented on changes that were occurring at head office. These changes affected him directly. He was called *the pearl* (which rhymed with his given name) by his white colleagues in head office for good reason. Some young upstart, in his words, was being promoted to be his boss. In his estimation the fellow knew nothing about Africa or India but was already lecturing him on what needed to be done to improve performance in the division. It so offended him that he reached back into the contradictory history of his coming to the region as the VP. Perhaps the single most remarkable thing, in his view, was his being made an honorary white person so that he could have white South Africans report to him. I believe that what was happening to him on a personal level was being juxtaposed in his own mind with the madness of his South African experience. Together they were driving him crazy. He was an exceptionally brilliant man and I am sure that he was not unaware of the role color played in America and as I would soon learn, in our company. Certainly, he was now realizing that while his place on the color-class continuum had been helpful earlier in his career it now had outlived its usefulness and no longer offered even the slightest of advantage. To the contrary, it may have become a distinct disadvantage. Not long afterwards he left the company.

The feelings I was now enduring, though not baseless, would not overwhelm me. My 'J' rule would be my comforter. I vowed to resist, confront and change the dynamics of my situation. I was convinced that justice and the evidence were clearly on my side. I would prevail. Accordingly, I set about devising a plan of attack. I would raise my concerns directly with the VP of Manufacturing for the American Division. After all, I was now a part of the manufacturing cadre for which he was responsible. Eventually he arranged for me to be placed in a line function at the site. I was put in charge of the plant that made toilet soaps and shave cream. In terms of people this plant had the largest workforce but there were plans afoot to mothball the operation. The company was in the process of rationalizing its factories and this factory was on a short list of plants that would be closed. One consequence of this plan was that no one would approve any capital spending for the facility. This in turn made routine maintenance a critical issue for the plant. These conditions made it almost inevitable that the plant would not survive.

Team work, as a management philosophy in the work place, was coming into vogue and the company had been expressing the view that implementing team work in my plant was perhaps the only thing that could save the facility. My plant would be a demonstrative laboratory for rescuing an old, dying facility. At the time, all over America, union rules made it impossible to be innovative in how labor was used. For example, an electrician was not allowed to relieve a line operator even if he had worked on the particular pieces of equipment for years and probably understood them better than the operators. The list of caveats in our union contract and job descriptions against this type of flexibility was endless.

Naturally, I had a serious vested interest in saving the facility. I approached the union with a proposal to transform the facility into a showpiece for team work. While the workforce as well as the union delegates in the plant itself were favorably disposed to the idea, the union executives and the rest of the site were automatically and vociferously opposed. This was not a bad sign in my estimation. It was a matter of how one was willing to see the proverbial glass, whether as half empty or half full. To me this was a good and useful start to a process I knew would require unusual trust, patience, courage and faith.

The years went by and I continued to work with the union and my plant workforce on saving the plant. As I expected, there were many troublesome issues in the interim. Workforce morale was on a steady decline as workers felt that they were powerless to save the facility. In their view, the company had already decided it would be closed. This view was supported by the verifiable fact that no funds were being allocated in our plant budget to improve equipment or support the type of maintenance effort that was obviously required. Just then a manager from the subsidiary in Singapore arrived at the site on a training program. He was Malaysian and spoke English well enough to be understood with some effort on the part of the listener. His family accompanied him and he was going to be at the site for some time. After several weeks of orientation he was inserted between me and my manager. I would now report to him directly.

While this was somewhat troubling it was an interface I was certain I could manage to good advantage.

He was Chinese in appearance and many at the site simply saw him as Chinese. I knew, understood and respected the difference and was very protective of him, especially as most of the staff around him disrespectfully ridiculed him even to his face at times. He lived in a house in the subdivision next to mine. In an attempt to be helpful I suggested, and he agreed, that we car pool to work. His children also attended my children's school. My wife, of course, did everything she could to assist his wife in getting around and in understanding the new and quite different culture in which she now found herself.

The more I attempted to convince the union leadership to support the effort being made by my plant to transform itself, the more pressure was brought to bear on the Malaysian and myself to improve housekeeping, product quality and the efficiency of the facility. In his culture it is traditionally disrespectful to question, let alone visibly oppose, those in authority. Because of this he absorbed all the criticism he received from the site director and others who were, or appeared to be, in authority. I saw much of the criticism somewhat differently as not all of it was justified, given the status of the facility. I pointed this out to him and I believe that, against his better judgment, given his culture, he must have raised the matter with the site director. He was directed to have a review with the Human Resources manager about the people issues in the plant. Thereafter our relationship was never the same.

We ceased to car pool but remained civil with each other at all times. I succeeded finally in reaching agreement with the union that allowed a reassessment of jobs in the plant. The objective was to permit entire lines in the plant to operate as de facto teams so that individual employees on each line could freely switch places and relieve one another for staggered breaks. The teams included the assigned maintenance personnel.

This allowed us to accomplish what was at the time a revolutionary step: but for break downs or scheduled maintenance, selected production lines would operate continuously through an entire shift. On this basis we recovered an entire hour per shift on the affected lines. Over an eight hour shift this was more than a twelve percent improvement in production time at no additional cost to the facility. One would have thought that this was an accomplishment worthy of singular recognition. Instead the accomplishment only received passing reference. At least in theory, the new procedure could be applied to the rest of the site to potentially remarkably good effect. It was therefore a matter of great concern and much astonishment when my performance appraisal was done, that my performance was rated as fair. This was especially disturbing when viewed against my previous appraisal which was competent.

Frankly, the entire performance appraisal process was essentially flawed and open to abuse. It went in gradation from best to worst on the following scale: Outstanding, Commendable, Competent, Fair, Unacceptable. Even the traditional Bell Curve distribution of these ratings provided little if any comfort. It was never the less all that was available as a tool for assessing individual performance. I obviously recognized this reality. I was however unwilling to be abused by it. I therefore responded exhaustively to my appraisal. It was apparent that I was on a contrived slippery slope on the way to unacceptable and ultimately to extinction.

Following my request for a face to face review of my questionable appraisal I was invited to my supervisor's office only to be confronted by him and the HR manager. I rebutted each point of disagreement and indicated that I would subsequently put this in writing. My rebuttal is reproduced below. This was 1987. In retrospect it seems incredible that, in light of subsequent events at the site and what is currently occurring in America, confronting blatant injustice is often hazardous.

Re: Performance Appraisal of 2/18/87

Once again it is necessary to respond at some length to my overall performance rating. The previous rating was "competent". The present rating is "fair". What does this mean? In the words of the performance rating sheet: "Gets the job done with considerable direction and guidance". Since in fact you give the barest minimum of direction and guidance and less than minimal support, not just to me but to the entire Toilet Soap Department, the rating of fair is totally baseless. In fact, you will recall the public outburst of one member of supervision at our recent breakfast meeting regarding your total lack of support for the department. Even the unionized employees share this view.

One glaring example of your lack of support involves the pointless hold of over thirty thousand cases of product for improper sealing of cases. A very small proportion of these cases was inadequately sealed. However, quality assurance went through scores of pallet loads forcibly opening sealed cases to prove they were not satisfactorily sealed. Our appeal to you generated no positive response. Since the problem was mechanically related I appealed to the maintenance manager for help. Not only did he help mechanically, he also had quality assurance release thousands of held cases by simply appealing to reason. The question is, could you have done this yourself? This is one area for which a rating of fair has been given.

In regard to cost improvement: After several meetings with the union, the involvement of the Industrial Engineering Department and our former savings committee it was agreed by no less a person than the site director that under the circumstances (union contract implications) we may have gone as far as we can with attempting to change the method of calculating palletizing points.

Automating our soap mills: This was not implemented on time because, as you are very much aware, the *department is at the lowest level of priority for engineering and maintenance attention. In neither case was implementation due to inadequate effort on my part. A reasonable and realistic assessment of this situation would certainly result in better than a rating of fair.*

Career Path: You will recall my meeting and discussion with you and the HR manager in April of 1985 at which I expressed incredulity at his solemn undertaking that someone from corporate HR would meet to discuss my career path with me in six months. After all I had been trying without success to have such a discussion for several years now. When such a discussion failed to materialize, I requested and got your intervention. You indicated to me that you had brought the matter to the attention of the HR manager but had no idea when or if anything would be done.

My insertion of a career path objective in my 1986 objectives was partly motivated by a desire to further stimulate some positive response from management. Alas, even after over eleven years of trying and not a single meaningful response from the company, my abandonment of this objective is seen as being due to my not wanting to pursue this "badly enough".

In a meeting with a representative of corporate HR in April of 1985 she admitted that the company was failing in this area of its responsibility to employees. The company, it seems, continues to fail.

Skills Assessment: Regrettably, one has to assume that insufficient thought or attention was given to the preparation of this area of the appraisal since certain basic skills that must be mastered on an ongoing basis, even at the level of first line supervision, I seem capable of merely to some extent. This entire area of the appraisal along with the overall rating of fair seems so contrived as to lead one to wonder at the motive behind such contrivance.

Finally, I again emphasize that my abiding goal is to be a positive influence for outstanding performance in the department even under the current condition of stated operation phase out. I also ask again to have problems brought to my attention prior to end of year evaluation so that together or singly we may overcome these on a timely basis.

Perhaps upon reflection you may now wish to reconsider and revise the appraisal and skill assessment ratings to more accurately reflect reality.

My response was sent to corporate and the rating was subsequently adjusted to commendable. This is not an insignificant thing and was surely done over strong objections from the local site HR functionaries. After all, this change in rating signified that a serious problem did in fact exist. Bear in mind that not only are salary increases directly affected by performance ratings but these ratings also influenced the possibilities for promotion. Given the far reaching impact of this defective system no employee should simply accept any rating that, in his view, is suspect.

The Outsourcing
Stratagem

What I am about to relate is based purely on deduction from a very unusual set of circumstances, none of which was remotely related to any action on my part.

In all my time with the company not once did I ever attempt to initiate contact with a recruiter or head hunter. Yet, shortly after my appraisal confrontation I started to receive almost daily telephone calls from head hunters wishing to arrange interviews for what appeared to be lucrative positions for which, on the face of it, my qualifications, experience and exposure made me an attractive candidate. Each time I enquired about the source of the information the caller obviously had, I was told that the source was confidential but highly respected. One such caller insisted that I meet with him in the Louisville airport while he was intransit to his offices in Chicago. I was very reluctant to accommodate him but he was so insistent that I was overcome by my curiosity and met with him as requested.

He was representing a large, national chemical company whose head office was in Chicago. I came exceptionally highly recommended, he revealed. Naturally, his source was confidential and could not be divulged. The position was for a Plant Manager. I asked how many managers who looked like me were employed at that level in the company he represented. His cheeks became cherry red and I knew what his answer would be. There was none. I enquired why me and why now? He responded that the company was finally attempting to integrate its management ranks and was very impressed with my résumé and thought I would be an excellent candidate. While this was flattering, I told him, I could not consider accepting the opportunity. He was very persistent until I told him that I was convinced that it made more sense for me to deal with the devil I knew than with the one that I didn't know. I was not willing to relocate to a new and unknown battlefield. He tried to convince me to reconsider by admitting that my concerns were not unfounded but he could assure me that I would have direct access to the CEO of the company because the company was absolutely committed to making its integration plans work. I thanked him and we parted company.

I am convinced that my company had implemented a strategy to outsource me. I must admit that it was a very resourceful move. I could accept a position commensurate with my qualifications, experience and exposure, improve my employment status and income but simultaneously put myself at the greatest possible risk of termination which could very easily occur during the obligatory period of probation in any new job. At the same time I would have let my company off the proverbial hook. I had no doubt that my departure would have been seen by many in the company as the result of a brilliant maneuver that won a war using a howitzer with a silencer. I was not about to surrender or even temporarily withdraw from the field of battle.

At around this time the Malaysian left the site to return to his home country as a plant manager. I was once again in a direct relationship with the manager for my plant. As time went by I started to feel that there was a kind of conspiracy of silence around me. People seemed to be friendly yet distant. I was at times beginning to wonder if I were becoming paranoid. I gave myself the benefit of the doubt and paid close attention to everyone and everything around me.

One day I received a hand written note in office mail from the HR Manager. The note revealed that "people" with whom I communicated regularly were complaining that my communications skill was poor. The note offered no details or examples or advice as to how I may address the matter. It simply said that I should be aware of this issue and bear it in mind whenever I was in discussions with my colleagues. This was laughable. I decided that I would communicate with everyone in writing as far as possible and I would follow up telephone conversations and face to face discussions with written confirmation of these conversations and discussions. Very shortly I received another note saying that there were complaints that I was documenting too much. The issue was never raised again and died a natural death under the weight of its own folly.

The Buy-out Ruse

The company was nothing if not persistent. In response to another inquiry I made to head office about my status, I was asked to meet with the corporate VP for HR in New York. We met over late lunch in a restaurant at the Waldorf Astoria. After ordering lunch and exchanging pleasantries she went directly to the point of our meeting. The company wished to make me an offer in exchange for my amicable separation; a golden handshake as it were. Would I be willing to accept this? Without the slightest hesitation I refused the offer without even wishing to know what the offer was worth. I explained that I would never give the company the pleasure of celebrating my departure by accepting any such offer. Can you imagine, I thought, the celebration that would ensue after I departed the company? To her credit she never pursued the matter further. We finished lunch, shook hands and went our separate ways. I now decided to keep meticulous records of all meaningful correspondence or telephone conversations in anticipation of a stormy future.

A Lesson from a Good Ol' Boy

Although my plant continued to survive, the company was proceeding with its restructuring plans. An early victim was the maintenance division which had a central office and workshop from which all maintenance personnel were dispatched to each plant. It was clearly an inefficient operation. Maintenance personnel punched their time cards at the central workshop. This meant that they were on the clock no matter what time they eventually arrived at a particular plant location. Needless to say, the procedure was grossly abused. This abuse was reflected in a number of plants losing a lot of operating time because of their late arrival on site, especially at the start of a shift. Maintenance would now be decentralized and each plant would be assigned its own maintenance crews. Time cards would be punched at the time clocks in the plants to which maintenance crews were assigned. Crews would be accountable now to the person in charge of their particular work site.

The maintenance supervisor generally regarded as the best at the site was assigned to me. Whether the motive behind this potentially good fortune was pure or tainted I will never know. At best, it was suspect, given the concern expressed by many at the site. The reason was that it was common knowledge that this good ol'

Indiana boy was known to be racist. Several white employees openly commiserated with me over what they assumed was my impending doom because of the problems he would more than likely cause me. In fact, I discovered that upon learning that he was reassigned to work for me, he promptly went to the site director in protest. He was told that based on company policy he had two choices: he could work for me or he could quit. He decided not to quit. Instead, he chose a rather self indulgent option. He would confront me and enlighten me to what I should expect in our relationship. I shall call him Goby.

Goby arrived at my office one afternoon to request a meeting. I purposely refused to accommodate him at the time but indicated that he could come to see me at seven o'clock the next morning. As expected, Goby was on time. I welcomed him and led him to a small conference room next to my office. I invited him to sit and proceeded to ask what I could do for him. He was direct and to the point. It was impossible for him to work for someone like me, he indicated, in a voice as calm as someone broadcasting the news. "And why is that?" I asked in turn. He indicated that I should understand. I certainly did not and I told him so. I then asked if he had a problem with my funny Kentucky accent. This elicited a faint smile but no response. I proceeded with a number of basically rhetorical questions. Among them: Is it because my hair is white? Is it because I dress a little differently? Is it because I am a relatively short person? In the end I forced him to tell me that it was because he was brought up a certain way and was too old to change. He was an honest person and wanted me to know that he could not imagine himself working for a black man. "There, you said it," I remarked cheerfully. I could see that my response confused him. It quite obviously was not what he expected.

I proceeded to explain to him that there were black people I did not like myself, just as there were white people I did not like. The difference, I indicated, is that my dislike had nothing to do with their skin color but with their behavior. The truth is, I told him, all of us dislike many around us for a number of reasons. Most of these are explainable rationally. Discrimination based on skin color is not only irrational but is absolutely indefensible and cause for termination in our company. The fact is, while I understood his prejudice it was unacceptable and would not be tolerated. Moreover, if his behavior on the job reflected his racist views or was in any way disruptive, he had to understand that I would have no hesitation whatsoever in terminating his employment immediately. This was company policy.

I emphasized that as far as I was concerned I was solely interested in his skill as an exceptional mainte-nance professional; nothing more nothing less. I went on to tell him that I did respect him for his bold honesty. We both knew that there were many others on the site who felt exactly as he did but would never ever be bold or honest enough to express this feeling. I indicated to him that I needed confirmation from him that he under-stood my position as perfectly as I understood his. He confirmed that he did understand my position. Since I clearly understood his and he clearly understood mine, I told him, we would get along like a house on fire. We did.

Shortly after our heart to heart I had reason to test Goby's mettle. We were about to discard several pieces of stainless steel tubing. The plain iron post for my gas lantern by my driveway at home was in need of replace-ment and a stainless steel tube would be perfect for this. I provided Goby with a diagram and dimensions for the post and asked him to do me the favor of using one of the tubes to make a replacement post for me. I further told him that it was not an urgent matter so he could make the post whenever it was convenient. The very next morning I arrived at my office to see Goby's gleam-ing handiwork by my door. I was pleasantly surprised and went to find him to say thanks. He brushed my expression of gratitude aside and told me that I should not hesitate to ask him for any favor as he would be only too happy to accommodate me.

As I anticipated, Goby was very good for my operations. My plant efficiency improved by several points within a few weeks of his arrival. He read the riot act to his subordinates and warned that if they failed to perform as expected they would pay a price. He was a very proud and meticulous man. He always wore black pants and white shirts. Remarkably, although he worked on equipment all day his clothes were never soiled. He did not go to the barber's; he went to the hairdresser's instead. He was always impeccably coiffed and could lean over a machine without a strand of hair falling out of place. Above all, he was known to change his Z28 Camaro every two or three years and never failed to openly criticize his colleagues who drove rusted, unattractive cars to work.

Intervention and Alarm

My plant's performance continued to improve and I anticipated a very successful annual pre-budget cost of sales review. The review team arrived soon enough from head office. There were six or so people on the review team. I was asked to join the team as a local representative. I suspect that I was asked to do so for exposure. The experience turned out to be anything but uneventful.

There were three black supervisors and several white supervisors who would make presentations of their operating budgets. The deference shown to the white presenters versus the black presenters was obvious to me. The first two black presenters were constantly interrupted during their presentations while the white presenters were allowed to complete their presentations before being questioned. I asked for a break in the presentation schedule so that I could address this disturbing observation. When I raised the issue, all but one member of the review team were offended by my observation and its implication. But for my presence the review team was entirely white. The one member who seemed not to be offended agreed with my observation and asked the others to think more carefully about my contention. I also indicated to them that I did not believe that they were aware of their behavior. They all finally agreed and apologized. The review concluded without any further incident.

During a cocktail party in a downtown hotel to celebrate the end of the review, I was pulled aside by one of the black supervisors who had heard of my intervention during the review. He expressed more concern than appreciation for what I had done and asked if I were not afraid of being fired for being too uppity. I laughed at his comment and told him that this was absolutely out of the question. He implored me to imagine that it did happen. Then what would I do, he wanted to know. I told him that I would perhaps engage a lawyer because there was no doubt in my mind that such action as a result of my intervention was clearly unwarranted. He remarked that while this may in fact be the case it could still happen. He then wished to know what I would do in the meantime for income. My response was that I would find another job. "What if you couldn't?" he persisted. He then reminded me that the outcome of any litigation could take years. He was insistent and wanted to know what I would do in the end.

More out of a desire to end the interrogation than to provide a serious response, I indicated that in the end I could always return home to Jamaica. It was perhaps the most remarkable *ah ha!* moment I had ever witnessed. His expression was as if fireworks had gone off behind his wide open eyes. "That explains it," he exulted. I was clearly perplexed. He explained that I could afford to behave in the manner I did because I had a home to return to. I pointed out that he was already at home himself. His response was immediate: "How could I be at home and be treated the way I am treated?" He never expected an answer and I could not have provided one. His eyes welled with tears and I felt his pain. For a moment I too was overwhelmed and excused myself for an escape visit to the men's room.

The following week three interesting things happened.

The first was my boss telling me that someone had paid me the most wonderful compliment. In a discussion he was told by an employee that I was the most intelligent black man he had ever seen. I laughed uncontrollably at this. My boss wished to know why I thought this was so funny. First, I explained that Goby obviously had seen few black people; second, he should simply have said that I was the most intelligent person he had ever seen. My boss was now unable to control his laughter and wanted to know how I knew that Goby was the person in question. I confessed that I was certain that only Goby would make such an outrageous statement in earnest.

The second event was my being cornered by the black supervisor who had accosted me at the cocktail party. He wanted to know all about Jamaica and how I was brought up as a child there. I basically told him my life story, including the very meaningful fact that no one in Jamaica even if illiterate, would ever succumb to intimidation by anyone because such a person was white or had some authority, especially if such authority were being abused. It was then that he told me a number of the black "guys" in the plant was aware of my problems with the company. I denied that such problems existed. He did not believe me and indicated that he would speak with me about this again.

The third revelation was that my boss was being transferred to the Philippines in a few months. To my mind this was of significance. The Philippines at the time was a very uncomfortable place for Americans. They were often kidnapped and held for significantly large ransoms. Most of those kidnapped were executives of large, multinational American companies. Rightly or wrongly, I suspected that this move was in part punishment for my boss being too "helpful" to me. Even so, this suspicion would very shortly be the least of my concerns.

Creating Options

My wife and I agreed that given the rather confusing, if not uncertain, situation with my job, we needed to create some alternatives that would allow us to remain in America were my work permit not renewed by the company at any point. The company had to finance the periodic renewal of my permit. If at any time it was decided that this could or would not be done, I would have no alternative but to leave the country. This was definitely not a situation we relished even as a remote possibility. My wife suggested that I approach the company with the proposal that it would make much more sense if I were made a resident. Over time the cost of doing this would be less than the continual renewal fees for a work permit. I was doubtful that the company would oblige but my wife insisted. What did I have to lose by approaching the company on this very reasonable proposal? It was clear by this time that neither the company nor I knew just how long I would be in Indiana. My eighteen to twenty four months time line had long expired. Surprisingly, the company agreed to my proposal and we set about finding an immigration lawyer.

Simultaneously, my wife immersed herself in the study of immigration law at the local library. She literally became an expert on the subject overnight. Our lawyer was a senior partner in reputedly the best local immigration law firm. He indicated that converting my status would require that the company advertise the position nationally and find no qualified American who could do my job. My wife, the new expert, told him that this was in fact not the case. She was absolutely correct. She had discovered through her research that because I had been with the company for a number of years and had spent at least the last two consecutive years in basically the same capacity I would be exempt from this requirement. I would qualify under the classification of *professional*. This was the classification under which doctors and professional engineers, for example, were given high residency preference. On this basis my residency application would take very little time to be approved. We easily forgave the lawyer's ineptitude because his embarrassment was so obvious. The usual process for gaining residency ensued and our residency documents were in hand in just a few months. We had successfully created our first option.

My wife convinced me that we needed to initiate steps that would allow us to survive, if for whatever reason I had to separate from or be terminated by the company. After a brief period of investigation we agreed on the idea of starting a catering business. This business would showcase Caribbean style cuisine with an international flair. A signature feature would be the introduction of Jamaican beef patties to Louisville. In Jamaica and large city centers like Toronto, New York, Atlanta and Miami, Jamaican beef patties are almost as popular as hamburgers. In Canada and America the popularity of the patties had crossed over from the immigrant population into the mainstream.

We contacted the appropriate local authorities, including the Department of Health, to learn exactly what we would need to do to set up our business. One health official suggested that our idea would be better served were we to also start a restaurant. This would allow the local folks to try our food. He convinced us that since our potential clientele was essentially meat and potatoes people and not predisposed to being adventurous, this would be a great way in which to introduce our menu. It was a very attractive idea but would require much more funding than our budget would allow. We never the less did not discard the idea even as my wife experimented at home with recipes for our Jamaican beef patties. We used friends and neighbors as guinea pigs to great effect.

At the same time we had become quite disenchanted with our rented house. It was our second rental because the owner of our first had returned from abroad and needed his house. Given our already extended stay and the fact that we were now residents we agreed that it made sense to purchase our own house. We decided on a house in the neighborhood in which we had first rented. This house was a later but very similar model and had been the model house for the subdivision. It was on a postcard perfect cul-de-sac of no more than a dozen or so houses. We loved it and settled in very quickly and comfortably. Our neighbors on either side of us were friendly. One neighbor was a physician and his wife and the other was an elderly, retired couple. We re-established our routine and continued to work on all fronts to ensure our family's survival with or without my employer. We obtained all the necessary approvals for our restaurant, found a building in a historic district ten minutes from down town Louisville and fifteen minutes from the plant site across the river in Indiana. We proceeded to renovate the rented property.

Not so surprisingly, there were a few Jamaicans residing in Louisville. We naturally became friends with a number of them, including a banker and her husband and a handy man who owned an apartment complex which he maintained himself. It seemed that Jamaicans could be found anywhere. In fact, someone once said that he was sure there was a Jamaican on the moon when the Americans first landed there. They just did not see him. With their help we set about converting the building into a restaurant. We also had significant financial assistance from one of our closest friends who resided in Jamaica. We agreed on a name for our sub-chapter S company: *The Caribbean Gourmet*. We fine tuned our business plan, developed our menu and created a business logo which an artist friend graciously finalized at no charge. We passed all the required government inspections and started our restaurant and catering business.

It was not easy. The entire family was involved intimately with the endeavor. I assisted my wife every day after work, the children bussed and waited tables on week-ends and my wife easily worked twelve to fourteen hours a day just about seven days a week. But the hard work and long hours were beginning to bear fruit as more and more people became aware of us and a number of companies and public institutions became patrons. Eventually we had a very flattering review by the local newspaper. We were not prepared for the aftermath and were overwhelmed the week-end following the review. Diners came from as far as Cincinnati, ninety miles away. It was a heady experience. Our second option was successfully in place. By this time many people at the plant site were now aware of our restaurant and quite a few of them came by to dine. We started to consider phase two of our business plan which was to expand the Jamaican beef patties part of the business into franchising.

In a sense, the restaurant became a little piece of the Caribbean in Kentucky. Diners were always fascinated by our presence and would never fail to ask why we decided to start this type of restaurant in a place like Louisville. Our response was always the same: my job took our family to Kentucky; my wife loved to cook, and there was nothing like *The Caribbean Gourmet* within hundreds of miles. We thought it was a great idea. We were spreading Caribbean culture through the restaurant as well as by our presence in the community in which we lived.

We maintained our Jamaican sensibilities and made sure that our children did the same, in spite of the inevitable assault of peer pressure at school and elsewhere.

For example, we never gave our children an allowance and never paid them to do chores. But they were aware that their friends enjoyed both. We discovered once that our elderly neighbors were unable to cut their lawn for sometime. We directed our sons to cut their lawn when cutting our own. The neighbors were effusively grateful and offered to pay our boys. They both refused to accept payment. Our sons confessed to us that their refusal was not painless. We told them that we understood and that this fact made us even more proud of them. The neighbors called us in protest and wanted to give us the money so we could pass it on to the boys. Of course, we also refused and explained that in our home country no one gets paid for being a good neighbor.

On another occasion, this time at the restaurant, a homeless white man came to ask my wife if there was anything he could do in the restaurant for food. He had been driving from Tennessee with his family in an old battered car looking for work but could find none. My wife explained that she already had employees doing everything that needed to be done. Just then my wife observed that his family, his wife and two little girls, was in the car outside just a few yards from the entrance to the restaurant. This convinced her that his story was credible and she offered to give him food for him and his family. He protested because he did not want to be fed for free although he had no money with which to buy food.

In the meantime my wife had prepared enough food for him and his family. As he continued to protest and insist that he wanted to work for the food his two little girls ran into the restaurant. They were obviously hungry, in need of baths and clean clothes. My wife was overcome. She asked him whether he had tried to get into a shelter for the homeless in downtown Louisville. He had, but the family would have to be separated as only the mother and children could be accommodated together. He would be placed in a separate shelter. He would not agree to this. The man then asked her why it was that she, a foreigner, could come to America and get money from the government to start a restaurant and he, an American, could not find a job to take care of his family. My wife explained as best she could, that the government did not give us any money; that all the money used to start the restaurant was our own money, some of which we brought into America from our own country. Whether he believed this or not we will never know. As he thanked my wife and turned to leave he promised to return and pay for the food as soon as he had money. Although we never saw him again his story remains with us and we too wondered why such severe poverty exists in the wealthiest country on earth.

The Good Doctor

At the restaurant we met some very engaging and interesting people. There was a diner who came by after he had read our favorable newspaper review. Despite the warning that the Jamaican hot pepper sauce was "high octane" and should only be used very sparingly, he decided that his familiarity with Tabasco was ample preparation for using any hot pepper sauce. He was wrong, of course. To our consternation, after trying the Jamaican Scotch Bonnet hot pepper sauce in excess he hyperventilated. In another incident an avuncular guest teased our younger son about reporting him to the authorities for working while under age. Our son responded defensively that he couldn't be reported as he was the owner of the business. Just in case this defense failed, he quickly alerted his mother to the perceived threat. He was, of course, put at ease and filed the experience away as one to be remembered wryly. But the most unforgettable diner of all was our very regular black American physician patron. He dined nearly every Friday afternoon and loved our curried chicken and fried plantains. We would have brief, casual discussions on a variety of subjects.

On one occasion we both realized that we did not live very far from each other and that our children attended the same schools. I told him I thought I might have visited his neighborhood a number of times when I took my sons there to some of their classmates' birthday parties. He asked whether the parties were on the white side of his neighborhood or the black side. I was much surprised by this and asked whether there really were such a division in his neighborhood. He assured me that this was indeed the case. I asked why and was told one of the saddest stories I have ever heard.

The physician was probably a few years younger than I so the story he was about to relate would not have been about events of too many years earlier. He recalled his white teacher asking each student on the last day of school in his senior year, what his plans were after graduation. He indicated that he intended to go on to college and ultimately become a doctor. His teacher promptly advised that he should not set himself and his parents up for such great disappointment. Instead, she advised, he should think more realistically about being a tradesman or even a teacher. As he related the story I could see the fire of anger masked by pain burning in his eyes. His face tightened and his voice broke as he told me that at that point he knew that if it cost him his life he had to become a physician.

He had obviously done well in school and his mother had given him a graduation gift of ten dollars. This was more than a pittance in the early sixties for any kid, especially a black kid. He proceeded to the ritziest store in down town Louisville to make a purchase in celebration of his graduation. As he stepped into the store he recalled two white clerks shadowing him. Eventually one approached to enquire what it was that he wanted. He explained that he was interested in buying a cardigan. He was told immediately that niggers were not sold anything in the store and he should leave. He refused and continued to shop. Within minutes two white police men arrived and escorted him to jail. He was allowed a phone call to his mother who later came to collect him.

I commiserated but suggested that living in a completely black neighborhood did not seem to me to be an appropriate response to the terribly painful experiences of his youth. For a start, I pointed out, property values either remain stagnant or decline over time. Secondly, to my way of thinking, such a separation could not possibly be helpful to black children who would inevitably have to relate to white people in their later life in any number of ways. This was basically unavoidable. He interrupted my challenges impatiently by admitting that what I said made sense. He just could not afford it. I asked why, since it was very obvious that as a physician he could live wherever he wished. His response was deeply bitter and final. He simply could not afford to subject his children to even the slightest risk of encountering the kinds of insults that he had suffered as a youth.

He informed me that he owned a shotgun and if a white neighbor ever harassed or insulted his children, he was more than prepared to blow such a person away. His language was much more expressive and colorful and its intent impossible to misconstrue. He continued to explain to me that not a lot had changed since his days at school in Louisville. Even at medical school, at professional conferences and in his practice, he could still feel the indignities of racism. For example, he revealed that he could not have set up his practice any where between Louisville and Cincinnati unless he wished to starve as there were too few, if any, black people along this corridor. He admitted that he did have some white patients but mainly because of the convenience of location and nearby companies whose health plans allowed employees to see him. Even so, he observed, once he confirmed to a white patient that she was pregnant he never saw her again. I asked why and he asked me in turn why I thought this was the case. I believe I understood.

I inquired about his mother and listened to yet another remarkable story. His mother was in her seventies. For a long time he had tried to get her to retire but she steadfastly refused. She worked as a nanny and housekeeper for a very wealthy family in Louisville. She had effectively raised this family's children who now had their own children. Her contention was that she could not abandon the second generation of children as there was no one else to raise them. It was a very complex relationship, he told me, between black people like his mother and white people like the family she honestly felt she could not abandon. I thought of this in terms of two magnets whose polarities are constantly being switched so they are inseparable at times and repel each other vigorously at other times. The complexity did not escape me. It also occurred to me that, as a rule, black Americans always appear to be so much more concerned about the welfare of the white people they serve than the vast majority of white people appear concerned about the welfare of the black people who serve them. Given the one sided history of abuse in the relationship, this kind of consideration on the part of black Americans has always seemed paradoxical to me. In fact, the genesis of the doctor's purposely segregated neighborhood came about in a very calculated and ironic way.

In the days of segregation, white families lived in and around the city of Louisville. Black families lived outside of the segregated city but close enough to facilitate easy access to this black labor pool. This was very convenient for the white gentry. Domestic workers could walk to work. When segregation was outlawed and blacks started to move into the city, the white people fled to the suburbs, miles away from their labor pool. In order to address this real inconvenience they built servants' houses on the opposite side of the main drive across from their estates. Black workers were housed once again close to their employers. In time these servants' houses were sold to the residents who were all black. The good doctor's mother owned one of these houses in which he now lived by choice.

Try as I might I could not stop thinking about what all of this meant. Is there any lesson to be learned from my interaction with the good doctor? I think so. I was deeply moved by the fact that segregation was actively chosen by a person who had endured forced segregation much of his life. To me this was equivalent to choosing pain over the possibility of no pain because you had learned to tolerate high levels of pain. But looked at a little differently I can see how choosing the pain you had learned to endure could be less painful than the new pain of the hostility which inevitably accompanies desegregation for desegregation's sake. It was clear to me that the psychological scars of slavery and racism are significantly more harmful than the strongest memories of physical bondage and abuse. I never the less continue to have great difficulty understanding why a physician would be unable to move beyond the hurt of his past and was so intent on building a gossamer wall to insulate his children from anticipated racial discrimination. I doubt very much that we can escape the quagmire of the past by quarantining ourselves there.

This interaction made me reflect on the survival psychology of former slaves and indentured servants and their descendants in Jamaica. Perhaps the single most influential fact in our case was the reality of our overwhelmingly superior numbers. The ruler class had very little choice in how it could respond to the abolition of slavery. This was the truest possible case of adapt or die; remain and be absorbed. Accordingly, the damaging psychological hangover from slavery and its diabolical progeny, racism, was relatively short lived. Unfortunately, this was never likely in America. In fact, the opposite was the all but inevitable outcome. And this is indeed the case. Looked at from this perspective one is forced to be much more understanding of, and even sympathetic to, the dilemma facing my friend the good doctor. Yet, this does not mean that Americans like the good doctor should feel hopeless. We may at times feel as if it is pointless to attempt to escape from our worst nightmares but there is always a chance that the future could be better than the past. It is a risk worth taking. And there is perhaps no better place in which to take this risk than America. We should never lose hope as the poem below suggests.

Toward A Nearing End

Jack and Jill
Went up the hill ....

Where once there was a gurgling stream
Where primordial carpet grew thick and green
And the jibbing air preened with lilied fragrance
Pulled forth a thousand sniffs
Where they wont would swirl the water
With accustomed toes or twirl a twig therein
Or cast a handful of plucked buttercups
Then watch them bob downstream
Some upside down, inverted crowns
Some right side up, simply buttercups.

They drop their pail
For there is no stream
Just jaded rocks without their natural slime
Or ivy-like morass.
In shocked concert they pointed
The cracking joints of knotty fingers
Making curious antiphony.
Endless waves of besieging sand
Lay like a sculptured, frozen sea
Uninhabited above uninhabitable below.

In hopeful disbelief they look to each other
Cinderella at midnight
Orpheus after the Maenads
Mangled but alive.
Where is the golden slipper?
Where is the golden song?
Jack fell down ......
And Jill ......
Like common curs they lick the sand
And scramble on all fours, on knee and hand.

Pockmarked limbs leave trails of red on cruel sand
Is this the Promised Land?
Their glazed eyes they raise to heaven
But empty heaven cannot weep
And kind Aeolus seems sound asleep.
It is not night but there is no day
It is not life but there is no death
In the stark exacting wilderness
Where no vultures lurk
And cacti do not grow.

Their rags but so many growing pains
Which but for frayed edges
Are naught but life's red stains
Vacuous unfeeling bellies
Bloated distortions
Gouge the barren land
A turtle would have been more grand
Tunneling a hole
Mercy - a hole
Salvation - death

Are we alone we two or are there others who ....?
Insulted earth shudders in the pain of its own fever.
Torn figures squirm a painful inch then lay flayed
Trampled petals on a doormat. Stilled.
Time becomes an imperious instant
Capsule of all hope, boundary of all faith.
Not far behind though they had not seen
A desolate palm stood gaunt but green
Cheerless supplicant to deserted heaven.
The landscape now a painter's dream.

Assistance from a Likely Source

My black supervisor-protector came to my office one Friday afternoon accompanied by three other black supervisors. They each worked in different areas of responsibility, from quality assurance to purchasing. They wished to know how they could be of help in my attempt to address my problems with the company. I continued to deny that I had any such problems. Soon enough I realized that they in fact had more information about what was happening than I thought. It became apparent as well, that a number of people throughout the site was also aware of the issue. This was surprising since I had not revealed my situation to anyone at the site except selected site management and only on a need to know basis. My potential supporters indicated that the site HR department appeared to be the publicizing source. It was futile to continue in denial.

Up to this point I saw my problem with the company as a strictly personal one. I was convinced that I could address it effectively on this basis. I was very concerned about involving others and running the risk of losing control of a process I was convinced would work quite successfully on my behalf. In addition, I was very conflicted in my views regarding employees who had been subjected to discrimination over what appeared to be a protracted period but seemed to have done little about it.

After some discussion I was convinced that, under certain specified conditions, the group and I could in fact work together to help each other. The most crucial condition, in my view, was that the group, to a man, take the week-end to think about the possible downsides to confronting the organization on a matter as incendiary as racial discrimination. I demanded that they discuss the entire matter with their wives and get their wives' commitment before I would be willing to proceed with their involvement. We agreed to meet again in my office after work on the following Monday. My wife and I spent much of the week-end discussing the likely permutations of what the involvement of this group of partisans could do to the tone and outcome of the approach we were committed to take in addressing the issue with the company. In the end, we agreed to play it by ear and to let the group's involvement run its course for a little while.

In spite of my ambivalence about the involvement of the group, I was quite excited at the prospect of what I thought they might bring to the table. We met as agreed. They had all discussed their involvement with their wives and had received their wives' unconditional blessing. I challenged them with the issues my protector had raised with me regarding the possibility of termination in the middle of things, regardless of how remote a possibility I genuinely thought this to be. They convinced me that this was of no moment to them and proceeded to tell me how much information they had about the company's discriminatory treatment of black supervisory employees over time. They recounted one story that was the most moving of all.

There was a foreman in the warehouse, whom they knew I had met, who was the very first black first line supervisor to be hired by the company soon after affirmative action became law in 1964. I believe he was a graduate of Kentucky State University. It was nearly twenty years since the company had taken this bold, commendable, ground breaking step. Yet, the foreman had remained in the exact same position in the same warehouse ever since. During this time he had trained a number of white employees who had since moved on to very senior positions. They identified one such employee who was now a vice president. I was enthralled by this revelation and wanted to know whether the foreman had had poor reviews or had raises withheld because of poor performance or disciplinary failings. They were emphatic in their response that the foreman was in fact considered an exemplary employee who always had favorable reviews as well as satisfactory salary increases. I was probably as apprehensive as I was amazed by this story. How could this be? I wondered to myself. Instinctively, it seemed so unlikely, I demanded substantiating evidence.

My demand for evidence was apparently anticipated and I was told that they had already started to collect data which would substantiate every claim that they would make. I congratulated them on this approach and advised that they put it all in writing. I could hardly contain my excitement. I was beginning to understand and appreciate the potential power of this collaboration. Although I had never once doubted the moral force of my own case or my unshakeable conviction that I would prevail in my address of it, having the kind of supportive data that I now anticipated was icing on the proverbial cake. It also occurred to me that, in the case of my collaborators, justice delayed may not after all be justice denied. I proceeded to document my own personal experiences since arriving at the site in Indiana with much greater zeal. After all, I could not demand less of myself than I was demanding of my collaborators.

As we continued to accumulate data, the more obvious it became that the extent and depth of now visible bias in the company exceeded my worst fears. There was a young white male in the HR department with whom I had worked when he was an engineer in the IE department. Astonishingly, he seemed sensitive to the issue of bias at the site and often surprised me with his candor.

Every now and then he would hint at what the prevailing thinking of the site director and his own boss, the HR manager, was on the matter. At first I was very wary of him. I thought that he may just be using subterfuge to obtain useful information which could be used to blunt the impact of what my collaborators and I were doing. I expressed this concern to the group. To my surprise I was told that our HR colleague was a genuine sympathizer and could be trusted.

After about three months, I had collected and systematically organized enough meaningful data into a small booklet. I had treated the data just as I would treat normal business data were I planning for a business review. I organized the data to best demonstrate the comparative progress of white employees versus that of comparable black employees who had made no progress whatsoever. The data also revealed the depressing impact this discrepancy had over time on the earnings of these employees. By any standard of measurement, the data was a damning indictment of the company's behavior in regard to its qualified, experienced black employees. I provided each member of the group with a copy for review. When I was satisfied we had all adequately reviewed the document, we agreed to meet off-site to develop a plan as to how we would approach the company with our findings.

Predictably, some non-management black employees became aware of what we had done and came to me with a request that they be allowed to participate in the exercise. I explained to them that this was not a possibility as their involvement would likely do more harm than good. They made the point that already most people in the plant were aware of what we were doing and were making outrageous assumptions about our wanting to sue the company and shut down the site. They felt that they could be helpful in squelching such rumors with facts. We came to a compromise and agreed that two of the non-management black employees would be allowed to attend our off-site data review meeting. One

165

was a union delegate; the other was a line worker smart enough to have been a line supervisor.

It was not surprising that some of us were angrier and more impatient than others. There was a small faction of the group at the meeting that wanted us to lodge a formal complaint with the EEOC. The two line employees, not unexpectedly, were firmly in support of this view. I was firmly opposed to it. In all likelihood this would move the issue into the public arena. This is exactly what I wanted to avoid at almost any cost. I was absolutely convinced that this would not serve our purpose in any effective way. The counter argument was that, were we to file a complaint, the company would not be able to penalize any of us in any way as long as the filing was active. While this was apparently true, it would have created an unhealthy atmosphere in which to work with the company in any attempt to resolve the issue. I finally had agreement to a compromise. We would visit the EEOC offices for a discussion but we would not lodge an official complaint. In spite of this compromise, I was certain in my own mind that as soon as we showed up at the offices of the EEOC the news would get back to the company. I have no proof that this did in fact occur but I have to admit that I believe that it did.

We agreed that I would follow the company's chain of command in addressing the issue and that I would be the spokesperson for the group of management employees. Accordingly, I requested a meeting with the site director and presented him with the document. I explained to him what was in the document and what I believed this revealed. I urged him to study the document and to treat the matter with the seriousness it clearly deserved. I emphasized that this would be in the very best interest of all concerned. He said very little but his body language spoke volumes. He perceived the document and my contention as little more than a nuisance. He never the less told me he would certainly read the document. I reported back to my colleagues and indicated that, in my opinion, we should not expect much of a response from the site director.

In short order I received a call from the site HR manager asking that I come to a meeting with him and the site director in the site director's office. I quickly alerted my group and set about preparing for what I anticipated would be a most interesting meeting. I arrived at the office to see the two principals as well as our young HR sympathizer. They each had a copy of the booklet. It did not take long for me to realize that they had studied the findings. I was able to see highlighted sections of pages, circled and underlined words and sentences and bracketed tables. To my mind this was a good sign. The HR manager was the first to speak. He expressed the view that there appeared to be much misunderstanding surrounding the claims my document made. I asked him to explain. He responded by questioning the source of the data. I asked him if he had data that would contradict the data presented. He admitted that he had not. I then pointed out to him that even if my data were only 90% accurate there was a very serious problem that needed urgent attention.

The site director advised that I should be very wary of the group of black supervisors with whom I was consorting as, if they had issues, those were certainly different from mine. Our sympathizer said nothing. I suspect he was smiling on the inside of his face as he had in fact validated much of the data in the document from HR files. I advised the meeting that, in my estimation, it may be necessary to seek the involvement of head office. I felt that the problems identified in the document may very well have implications beyond our site. All along, my assumption was that head office had already been notified. More likely than not head office had advised site management to see if they could deal with the issue as a strictly local matter. Even in hindsight I am unable to tell whether the site management's failure to address the issue effectively was due to incompetence or indifference. The ball was punted to head office.

In the meantime the site and the rest of the U.S. manufacturing operations were continuing with an extensive rationalization program. At the Indiana site a number of plants was now at risk in addition to my own. Needless to say, this precipitated very serious areas of distrust between site management and the union as well as between site management and head office. The site director was caught in the middle. As morale continued to fall the incidence of product quality problems increased almost proportionately. It is my opinion that between the quality and morale issues the site director was so compromised that the company thought it best to relocate him. He was replaced by another son of Indiana who had done well for himself and had become the VP of manufacturing for our very large subsidiary in Brazil. He was very highly regarded. It appeared that the company felt that, with his exposure to a diverse society and workforce, he would be good for the Indiana site. Of course, I knew enough about expatriate life and about Brazil not to be as optimistic as the company appeared to be.

In many ways the new site VP reminded me of the Canadian experience with the attempt to relocate the manufacturing executive from the Philippines. This executive was also married to a native Brazilian woman whose family was very wealthy. The story is that she never really wanted to leave Brazil and neither did he. While the new VP appeared to be settling into his new assignment, people who knew him well indicated that he was not at all happy and regularly expressed a desire to return to Brazil. He had inherited some very difficult problems. He made it his number one priority to improve quality and housekeeping at the site. I am sure he had hoped that site morale would be favorably affected by improvements in these areas of priority he had set himself. Subsequent events would prove that this approach was deficient. He was clearly very focused and a lot was expected of him.

Help from on high - the Black Court Press

Head office help arrived in the form of a one man cavalry. He was tall; he had presence; he spoke well. His easy, comfortable, assured manner said, "I can take care of the problem." And yes, he was black. He was a former NBA professional. This fact could easily have been assumed from his height and athletic build. We met alone. He repeated what was about to become the mantra of rebuttal: there is much misunderstanding surrounding the data in the document. He was certain we could easily and amicably address what I saw as very troubling problems but he saw as simple misunderstandings. I asked whether he had studied the document. He confirmed that he had. I asked how long he had been with the company. He indicated seven months. This surprised me. I wondered what would cause the company to insert a new hire into the thick of things. He simply would not have been around long enough to know the history of the company or even to begin to have a sense of the environment at the site. I explained to him that it was doubtful that he knew or understood the company as well as I did from the perspective of my nearly seventeen years versus his seven months.

As I listened to him I realized that behind the strategy of the company was the hope that this rather imposing black man would be able to convince me that my concerns, while not totally baseless, were not too far from being so. It is not without irony that the company obviously felt that, on this occasion, this imposing man's black skin would somehow be an asset in resolving the problem. I asked him whether he was in a position to decide or agree on anything with me. He admitted that he was not. I warned him that he should be very careful of being used by the company as a sacrificial lamb since it was very clear to me that he could not effectively address the issues at hand. I suggested that he return to New York with the message that I was only willing to have further discussions with someone who was able to make decisions on behalf of the company. I learned later that he was hired on the understanding that his continued employment depended on his resolving the issues I had documented. He never had a chance. I saw him a few weeks later at a company event. He approached me and apologized for his approach at our recent meeting and indicated that he now understood much more clearly the real issues I had documented. He then dropped a bombshell: he would be leaving the company at the end of the month. In less than twelve months he had come and gone.

It was now necessary to move the discussion to the next level. I continued discussions with the company about my own situation as well as the circumstances pertaining to the other members of the group of five (which I shall now identify as the G5). I sent a copy of the G5 document along with a cover letter directly to the President of the North America Division. In my letter I expressed incredulity that after many months of attempting to resolve what was clearly a very serious problem, I was left with no choice but to bring the matter directly to his attention. I indicated that it was my hope that, unlike those before him, he would not view the evidence presented in the accompanying document simply as misunderstandings.

Negotiations and Accommodation

I received a telephone call in my office late one afternoon. It was the President of the North America Division whom I shall call Felix. He wished to know if I were alone and could speak with him. I thanked him for calling and indicated that I was alone in the office and would indeed be delighted to speak with him. He confirmed that he had received the document and my note. He had studied the document and would love to meet with me to review and discuss the material. He also indicated that the VP for HR was on the line with us and introduced him. Our three way conversation was very conciliatory. Felix insisted I keep our telephone conversation confidential. I agreed. He went on to ask if we could meet the very next afternoon in the Brown Hotel in down town Louisville. Again, I agreed. He would fly in on a private jet. Our meeting would also be held in the strictest of confidence. He would fly into Louisville just for our meeting and would not visit or see anyone at the site. For the very first time during the entire episode following the distribution of the G5 document, I felt that action was about to be taken to address the painful issue of bias and its effects at the site and, I suspected, in the company at large.

Felix was a lanky, athletic looking man, perhaps a few years older than I. We had met at company meetings before but he was not someone I saw frequently. I had to control my urge to laugh on seeing him in the hotel suite he had reserved for our meeting. When he let me into the suite he had already put aside his ubiquitous jacket and loosened his neck tie. There were trays of fruit, biscuits and cheese, coffee and a pitcher of water on a table with cups and saucers, spoons and glasses. The sharp afternoon sunlight filled the room. The surprisingly thin material of his charcoal grey trousers was like a filter and I could see his boney knees where his knee cap had clearly worn away much of the material of his already very thin trousers. It made me wonder if this were the only pair of trousers he wore to work. I was certain that this could never be the case but just the thought was sufficient to make me want to laugh aloud.

Felix reminded me of another corporate company executive I had met many years earlier when I worked in the Caribbean. He was so focused on work that he never married and as far as any one could tell, never had a girl friend. The male side of his family was prone to heart failure. His own father had in fact died from a heart attack at a relatively early age, as had an uncle. This made him paranoid about his health to the point of obsession. He ran five miles every day of his life regardless of where he happened to be and all he ever had for lunch was a single ripe banana. He was a small man, probably just over five feet. He was so spare you could see nearly every vein in his face, arms and legs. I guessed that his body fat index must have been zero. His two obsessions in life: his work and his health. The story is told that when his promotion to Executive VP was announced his friends in head office forcibly took him from the office to purchase a new suit for him to wear to his celebratory cocktail party.

Felix was accompanied by the corporate VP of HR who, amusingly, had remained in full executive garb. He invited me to sit next to him and beckoned to his VP to join us at the table. Each had his own copy of the G5 document in front of him on the table. I removed my own copy from my file folder. We exchanged pleasantries for a few moments before getting down to the business at hand. Felix readily admitted that there was indeed a problem and indicated with conviction that he fully intended to address it. I commended him for his refreshing candor. He expressed great admiration for the manner in which I was handling the potentially inflammable issue and wondered if I had thought about how he might address it. I told him that while I had not spent much time contemplating this, I did have some ideas. He was anxious to hear these.

First, I said, apart from the issues raised in the G5 document we should all realize the true extent of the problem. I implored him to think about the fact that he, the President of the North America Division, was meeting with me in a hotel room in Louisville over a matter that probably a dozen or more people in between us should have been able to handle. This, I pointed out, is itself a very significant aspect of the problem. He agreed. Secondly, I did not think that the management of the site could be left with the responsibility to address the problem, even if it were given direct marching orders, trained to do so and provided with on site professional assistance for support. He wondered aloud why I thought this to be the case. I referred him to the statement recorded in the G5 document that was made by the previous site director that, in spite of my experience and qualification, no one in the company would allow me the opportunity to manage at a level commensurate with my abilities and experience. In my opinion, I indicated, the degree of insensitivity, indifference and malice among site management disqualified them from any consideration of being able to execute such a task with even a modicum of credibility. They were in fact a large part of the problem and very unlikely to be an effective part of the solution. Felix then wanted to know what I would suggest as an alternative.

I had not thought of this before. In an instant, it occurred to me that the only meaningful way in which to address the root of the problem was to have the entire site work force together in one place to speak about the issues as well as confirm and emphasize the company's policies regarding bias of any type in hiring or promoting employees. To my great surprise Felix agreed to this idea immediately and directed his VP to arrange such a meeting. He indicated that this should be done off site. I was very impressed with the decisiveness of his approach and his willingness to accept and act on my idea. He also felt that this meeting should take place at the soonest opportunity. I agreed with him. Any protracted delay would not be healthy for site morale which was already in serious decline. I was convinced that no matter how we tried, there was no way in which we could contain the inevitable rumors that would arise from the prospect of such a meeting, especially when it was to be held off site.

Felix then turned to my own personal situation. He requested that I allow him a few weeks to think about how exactly to address this and, unprompted, indicated that he would confirm our meeting and discussion in writing within the next twenty four hours. I cannot even guess at how long our meeting lasted but its duration was immaterial. What was certain was that much had been accomplished. We now had a plan for action which was sure to make a serious impact on the entire site population and would certainly change my own circumstances. It was my hope and expectation that the circumstances of the other G5 members would also be affected favorably.

True to his word, Felix' confirmation letter arrived the very next day in the mail at my house. I was very impressed. He must have written the letter immediately after our meeting and mailed it before leaving Louisville. There was no reason not to have faith in this man's word going forward. I invited the G5 to have lunch with me the following day and revealed the facts of my meeting and discussion with Felix. I asked that these be kept in the strictest confidence until at least after our off site meeting was held. They were all delighted to hear this but wondered at the extent to which such a meeting could effectively change the realities of site culture. I encouraged them to be optimistic. I believed that this was a very exciting start on a journey of intervention that could only have positive outcomes.

Corporate
Commandment

    Within a week the moment of truth arrived. The site was informed that the entire facility would be shut down for an off site, all day meeting at the French Lick resort in Indiana. Employees would be transported by luxury coaches to the resort. Speculation was rife as to the nature of the meeting and the reason it was being held. Understandably, there was no useful way in which to communicate the real reason for the meeting or the substance of what would be discussed. One thing became clear immediately after the announcement of the meeting, however. The most commonly held view was that I was the reason. A number of white employees came to my office to tell me exactly this and to let me know that I had suddenly become the single most powerful person on the entire site. Of course, I attempted to debunk this outlandishly silly notion but with no visible success. Interestingly, the site VP never said a word to me.

    The meeting site was quite new and impressive by any measure. It was an upscale resort with exquisitely manicured grounds. The company had taken over the entire place. We would be there for breakfast and lunch. The inevitable buzz around the resort, once we all arrived there, was electrifying. I could not avoid sensing that I was a focus of attention. It was apparent that Felix and the VP of HR had arrived the evening before and had stayed over night at the resort. A number of small meeting rooms was also available. The thinking was that some employees would wish to have discussions in small groups with their managers or supervisors after the main presentation by Felix. The Indiana site population numbered in the hundreds and easily filled the main meeting hall. After introductory remarks by the site VP and the head office VP of HR, Felix addressed the meeting.

Felix was blunt. The audience was as hushed and anticipatory as could be expected under the circumstances. There is more than ample evidence, he intoned with unquestionable authority and conviction, that prejudice, bias and discrimination existed at the Indiana site. The policies of the company explicitly forbid this. His tone was almost angry. My view is that he was furious that he was forced by unacceptable circumstances to do what he was doing. By any stretch of the imagination, it was not a pleasant task. It was clear to me that Felix felt that the discomfort he was enduring deserved to be shared with those who were certainly more culpable for the precipitating circumstances than he was. He made it clear that, regardless of position in hierarchy, anyone who could not live with the very explicit policies and rules of the company should voluntarily resign or face termination. There would be zero tolerance for discrimination on grounds of "race, religion, national origin, color, sex, age, veteran status, marital status, or handicap."

There was going to be no accommodation for behavior which was at variance with these policies and rules. These policies and rules had been seen by all employees as every employee had been given a copy of the company's code of conduct from which the preceding grounds statement was taken. Certainly, no employee had ever heard this policy repeated to them like an inviolable commandment. There could be no doubt whatsoever that what Felix said Felix meant. He took no questions and indicated to the audience that if anyone had questions or concerns these should be directed to his or her supervisor or manager. Every supervisor or manager was obliged to address such questions directly without exception.

Felix indicated that plans were being developed to have employees at the site go through sensitivity training. This would be company sponsored and mandatory. Local management would shortly provide the details. The entire program would be monitored very closely by head office. It was his hope that a meeting such as this one would never again be necessary. He emphasized the real value of diversity in the organization as a competitive weapon that must be encouraged and nurtured. His address was decisive and moving. No one present could possibly have the slightest doubt that variant behavior at the Indiana site would be very risky business.

After the meeting I was invited to a meeting with the VP of HR from head office. He, and I guess others at head office, were very concerned that I may initiate litigation against the company. By inference, it was now public knowledge that I and others had been the victims of bias at the site. The VP was very direct in his comments. He wished to know what I thought of Felix' presentation and what my intentions were having heard it. I was unstinting in my praise and admiration but remained very concerned about next steps. He warned against pursuing litigation on the matter as this could be self defeating and would, without a doubt, take much time. Ultimately, in his view, neither the company nor I could be certain of the outcome of any such litigation as each side had an equal chance of success or failure. He implored me to be patient as Felix was firmly committed to making things right. This would take a little time, however, as any action taken was bound to affect other people in the organization. I admitted that I understood this but never gave him the comfort he sought - that the possibility of litigation did not exist.

Similar meetings were held with the other members of the G5. Most went well. One did not. There was one member of our group, whom I shall call Ted, who was overcome by emotion. He was so deeply hurt and offended by the price he had paid because of bias, he was unreservedly offensive in his language. He made it known in no uncertain terms that the company, through people he named, had robbed him of years of wages he should have earned. As a result, not only did he suffer but his family had suffered as well. He had lost faith in the company and its management and did not expect much to change. Accordingly, his only interest was to be compensated retroactively for his financial losses. This was not an unreasonable position to take. However, while this vented, unbridled hostility might have made Ted feel better at the time, it was not at all helpful ultimately. I came to learn that Felix and corporate HR had decided that his individual case would not be addressed. Corporate was so offended by his behavior that they were willing to face the possibility of being sued rather than appear to cave to his demand for retroactive compensation.

This saddened me immensely as Ted was a wonderful person and had truly worked his heart out on his job, fully aware, that in order for him to get ahead or even keep up with his white colleagues, he had to do much more than they at every turn. He was a college graduate but watched white non-graduates move ahead of him without much effort and certainly little to no evidence to justify their promotions. I have no doubt that Ted's hypertension was related to his job and his feeling of powerlessness to change or improve his circumstances. It was abundantly clear to me that of all of us he was the most deeply scarred by his experiences at the site. Even more regrettable is the fact that he eventually fell ill and had to be hospitalized a number of times for multiple illnesses. Ted passed away a few years later. The entire episode appears so unfair that one is forced to wonder whether justice can ever truly rise to the challenge of experiences such as those he had endured. Still, there are ties that bind and memories that will never leave.

The String

The string of life is fragile, brittle.
Yet stronger than tensile steel
The ties we make
With others and with ourselves.
We laugh, we cry, we say goodbye,
We remember, we forget.
We regret not saying this
Not doing that
Before we disappear.
We beat our chests and scream to heaven
Each time the string is broken.
Death we expect if always unprepared.
Confused, we wonder why
The mystery only deepens.
In the end we cannot comprehend
But will not accept
Life's riddle or death's question.
From whence do we come?
Where do we go?
And what of the in between?
We struggle with our coming and going
No less with our existence.
In the end we are the question
Expressed or not
The answer as well
Provided or withheld.

I recall a number of memorable occurrences following the Indiana off-site meeting but two of these stand out above the others. One was my participation in one of the sensitivity training sessions. The other was the departure of the site V.P. He returned to Brazil.

As decreed by Felix, the sensitivity training sessions were coordinated with head office who had commissioned a firm of consultants to execute the program. Attempts were made to ensure that each group session was diverse and included whites, females and blacks.

My own group met these criteria. The consultant went through the usual overview of what diversity meant, why it was valued and the fact that diversity would only increase not diminish. The real highlight of the session came when each participant was asked to explain what prejudice or bias was and to relate examples he or she may have witnessed. Most had no problems up to this point. The gut wrenching question was the question asking whether he or she had ever exercised prejudice or bias. At first, nearly everyone denied ever being prejudiced or biased. The consultant was the consummate professional at what he did. He explained that it was perfectly normal to see others as biased but not ourselves. Based on his professional experience, he revealed that nearly everyone eventually admitted to some behavior that was essentially prejudicial or biased.

This revelation allowed him to continue to insist that participants provide more honest responses. The result of his insistence was remarkable. Several white employees broke into tears as they related behavior that they now recognized as prejudiced and biased, mostly on account of color and to a lesser extent because of sexuality on the part of a number of male employees. Women seemed to have far fewer issues with prejudice than men among the members of my group. Without any suggestion from the consultant, it was amazing to witness white employees in the intense pain of contrition being comforted by black employees. This was without a doubt the most intensely moving aspect of the entire session. It is very difficult for me to imagine a more powerful demonstration of compassion than this. Yet, as my friend the good doctor said, it is a very complex relationship. It certainly is never a very settled one. Several weeks after the sessions a number of those who confessed to showing prejudice and bias readily admitted that they had felt somewhat pressured during the session and were now having second thoughts about their contrition.

The advantages of life as an expatriate more often than not far outweigh the disadvantages. When an

Indiana boy from humble beginnings is married to a wealthy Brazilian woman, has Brazilian children, speaks the native language and lives like royalty in a country like Brazil, it naturally takes much more than most companies are willing to give to get the Indiana boy to become an Indiana boy once again. So it was with the departing site VP. In the end there was nothing the company could do to keep him in Indiana. It is my understanding that he returned to his old job upon his return to Brazil and even resisted the enticement of a corporate position in the process. Brazil was home. The lesson: the company provides a living not a life. It is essential that the difference is understood. It is crucial what we choose.

Resolution

Two are on a quintessential journey
One certain only of the direction.
The other convinced the destination.
One is still though moving company
Knowing well the lay of the land
Across which they must travel.
Mapless, underfoot primeval gravel
Are we on the way to Samarkand?

A place along the way we visit
Quite often but unaware,
Not too distant not too near
And never at all explicit,
Seldom acknowledged Uncertainty.
One settles for extended residence.
The other denies its very existence
Fears legion and of vague paternity.

We move to meet imagined fate
Now and then secure
In blankets, lace guipure
Weave of recent unknown date.
Surely we have many reasons,

Beginning with faint heart
Set to turmoil from the very start,
To fear life's daunting seasons.

As seasons writhe and yaw
We refuge in forgetfulness,
Timidly explore time's largesse
As we grapple tooth and claw
With the echoes of our dreams.
Confused what to believe
Subvert reason for reprieve
From uncertainty's stout streams.

Religion's sandbags pledge relief
Labels illegible from midstream
Or squinting from roof's beam
No less harbingers of hidden grief
Certain outcome of our circumstance.
Sandbags intended to protect the shore
Make fat stream's passage more secure
And fear, hope in tow, scuffle and dance.

Left with that which is all we truly own
The marker of self-conscious existence
Choice then, choice now, choice hence.
Faint heart, weak mind, dark soul disown
In unity their unique and certain obligation.
Cowering in fear of anticipated finality
They give up choice's seminal reality
Seduced by vain chance for sly salvation.

Christian, Muslim, Hindu, Other,
Exclusive paths to virtual heaven
Or hell for the lost and the craven.
At times each seems the other's brother
But one man's heaven's another man's hell
And the Promised Land is without shore
Regardless of large promise's bold allure.
Where paths end in the end one cannot tell.

Life in concert with the good and grand
Harms not nor cheapens life's intrinsic worth.
It hardly matters, our circumstance of birth.
Matters more, that for which we stand,
For freedom, the right of all to choose,
Even the false promise of religion's call,
Even the myth of the great eternal fall
From grace that bet non-believers lose.

'And what of sin?' the other says to the one
Who is content with what has been, is, will be.
'What of it my friend? What is it you do not see?'
The other is pained for fear a friend undone.
There is no deeper, darker calamity
For the wages of sin is certainly death.
Who dare disagree even at last breath?
Yet there surely is a greater tragedy.

Where the logic or the sense in trusting God
But not his eternal, beneficent omnipotence?
Forsaking testy reason for feigned innocence
And faith that evil and folly with wink and nod
Are always forgiven by a deity allowing choice
But defeating enabled reason that he endowed
The rich and poor, the powerful and the cowed.
Still all's not lost; repent, be baptized, rejoice.

Why is sin perfection's gift to me and you?
Forgiveness unfailing saps sin's substance
More so given always in great abundance.
Not a trifling matter for the great Pan Gu
For herein lies the greatest of conundrums:
Why should perfection's issue be imperfect?
Why to dense commandments we genuflect?
Why banished, diminished, hope still drums?

No need surrender to the myth of Eden
Unless our choice is to deny choosing
Concluding we cannot win for losing.

In the grand scheme we're made uneven
By limits to our future artful in disguise.
Disciples, surrogates, rogues and raptors
Holy men with their holy books, captors
Sanctimoniously grave, magnifying lies.

Beset by choices all around as wanton fear
Sets up walls 'tween heart and soul and mind.
We doubt, we hope but are most of all unkind.
Sorry lot left hugging sodden pillows of despair
Pitiful shadows of potent selves emasculated
Pleading to be rescued from myriad maladies,
Self inflicted wounds and fleeting parodies
Of reconstituted self no longer dissociated.

Those who choose faith all else must abandon
Harbor no regret, be sure to also understand
Faith its own justification, plays its own hand,
Only by non-compliance and discontent undone.
In the end each arrives at his unique place
Where by fortitude and purpose he abides
Taking comfort in choice that like the tides
Leaves clear evidence as lines upon the face.

'And what of resurrection? Can we atone?
We do not live forever but forever do we die?'
'Tis the crux', says the one. 'Tis the reason we cry
Forever in the wilderness bearing Sisyphus' stone'.
Resignation no more no less our celebrated lot.
Faith thrives where information sparse, hidden
Greets companion fear like ardent lover smitten
Not recognizing life's blurred yet complex plot.

Life and death and resurrection in any event
By definition cannot arise one from the other
Save in a world where evidence does not matter
And unbridled choice allows us to circumvent
Our defect, refusal to see what we have chosen.
In truth matter cannot be created or destroyed

Though in many ways manipulated or alloyed
With choice the fabric in which all are woven.

Indeed science has its own rules of faith
Predicated on evidence, outcomes anticipated
Theory, formulae and reality much debated
Resolved as fact or fiction on reason's lathe.
Why not mutually exclusive these sturdy two?
Can parallel universes be common highway?
Can we trust science yet blissfully pray?
Always there is room in choice's curly queue.

'I need must pray for you', says the other.
'There is no need unless for your own good',
Says the one unyielding where he stood.
'Life is nothing but choosing over and over.
Celebrate your choosing be wary your choice
For others choosing differently will survive
Your choice's singular certainty and thrive,
Rejoicing likewise in bold stentorian voice'.

Choice and consequence conjoined twins,
Sole arbiters, brackets of our existence,
Bring balance to life's fickle sentence
To a contest neither loser nor victor wins.
These twins the masters of our universe
Forever indifferent to our pain or regrets
Parade through time like furtive ferrets
From sunrise to sunset blindly obverse.

Life teaches lessons very difficult to discern.
Choice, reliable warrantor of our humanity
Provides no secure harbor for venal vanity.
In the end we are confined to self made urn
Less than we could be, not as much as we are.
Dare we face the truth of self and existence
In a universe indifferent to life's insistence?
We choose even if simply wishing on a star.

The new site director was a former manager of Industrial Engineering at the site. He had been promoted to plant manager of the operations in the Philippines. My first boss, the former manager of the Industrial Engineering Department, was currently the factory manager for my plant. He was now being transferred to the Philippines to replace the new Indiana site director.

End Stage

My negotiations with the company now entered its final phase. Felix and I had several discussions regarding resolving compensatory steps which could be taken to address the effects of my stagnation at the site. I strongly suggested that he simply place me in my boss' job. He did not think that was a wise move for two basic reasons. One reason had to do with perception. He thought that it would be bad for the company to appear to have been blackmailed into promoting me to my boss' old job. My response to this concern was that, under the circumstances, whatever accommodation the company made could be seen in this manner. Naturally, this solution was one I preferred since leaving the site at the time meant closing my wife's restaurant. This was a step my wife and I were very reluctant to take. Felix' other reason was that, in his mind, remaining at the site might not be the best option for me. The history was not good and he was concerned that both he and I may have to fight battles against residual backlash which is perhaps inevitable whenever bias is addressed. I admitted to myself that this was a much more plausible argument. Even so, to me, such a situation was quite manageable. I finally agreed that I would seriously consider being relocated.

A major concern, of course, was the disposition of the restaurant. My wife and I decided that we would have to be compensated for the losses we would inevitably incur as a result. There was also a sense that we would be abandoning an opportunity we had created that had the potential for significant future income. By this time we had purchased the building housing our restaurant and decided that we would retain ownership even if we were relocated. In my next discussion with Felix I raised the matter of the restaurant and the unfavorable impact my relocation would have in this regard. He asked my advice as to how we may address this issue. I suggested compensation for all tangible losses and some compensation for lost opportunity on grounds that the company was not blameless in creating a need that led to my decision to craft a survival option independent of the company. He conceded the point and requested that I formulate and propose a methodology for addressing this particular concern. In the end we had agreement in principle on a compensation package which included an accommodation for our closing the restaurant. We were left to agree on the other less complex details of my move.

I was asked to look at the position of Plant Manager at a site in New Jersey that manufactured nearly all of the corporation's flavors and fragrances for world wide distribution. My wife and I did so together. We agreed that the site presented a real opportunity for a new and meaningful start. Our older son was then in his final year at Dartmouth College in New Hampshire and our younger was in his final semester in high school in Louisville. We had agreement that he would complete high school in Louisville. My wife would remain in Louisville until our son completed high school. We would each alternate commuting to each other's location every other week.

Relocation is always a mixed blessing. We were pleased with the outcome of the negotiations with the company and anticipated only good things of our new life in New Jersey. But we had to decide what to do with our house and the commercial property which housed the restaurant. The house was easy as the company would ensure that we would not be out of pocket on its sale. The commercial property would be solely our responsibility. The challenge was to find a good tenant. We were lucky to do so very quickly. If there is any truth to the belief that we make our own luck then I guess we had our own example of this. The tenant remodeled the place extensively to accommodate her California style restaurant with typically very eclectic style, finish and furnishings.

While my own issues had been satisfactorily addressed, I was uncertain of the company's real intent regarding the other members of the G5. Although our partnership was essentially over at this point, I never the less felt some obligation to make sure that justice was done. My enquiries revealed that the company intended to provide opportunities for the group to advance but would not consider retroactive compensation for past inequities in promotion and compensation as our colleague Ted had demanded. I believe that, in the company's view, the case against them on this account was not strong enough to make them fear the risk of any possible litigation which might ensue. The evidence indicates that the company acted on this basis without penalty.

As is customary there was a number of farewell parties and lunches to attend. At one party I was moved by a very emotional statement made to my wife by my reformed maintenance supervisor, Goby. He was very concerned for the future of my plant and perhaps the site, after my departure. He could not imagine how the place would continue to function effectively in my absence. He confessed that he had learned more from me than he had from anyone else in the company and he wanted my wife to know this. Goby had lit up fireworks on my behalf once again but this time without any trace of racial condescension. It appeared he had made some progress.

My Life's Mission

Just around this time I began to reflect very intensely on my relationship with the company and those around me and the real purpose of my life. I suspect that the circumstances and events which were assailing my life at the time were the catalyst for this intense reflection. I did not wish to simply think about this and decided that I would document my thoughts, refine them and make a commitment that whatever statement I arrived at finally would become the fundamental guiding principles by which I would live. As I read today what I wrote then, I am amazed at how faithful I have been to my mission throughout the most turbulent periods of my life. I share this with the reader to further facilitate a deeper understanding of my thinking.

THIS IS MY LIFE'S MISSION

To live a life based on the cardinal principles of **TRUTH, HONESTY, TRUST and HONOR** *in the unshakeable belief that the more my life's activities reflect and validate these principles the greater my integrity. The greater my integrity, the greater the influence I can have on my life partners and associates. I must be a force for good and happiness in the world and demonstrate by my own existence that goodness and happiness are possible under any circumstance if we, each of us, understand that our* *integrity is the fulcrum of our existence, the compass for our journey and the final bulwark against adversity. The beliefs below support this mission:*

1. *There are no substitutes for truth and fairness.*
2. *Always strive to do the right thing under all circumstances. This alone can safeguard integrity.*
3. *Co-operation is of significantly greater value than competition because we are all life partners with one overriding objective in life: to be happy.*
4. *Always balance short term needs against long term objectives.*
5. *Be courageous. Never be intimidated by persons or ideas.*
6. *Keep things simple and never shortchange common sense.*
7. *Constantly act to add value, eliminate waste and improve relationships.*
8. *Be flexible and responsive but always be guided by your vision of the future.*
9. *Be anti-bureaucratic. Refuse to be managed by systems, policies and procedures.*
10. *Act to eliminate artificial barriers so that each person may contribute over the short term as well as the long term.*
11. *Be persistent. Quit only when you are ready not when others say you should.*
12. *Never judge but if you must, judge people's behavior not their humanity.*
13. *The most important things dictating the quality of our existence cannot be touched, seen or measured, e.g. trust, honesty, fairness, truth, gratitude, courtesy, respect, hope, faith, courage, love, beauty, intuition, integrity. Moreover, these things are all integral to ourselves and cannot be bestowed. Therefore, never succumb to the view that that which cannot be measured or quantified is naturally less important than that which can be.*

14. *Always remember that "what motivates people is a vision of themselves in the future". Never obscure or deny this vision.*
15. *All persons are accountable for their actions and the consequences which result directly.*

It was a very happy coincidence that after arriving at my life's mission I came across a quotation from **Sun Bear, Member of the Chippewa Indian Tribe**, in a **Management Review** magazine: *"I do not think that the measure of a civilization is how tall its buildings of concrete are, but rather, how well its people have learned to relate to their environment and fellow man."* I do not think that the statement of my life's mission needs validation but I certainly take comfort in the connection I detect with Sun Bear.

Bequeathing Goby

One member of the G5 had endured severe maintenance difficulties in his plant. I thought that the best thing I could do as a parting gift would be to bequeath him Goby. Accordingly, I went to Goby with the proposition. He agreed immediately, commenting once again that I should know that he would do whatever I asked of him. As it turned out, Goby's agreement was the easier of the two I would need to have to make my contrived marriage work.

I understood very well the bitter history of the relationship between people like Goby and my G5 friend whom I will call Chuck. It was impossible to overestimate the level of animosity which existed historically between people like Goby and Chuck. I understood this perfectly. I approached Chuck with the proposal. He was clearly offended by my insistence that he consider my transferring Goby to work for him. I explained my own experience with Goby and how we had developed the best possible working relationship. I emphasized that regardless of what the general thinking was about him, Goby was the quintessential professional. He respected and valued his craft above all else. Chuck was adamant that he and Goby could never work together. In fact, were this to happen he was certain they would come to blows on the job. I ended our discussion with a plea that he not make up his mind at the moment but think about it for a few days and then call me to revisit the matter.

More than a week went by and I never heard from Chuck. My time for departure was fast approaching and if I were going to accomplish what I set out to do I would have to approach Chuck again and not wait for him to call me. I asked him to have lunch with me and confessed that I had an ulterior motive. He was not at all surprised. At lunch I again pleaded with him to reconsider his position on Goby. He continued to resist the idea. I then indicated that the maintenance problems in his plant would eventually lead to his downfall because there was no doubt who would be blamed for the plant's continued poor performance. I begged him to look beyond the history of bigotry and to think of how best he could improve his plant's performance; to think of Goby as skill without color. I implored him to simply give the idea a try. If he felt it could not work, he certainly could revert to his old arrangements.

To my great relief he agreed to speak with Goby and would let me know in a few days whether he would give the idea a try. I was ecstatic when Chuck called to tell me he had decided to work with Goby. For a number of months after leaving the site I called to get updates on Goby's performance. In less than six months Goby had effectively addressed Chuck's maintenance problems and had measurably improved the efficiency of his plant.

Very few things I did in Indiana left me with as much satisfaction as this did.

VI. AMERICA NORTH

World Class Facility

The plant for my new assignment was in the quaint little town of Burlington, New Jersey. It was an hour from the company's main R&D facility in Piscataway and an hour and a half from our head office in Manhattan. Although a relatively small facility it was widely recognized as being world class. It was in the forefront of facilities applying advanced team work techniques and the effective application of the very latest computer technology. The team work concept at the site was so advanced that technicians rotated among themselves each month as well as into selected jobs in the office. My initial impression on my earlier visit was somewhat discomforting. I was not at all certain what the job of the plant manager really could be. The plant appeared to run itself. Now that I was permanently on site I felt challenged to make a clear difference in the operation and visibility of the facility.

It would be six months before my wife, son and mother-in-law would arrive to reside permanently in New Jersey. In the meantime I had settled into temporary accommodations twenty minutes from the plant and had immersed myself in files of accounting, technical, logistics and operating data. In the midst of all this I reflected on the fact that, while I was consumed by all the dislocations occurring in my own personal and professional life, I never gave much thought to the one life that I had clearly caused to be dislocated directly. My relocation to the site meant that the plant manager I succeeded was hastily moved elsewhere. I subsequently learned he was transferred to the Indiana site in an engineering capacity as Central Services Manager. He had been at the Burlington site less than a year. I am certain he was quite unprepared for such an abrupt move. In a sense, if only indirectly, he was also a victim of prejudice and bias. I feel certain that this collateral consequence is seldom taken into account when the effects of prejudice and bias are considered.

At the end of my first month, my new boss, the VP of Manufacturing for the U.S., came to visit. His visit was two fold: to see how I was settling in and to deliver my first pay check. This was flattering on both counts. I opened my pay envelope before he departed and discovered that my check compensating for the closing of our restaurant was missing. I expressed surprise at this and discovered that my boss was oblivious to the arrangement. This meant that he had been purposely kept out of the loop on this aspect of my compensation package. Perhaps it was best that he not know everything. I asked never the less that he check with Felix about this as Felix was quite aware that there should be a second check. Upon returning to New York he called to say that an additional check would be in the mail and should arrive within a couple of days.

A significant portion of my wife's visits was spent house hunting. We discovered how relatively inexpensive it was to live in Louisville, especially in regard to the cost of housing. Houses in comparable neighborhoods in New Jersey and only two thirds the size of our house in Louisville, were selling for nearly fifty percent more. We eventually found a suitable house in the delightful neighborhood of Fox Run, in Mt. Laurel, no more than eight miles from the plant in Burlington. It was two stories like our Louisville house but had no basement and was faced with aluminum siding instead of brick. We were quite happy with the new house and anticipated only happy times there.

Our older son, Gordon, completed college and was offered a job in the retail business in New Jersey, not too far from home. Our younger son, Gregory, started college at Rutgers State University just over an hour from home. My wife, Icy, signed up with a temp agency and worked at her leisure from time to time. She decided some time later to accept a position as manager for a restaurant close to home that was a part of a national chain. This attachment did not last very long as she knew the business too well and was quite intolerant of the poor work habits of employees and the ineptitude of the management of the chain.

I was now very comfortably settled into my job and was beginning to make the presence of the company known in the community. This was integral to my intention to raise the profile of the plant and the company in general, in the immediate community and surrounding neighborhood. I was beginning to discover additional ways to "lead" the site. By its very nature there was very little need to "manage" the site but there was still ample room to lead. It is true to say that meeting traditional business objectives was the focus. However, the real heart of the business was people: people in the form of our employees, our customers, our suppliers and our community. It continues to amaze me, even in retrospect, that once success is achieved with the *people* part of the business equation the chances of success at the other aspects are multiplied.

I set out to imagine how I could improve the skill levels of employees and came to the conclusion that an intensive course at the local community college in computer science would add significant value to their overall skills base, self esteem and performance. The entire group of twenty technicians was enrolled and successfully completed the course. The college was among the fastest growing community colleges in America at the time and welcomed my involvement. I eventually was asked to serve on the Board of Trustees for the college. This was not just a personal honor but a direct reflection of the recognition of the company's involvement in the community. Some time later I was honored by the New Jersey Council of County Colleges with one of its Fourth Annual Excellence Awards. Progress at the site was being achieved on all critical fronts: internally, with external business partners and with the local community.

Still, many challenges remained. As the use of technology increased and the roles of everyone at the site were expanding, the need for a site engineer was clearly justified. After an extensive internal company search and with the participation of technicians and staff in the interviewing process, a white female engineer was selected. She would become the very first female plant engineer in the entire company. I was not at all surprised that this occurred at this particular plant. Given my knowledge and understanding of the over all company organization it was unlikely this could have occurred anywhere else. It was therefore quite a shock that one male technician made an issue of having a female engineer and went out of his way to be visibly offensive in his interaction with her. His behavior was obnoxious enough that he eventually was threatened with dismissal. After a public display of contrition and a written apology he was suspended for a few days instead.

This occurrence was very instructive to everyone. It could not have been anticipated. That such behavior occurred at a site like ours was almost inexplicable. This is an object lesson that it is all but impossible to overestimate the individually corrosive and publicly disruptive power of bias.

A similarly curious experience occurred during the selection process to hire a replacement purchasing manager. The interviewing process was, as usual, inclusive of a representative group of the site population. One candidate arrived for his interview and was directed to our conference room. He was instructed by the secretary to ask for Mr. James who was the plant manager. I made a point of never sitting at the head of the conference room table for interviews. On this occasion that seat was occupied by my white technical manager. I was the only black person in the room. Rather than asking to see me the candidate went directly to my technical manager, called him by my name and introduced himself. On discovering his error he was truly mortified and apologized ceaselessly. Needless to say his interview did not go well. He found it impossible to put his blunder behind him.

As the company generally, and its manufacturing operations in particular, began to seek greater cohesion and to recognize best practices, all directors of manufacturing and plant managers for the North America Division met once each month. Each director/manager took turns hosting each meeting at his home site. By this time Puerto Rico had become a part of the division. It was quite noticeable to me that the group consisted of only men. Once every six months the group met for breakfast with the chairman of the company. I shall call him Carl. At one such meeting he asked the group if anything seemed peculiar about the group. For a moment I was concerned that he might have been alluding to the fact that I was the sole black member of the group. This kind of singularity I did not wish to publicly exemplify.

Happily, this was not the case. Instead, when no one responded, he expressed concern that there was not a single female member in our group of ten. Carl then asked if anyone knew of any qualified female in the company who could conceivably join the group. When no one offered any suggestions I felt obliged to do so. I indicated that I thought there was one such person. This person had been formerly with our R&D facility but had been transferred to our plant in Mexico in a line supervisory function. She also, I recalled, held a PhD. degree. The chairman memorably removed his pen from his shirt pocket and made a note in the palm of his hand. He then had the VP of manufacturing commit to having a female manager in our group within a year.

It was very clear to me that were I not at breakfast myself and the question had been about a black employee no one would have known of one either. I still have the greatest of difficulty understanding why I was the only person aware that this obviously qualified employee existed. Still, it would not have been altogether true to say we were not making some progress. For example, the forced objective set by the chairman was met and the female I had suggested was in fact promoted to plant manager of our plant in Morristown, New Jersey. After a meeting of top executives held at the La Costa Resort in California I had reason to send Felix a note, a paragraph of which is reproduced below:

"It is hard to verbalize this but at crucial moments in our history, personal as well as professional, it says more about where we are than the numbers tell us when we can say that we not only dream the same dreams and have the same vision but actively participate in realizing them."

In 1994, at the insistence of Felix, it appears, I was nominated by the company as "Black Achiever of the Year" for the Harlem YMCA's National Salute to Black Achievers in Industry. I must confess that, generally speaking, I am not supportive of color coded awards and made my feelings known immediately to the HR executive who communicated the news. I did not hesitate in turning down the color coded honor. He was perplexed and thought my refusal to accept the award would embarrass the company. I also confess that this was not of great concern to me and had no effect on my eventual decision to reverse myself. My reversal was in deference to a telephone call from Felix imploring me to reconsider, if not on my own account, on the account of the number of hopeful, young black executives who would be influenced by my acceptance of the award. In any event, in his view, I absolutely deserved the award. He was certain that my acceptance would serve a really useful purpose. While I deferred to Felix' insistence I remain ambivalent about the long term impact of these types of recognition. I often think of them as I think of surges in our electricity supply. They are remarkable when they occur but unless they destroy a major household appliance or your computer they are quickly forgotten.

Frequently, manufacturing managers with identified high potential were funneled through the Burlington facility. Consequently such managers could be at the site for as little as one year or as many as three but seldom longer. My personal experience not withstanding, I cautioned myself against impatience. It was not until my fourth year at the site that I began to express concern that I observed no signs that I may be in line to be promoted. Just about this time as well, I received a note from Felix indicating that he would be leaving the company to become the CEO of one of the largest manufacturers of female hygiene products in America.

I saw this as a very bad sign on a personal basis. I had come to realize that no matter what company rules and policies professed, if people like me do not have a champion, and this is especially true in a large organization, their chances of succeeding are always in jeopardy. I called Felix on the phone to congratulate him but also to express my appreciation for all he had done to "make things right" and to let him know that his departure would leave the battlefield of prejudice and bias without a referee. He emphasized that he had great faith in the company and he felt certain that I had nothing to worry about going forward. I neither shared his faith nor his optimism. I later sent Felix a note of final goodbye. His response in a sealed, monogrammed envelope marked "private", was heart warming.

"Dear Owen,
Of all the letters and notes I received, yours was the nicest.
The nicest because it came from the heart and because it reflected our relationship over the past few years.
When I first met you in Louisville, I liked you and instantly knew that you were a good, capable and honest man.

Knowing that, it was easy for me to 'take a chance' on you. And you've more than repaid me and the business for it. You've led Burlington to a new level of performance and established yourself as a very strong manager. We couldn't have asked for anything more.

But even more important, you're a really good guy, despite your suspenders and ties. I've very much enjoyed working with you, and I just hope that our paths will cross again in the future. In the meantime, continued good luck, and to you as well, 'Fare Thee Well'.

Felix"

Because Burlington supplied product to subsidiaries all over the world I felt obliged to visit several of these subsidiaries. I could find no evidence that any of my predecessors chose to do this. My visits included India, Thailand, the Philippines, Hong Kong, Venezuela and Colombia. I also needed to visit a number of our critical suppliers in the U.S. in places like Idaho, Oregon, Washington and Michigan. Combined, these visits gave me very valuable insight into our complete supply chain. On a personal level, it opened up a whole new world of interesting cultures and personal relationships that I may not have been exposed to otherwise. Still, as interesting and valuable as the experience in Burlington was I knew that the time had come for me to move on. I also knew that I needed to behave like the proverbial squeaky wheel in order to bring this about.

World Class Disappointment

I saw and met with my boss, the VP of Manufacturing for North America, at least once per month. There was no doubt that my performance was outstanding. My performance reviews and supporting documented commentaries from suppliers and customers as well as senior executives in the company confirmed as much. I had made a presentation to the company's board of directors for which I was highly commended. I had elevated Burlington to an unusually high and well deserved standing in the company and the community. Its visibility, contribution and best in class status made Burlington an exceptionally highly regarded operation. Yet, in the end, all this appeared not to redound in any meaningful way to my own professional benefit or credit. Just as I feared, I had reason to miss Felix, my champion. In spite of this, or perhaps because of this, I knew I had to battle on just like Bob Marley's *Buffalo Soldier*.

Once again I prepared to attack the ramparts of prejudice and bias in an organization that had rules and policies which expressly outlawed these things. I was uncertain whether my current boss, a younger man than his predecessor, was aware of my experience in Indiana. Nothing in his behavior or our discussions revealed that he was. I assumed that he was not. He confirmed a number of times during our many discussions of my desire to move on, that I was among manufacturing executives on a list of people who were *"ready to move immediately"*. In fact, he confessed that on a number of occasions in the past and at a recent *"selection"* meeting with Proctor, now the Worldwide Executive VP for manufacturing, I was proffered as a viable candidate for promotion. To quote my boss, my candidacy *"was not supported by Proctor"*. He confessed that he was under the impression that Proctor had a problem with me. He had no way of knowing what this might be although it was clear to him that there was a real problem. He was visibly embarrassed and asked if I knew what the problem could be. I did not. To the best of my knowledge, no problem existed.

Proctor's rise in the company was impressively meteoric. Although I clearly knew him in his earlier formative years, I had made a point of maintaining a respectful professional distance, very mindful of the fact of my Indiana experience with the site director there. It is not unfair to say that he did nothing to facilitate my taking a different approach. I explained all of this to my boss and asked him if he thought it would be helpful if I were to approach Proctor myself on the matter. He was emphatic in his opposition and indicated he would address the matter himself.

Over the next several months I accelerated the frequency with which I inquired of my boss about progress with his intervention with Proctor. It was obvious that there were difficulties. My boss was frustrated and was showing signs of process fatigue. In the meantime, a dramatic piece of information would reach me that would aggravate an already troubling situation. I began to receive frequent phone calls from junior executives in our corporate office in New York, congratulating me on being promoted to Manufacturing Director for the Caribbean Region with offices then in Barbados. Not only was this speculation, I was absolutely unaware of such an opportunity. The more I indicated this view the more insistent the callers became. Understandably, they saw my refusal to confirm the rumor as company intrigue. Since there had been no official announcement, in their mind I was obliged to maintain confidentiality and therefore could not discuss the matter.

Eventually, I realized that the assumption my callers were making arose from a very legitimate expectation on their part. This realization triggered an investigation by me to determine if, in fact, such an opportunity existed or was contemplated. Rumors, I discovered, while very often inaccurate, are seldom baseless. The position did exist and at this point at least two white employees had already refused offers of the position. One of these employees was a South African I had helped to train in Indiana. I immediately sent off an e-mail to the VP of manufacturing for Latin America and the Caribbean expressing my interest in the position and requesting an interview. I had no response even after a follow up mail. This and subsequent related events remain incomprehensible even now. As unlikely as it would have to seem to any reasonable person, history was about to repeat itself in the most unseemly of ways. I would face yet another obstacle course.

Obstacles

The spits lay strewn along the way
In purposed disarray
I look around to see men flayed
Impaled prostrate
'Twixt earth and heaven
Soggy cinders smoldering in hot blood
Red reminders of Noah's flood.

I pray the obstacles would disappear
Those at a distance those quite near.
Prostrate cinders make my wish corrupt
They scorn my plea for deference

Why should I be spared the cup?
The common plight is understood
Even before the heart of the wood.

The shadow of the spits pendulous
Have slipped into the carnal pus
Unblooded yet, still not aflood, I marvel.
There is a secret we must discern.
Ignoring feet shod in another's blood
Thinking we stand on hallowed ground
We forget our reasoning is unsound.

In nimble dance I circumvent the spits
And wonder at the human bits
Realizing at a grievous bend
Progress is a dash toward the end.
I climb a spit then two then two
How many can there really be?
More than waves in a shoreless sea.

Finally there is clarity to the vision
Cast fear aside to behold the revelation
The final obstacle wrongly thought the last
Is merely the one that stops you.
Endless barbs still point to heaven
With treacled spaces in between
To trap the careless to strip him clean.

History Repeats Itself

I brought the entire stream of events to the attention of my boss who confirmed his support and the support of the HR director for the U.S. company. He promised to follow up on my mails to the responsible VP. I documented all of this in a file I started. After a few weeks without a response from any one who was even remotely connected with the matter, I approached my boss for what would be my last discussion of the subject before taking matters into my own hands. I alone could apply my "J" rule. Following a meeting in New York I had lunch with my boss. Over lunch I related in detail my travails with the company and suggested to him that he should now withdraw from further involvement as anything he may say or do could possibly hurt his career. He expressed some reluctance at this suggestion and I explained that I was now prepared to engage in a bare knuckle brawl with the company if this were what it would now require to address this entire inconceivable affair.

I was no longer prepared to be patient or respectful of hierarchy or protocol. The company no longer deserved this nicety. Accordingly, I sent a very explicit letter to the chairman of the company and prepared a document which covered all the critical aspects of the problem. The title of the document itself, *"A Personal Perspective from Burlington – Accountability, Performance and Concerns,"* did not hint at the personal or organizational turbulence it would eventually cause. My objective was very clear: Take the assessment of Owen James out of the arena of innuendo and conjecture into the arena of responsible, factual and professional dialogue. The document was composed under the following headings:

1. *Introduction - What does it take to get a fair shot at opportunity?*
2. *Reflections of Performance – Internal*
3. *Reflections of Performance – External (Business)*
4. *Reflections of Performance –External (Community)*
5. *Concern Triggers*

The letter to the chairman and the most immediately germane sections of the document referred to above are reproduced later in this discussion.

Strategy

I determined my rules of engagement and remained firmly committed to my "J" rule. There was never a time in my entire life when I was as committed to a venture as I was to this one. I could imagine no way in which I would fail. I could see no way in which I would not prevail. As I look back, this conviction must have been the only reason I maintained my composure as well as my sanity. My letter to the Chairman of the company is very instructive:

April 4, 1995
Dear Carl:
I write this letter with profound sadness. Such a letter should never need to be written but recent and not so recent events make this necessary or, more accurately, inevitable.
On February 28, 1995 I learnt, quite by accident, that there was an open position for a Director of Manufacturing in the Caribbean, stationed in Barbados. Indications are that by then two candidates had already turned down the opportunity. I immediately communicated my interest to Kevin Bell, the responsible Regional V.P., by e-mail. I also informed my boss, Dan Glover, of my interest and action. Dan assured me of his support as well as that of the Director of HR for the U.S. Dan was especially impressed by the fact that I had at one time been plant manager

for the Caribbean Group and still maintained very influential social and political ties in the area that could be of value to the company. He also informed me that I was one of a group of people classified as "ready to move immediately". On this basis he had submitted my name on three occasions including this one but Proctor Masters never supported any of these moves.

Since the 28th the only activity on the matter has been my initiatives to learn the reason I have not been granted the basic courtesy of a response to my expressed interest. I still have no idea why I have not been offered the position or even considered a serious candidate. In the meantime it is apparent that two additional candidates have been considered for the position, one of whom, to my understanding, has also rejected the opportunity. In short, four candidates have had a shot at the opportunity while I have been completely ignored. I have since notified Dan of my concern. Since Proctor obviously feels that there is no need to justify his ongoing actions to block any advancement on my part I am left with no recourse but to bring the matter to the attention of the highest authority in the company.

For the record, over the past two years I have raised the issue of my lack of movement with Dan. On every occasion he indicated that he needed to "talk with Proctor." Over this time I have come to realize that Proctor is the sole arbiter over all of manufacturing worldwide. He determines who gets promoted, whereto, when and the duration of assignments. I am now able to put Dan's perplexing query to me ("Have you had any run-ins with Proctor?") during our discussion of 2/28 in perspective. Consider the following comments by former colleagues of mine and others: "nothing happens in manufacturing without Proctor's consent;" "you need to talk with Proctor if you want to get anywhere;" "Proctor is the man;" "whatever you do don't get in Proctor's bad books;" It seems that the manufacturing side of the business is run like a fiefdom. This raises a few questions: How *did a single individual acquire such awesome power? Why has he been allowed to wield it in such a blatantly discriminatory manner for so many years? Is there no oversight to Proctor's area of responsibility? If so where does this reside in the company?*

I know that you are not unaware of my performance in Burlington but think it useful to attach two pages of some of my most significant accomplishments over the past 5 years as well as a listing of my major assignments over the years. This brings me to the not so recent events alluded to earlier. It would be surprising if you are not aware that in 1990 while I was working in the Jeffersonville plant, Felix, then President of the North America Division, had to intervene to resolve an issue similar in nature to the one at hand involving myself and others, all of whom happen to be black. The issue then is basically the issue now - fair treatment. No one listened early enough then. No one is listening now. And so here we are - again.

I have to tell you that the Jeffersonville experience continues to haunt me as the single most painful experience of my life. I am compelled to tell you that at my age and after twenty two years of service there is no force on earth that will make me, and yes, my family, suffer such pain ever again. The power brokers in the current situation are certainly aware of the Jeffersonville history as I was told then that the reason for my lack of progress in the company was because some powerful person "does not like you". I have ceased attempting to understand the reason for this. Regrettably no one but me seems to have learnt anything from the events of 1990. I agreed with Felix then, that we cannot recreate the past but we can most certainly ensure that the future is different. It is with intense sadness and some degree of bewilderment that I conclude that the future with the company will never be different from the past. My wife and I have been losing sleep trying to understand how it could be that 1990 in Jeffersonville is about to be repeated. Absolutely incredible, to say the least!!

It is not unreasonable to think that of at least five recent opportunities I should have been afforded one based strictly on performance, experience, exposure and service. These include: Puerto Rico, Cambridge, Moorestown, Kansas City and now the Caribbean. Interestingly enough, one of the persons who turned down the position in the Caribbean has since been offered another opportunity. It is clear to me that in the eyes of the power brokers Owen James is damaged goods - very damaged goods - that should be avoided at all costs. Can you understand how this makes me feel? How can I continue to perform effectively knowing this and knowing as well that many influential people in the company (God only knows how many!) must now see me as one to be shunned, professionally speaking? Where in the company can I now expect to advance? Certainly, all things considered, if I am not good enough for the position in the Caribbean I cannot reasonably expect to be good enough for much else. It is so sad that it should come to this.

I now truly believe that I have been cut off from all avenues for advancement in the company. I had made a commitment to myself and to the company (Felix), after my Jeffersonville experience, to move on, to leave the past behind. Little did I know that what I was able and willing to do and have in fact done, the company was not, is not and will not, as evidenced by the behavior of its officers. The degree of insensitivity exhibited here borders on being recklessly malicious and is certainly at variance with the corporation's own code of conduct. It directly injures both the company and me.

And so what are the options left me? How do I go on from here knowing there is no hope of advancement? Does anyone have an answer? Does anyone even care? I feel devalued, maligned and abused. I am sure that my ability to contribute in the future has been irretrievably impaired. It is true: if we do not learn from history we *are doomed to repeat our past mistakes. I think I have learnt a very valuable lesson which I will never forget. Who knows, maybe this time around even the company may find that there is indeed a lesson to be learnt.*

Owen E. James
BURLINGTON.

Following my letter to the Chairman the profile below was created to further make the point that my expectations were indifferent to the application of any aspects of any affirmative action program. I had never relied on this mechanism and did not intend to do so now. What was being demanded was simply a fair and equal opportunity at advancement based solely on qualification and performance. In short, I saw my demand as being based solely on merit. I was willing to place my qualifications, experience, exposure and performance against any other employee's in regard to the position in question. I remain convinced that by any objective standard, of the employees who were offered the position none was more qualified than I. I also believe that in the end the company itself so concluded but had so compromised its position that it had to manufacture reasons to explain why I could not be offered the assignment. I will address this conundrum shortly, because it presents a distressing example of how prejudice and bias can put an otherwise honorable organization at risk.

QUESTION:

WHAT DOES IT TAKE TO GET A FAIR SHOT AT OPPORTUNITIES FOR ADVANCEMENT?

If there were an employee in our organization who could be credited with the following would he not be among the most viable and attractive candidates for promotion and advancement? **Does such a person exist?**

1. Service/Experience/Exposure

Twenty two years of service. Germane blend of experience in international & domestic areas of the business. Assignments:

- Plant Manager, Burlington
- Supervisor Toilet Soaps Operations, Jeffersonville
- Director of Manufacturing, East Africa
- Industrial/Special Projects Engineer, Canada
- Regional Plant Manager, Caribbean Group

2. Exceptional Achievements over the past 5 years

a. Dramatic Reduction in Working Capital: Reduced average inventories of mint oils from $30MM-$40MM to $2MM over 3 years without impairing reliability of supplies.

b. Improving Corporate Profitability: Played major role in implementing Corporate Surcharge policy. Burlington recovers in excess of $10MM/yr. from international subsidiaries.

c. High Commitment Work System Model: Burlington is recognized as among "best in class" by some well known companies including National Semiconductor, Boise Cascade, Wiremold and Productivity Inc. Status validated internally by professional, corporate sponsored surveys (Guiding Principles Profile, 1993; Change Readiness Profile, 1995). This model is at the very heart of our worldwide strategy to be the "best global consumer products company".

d. Customer Service: Developed & implemented 3 dimensional service assessment tools to reflect internal manufacturing cycle, freight forwarder performance and direct customer feedback on level of service from customers' perspective. On the latter account service has improved steadily from 67% in 1992 to just under 90% in 1994.

e. *Inventory Management: Implemented Supplier Managed Inventory with KC and major supplier to remove over $500M of fragrance & fragrance materials inventory from KC books in 1994. In separate exercise Burlington intervened to reduce fragrance inventories at CMB by $1MM in that same year. Burlington has consistently averaged 14 to 16 inventory turns over the past 5 years.*

f. *Budget Compliance: Over the last 5 years Burlington has averaged less than a 3% variance against its operating budget.*

g. *Environmental Affairs: In 2 years Burlington went from being significantly out of compliance to being 100% in compliance.*

h. *Occupational Health & Safety: Burlington has maintained an unblemished record of zero lost time incidents. Easily among the best in the entire corporation and among the best in our industry.*

i. *People Power: In dramatic departure from traditional boundary limiting behavior Burlington unionized technicians are sharing administrative duties including accounts payable. This has allowed a reduction in force of one employee.*

j. *Business Information Sharing: Intensive & extensive routine sharing of business information among Burlington employees has made the team perhaps the most knowledgeable and effective business partners anywhere in the company.*

k. *Partnerships: Burlington has initiated & maintained effective business partnerships with Strategic Materials, Fragrance Technology and Corporate Sourcing to better manage selected strategic materials like mint oils.*

l. *SAP Implementation: Burlington selected to be first Company site to install SAP. Implementation plan on target for July 1 start up. Selection based on highest level of readiness and greatest potential for clear success.*

m. *Developed & Implementing First Burlington Long Range Plan: Perhaps a first for any plant site. Plan continues to guide site Capital Engineering Budget preparation and gives focus to its vision as a world class unit for essential oils production.*

n. *Labor Contract Settlement: Directly significant contributor to amicable, "win-win" 5 year labor contract with unionized workforce. Three years of the contract have gone by without a single grievance having arisen. Burlington is a model environment of industrial peace and effectiveness.*

3. Performance:

In spite of unusual obstacles his performance overall has been consistently above average to outstanding.

4. Company's Community Image:

He has enhanced the Company's reputation in the community through his Personal and Professional involvement in community organizations.

5. Professional Currency:

Constantly updates personal skills in areas critical to the business and its expressed "new" direction, e.g., completion of Harvard University Program on Negotiation; completion of Covey 7 Habits Leadership Program; completion of windows training; completion of training in diversity.

6. Personal Recognition:

i) *Nominated by the corporation as Black Achiever of the year 1994*

ii) *Awarded certificate of excellence by New Jersey Council of County Colleges for Service to Burlington County Community College.*

iii) *Member Board of Trustees, Burlington County Community College.*

iv) *Member First Advisory Council BCC/NJIT Engineering School Unification.*

To my certain knowledge the foregoing is TRUE of at least one employee in the company. In reality, after all, such an employee does exist. His name:
OWEN E. JAMES.

The company was now in a quandary. The chairman summoned the corporate VP of HR and Legal, whom I shall call Heidi, to inquire as to the authenticity of my letter. She in turn was miffed because I had communicated directly with Carl and did not as much as copy her on my letter. Carl's overriding concern: were the claims made in my letter valid? Of course, this would now have to be verified. I was once again asked to recreate my history with the company. Even in hindsight, it is very difficult to understand how after Indiana my personnel files had again disappeared. Were this fiction I would still find the story implausible. I complied with the request. Heidi provided copies of my reconstructed profile to Proctor, the worldwide VP of Manufacturing, and to Carl, the chairman. In a subsequent meeting with Carl and Heidi, Proctor's only response to the facts of my letter was that he knew me better than anyone else. In other words he had no sensible rebuttal.

It was clear to me, as it must have been to all who had heard or were made aware of Proctor's response, that at best he was maliciously indifferent or at worst recklessly biased or prejudiced. Whatever the reason, it was overshadowed only by his senselessness. But power has its privileges and I doubt that Proctor was penalized in any way for what I consider gross professional misconduct. Perhaps this is not entirely accurate. He was in fact marginalized in terms of his ability to affect my future movement in the company. It is also probably true that he was henceforth seen in a lesser light by the chairman and his colleagues. And so it was left to others in the company to resolve this potentially explosive affair. On my part I was left to wonder whether Proctor's behavior was due more to stupidity than malice.

The company's annual shareholders' meeting is held in May. Carl demanded that a resolution be finalized before the annual meeting. His concern was that I might raise the matter as an employee and share holder at the annual meeting. When this was revealed to me by a source involved with the discussions on resolution, I was appalled. After all, it should have been considered unlikely that I would set fire to a house in which I owned and occupied a room. My intention was not to destroy the company but to persuade it into becoming the company it expressly and constantly stated it wished to be. That this should be the thinking was understandable, however. I suspect that Carl probably put himself in my shoes and imagined what he himself might do under the circumstances. This was not really a totally unlikely reaction had my sanity deserted me.

I consider it no simple coincidence that I was receiving phone calls from nearly every single executive officer in the company enquiring what he or she could do to help to resolve the matter. While flattering to a degree, this made no impression. After a number of meetings and phone calls Heidi indicated that the company was requesting that I allow an extension to the deadline I had proposed for resolution initially. This was on account of the likely *ripple effects* of the proposal that would be made to me. I was intentionally reluctant to respond to this request but did agree eventually. It was now the end of April. The share holders' meeting was getting ever closer.

Conundrum and Risk

By this time three employees had turned down the job offer for Barbados. I learned that a fourth employee was given no option but to take the position. His career was in trouble and he had no bargaining power so he accepted the assignment. Like all of the others before him, he did not find Barbados an attractive place. All these white employees shared and voiced a common concern: they found it unacceptable to have their children attend a Barbadian school in which over 90% of the children were black. It should be noted that the literacy rate in Barbados was among the highest in the world. Obviously the quality of education was not the issue. The irony cannot be lost on any person who breathes: the one candidate who was the most qualified and willing to accept the assignment was the candidate to whom no one would offer the position. The company was now facing an intractable dilemma: I could not be offered the position because it had now been *accepted* by someone else and the position could not be filled because my situation had not been resolved.

With no more than a couple weeks to go before the share holders' meeting, I received a call from the COO of the company. We had met when he was a rookie VP and I was the Regional Manufacturing Manager for the Caribbean Group. We had been seeing more of each other than we had for many years as a result of my assignment in Burlington. He leaned heavily on the duration of our relationship and used this as leverage to ask that I take a trip to Africa to see if there were any opportunities there I would consider. I turned this down instantly and indicated that I had spent as much time in Africa as I intended to spend. I told him that there were other opportunities available and he should consider offering one of these. He did not agree with this contention and suggested that I make the trip to Africa as a personal favor to him. He suggested I take my wife along. Given my thinking at the time I saw this as a way to take my wife on a well deserved, all expenses paid vacation. I accepted the COO's offer and within days my wife and I left on our safari to Africa.

We visited Tanzania, Kenya, Zimbabwe and South Africa. In every location we were treated like royalty. It was exciting to see many of our old acquaintances from our earlier time in Kenya. Most delightful of all, I saw my former secretary who brought me up to date on many of the goings-on in the region. She had become the local GM's secretary. Tanzania was a great disappointment. It was absolutely a most unattractive possibility despite the significant extra compensation for hazard pay and bi-monthly R&R outside of the country. Kenya, though somewhat better in appearance than I remembered, was still suffering visibly from years of government corruption and mismanagement and the local subsidiary had not changed at all. Zimbabwe and South Africa were both very attractive places with great potential for an expatriate to make a mark and live at a standard only matched by millionaires in America. Even so I would not make any decision until I was good and ready.

As promised, I telephoned the COO the day after my return to the U.S. He was delighted to hear me and wanted to know what I thought about the trip. I indicated that it was quite interesting but that I would not be able to say more than this at the time. He understood and asked that I get in touch with him whenever I wished, as he would remain at my disposal to assist in any way he could with any decision I would make. In a subsequent meeting in New York with Heidi, she referred to my trip and the COO's comments after his discussion with me. She was particularly struck by a question he asked her: he wished to know, "Why does Owen remain with the company?" I asked Heidi what was her response to this puzzling query. She told him that, in her view, I remained with the company because I was not a black American. I am not at all certain what the thrust of the statement was but assume it was meant to indicate that I approached my relationship with the company from a very different perspective; that I was firm in my conviction that I would prevail in spite of my harrowing experiences, regardless of the apparent odds.

Heidi's statement reminded me of a telephone call I received while in Burlington. The caller was a young, black American marketing trainee who was seeking advice. It was not the first time I was receiving such a call. Somehow, young black American males, new to the company, were told to contact me if they ever needed advice. I do not know who is to be credited for this very flattering recognition.

This young man was an MBA graduate of Harvard University and had been hired by the company on campus. He was attracted to the company in large measure because of its elaborate and intense training program and the fact that he was assured of mentoring over his first several months on the job. In addition, he told me that the company's reputation meant a lot to him. When he called me he had been on the job about three months and felt that the company was failing to live up to its commitment to him. For example, he explained, he had not met with his white mentor since the first week when the mentor introduced him around the office. Yet, he had observed his mentor visiting the offices and inviting his white colleagues out to lunch but never invited him. I suggested to him that he should ask for a meeting with his mentor to discuss his concerns and specifically how he felt about his mentor's behavior. He was adamant that he could not do this. He was convinced that it was not his place to do so but his mentor's.

I explained that he should be careful not to jump to conclusions as to the reason for his mentor's behavior. I tried to explain that it was very likely that he was the very first black person with whom his mentor was asked to work. It could be that his mentor was uncomfortable and did not know how to address his discomfort. It could also be the case that a Harvard MBA was intimidating, especially when he was a young black American. In any event, I tried to tell him, he was the one in charge of his career and he was the one who needed to ensure that he received the training and mentoring he needed. I went on to introduce him to my "J" rule and emphasized that the three options of the "J" rule were the only options available to him. He had to choose. No one could choose for him. After about six months he left the company. It would be fascinating to learn what became of this young man. My hope is that he never jumped from the frying pan into the fire. The grass is seldom greener on the other side. It only appears that way until you get there.

Resolution

The time for the shareholders' meeting arrived. I was obliged to attend in my capacity as the manager of a site. I also wished to attend as a shareholder myself but mostly, I simply wanted to be quite visible, especially on this occasion, as a shareholder and employee. Just before the meeting convened the chairman saw me in the hall outside of the main meeting room and rushed over to speak with me. After the usual exchange of pleasantries he inquired whether everything had been settled. I told him not quite. He became visibly agitated and demanded to know why. I revealed that there were still some details that were unresolved. He immediately looked around the room and found the COO whom he beckoned over to join us. Carl enquired of me if I wanted him to get directly involved in the process. I told him I did not think this was necessary at this point as I felt the folks involved and I would resolve all outstanding issues very soon. He never the less expressed his disgust to the COO that the entire affair had not yet been completely settled. He made it abundantly clear that this should be done before the week ended.

The share holders' meeting was without incident. Afterwards the COO and I walked from the hotel to our corporate offices. He telephoned the VP of HR for the U.S. manufacturing division and told him that I would be coming to see him to review and possibly sign off on documents the company's lawyers had prepared. The VP was new to the position, having replaced my helpfully informative colleague mentioned earlier. He was somewhat perplexed by some few items in the document and wondered aloud if these inclusions were made in error. I was so put off by this that I stormed out of his office. He later suggested to Heidi that it appeared that I was taking out some of my frustrations on him. I later returned to his office and signed the documents after the intervention of the COO. I had agreed to accept the position of Regional Director of Manufacturing in Zimbabwe.

The Chairman Summons

Before leaving for Zimbabwe I was asked by the chairman to meet with him for about half an hour. I had no doubt what the subject of discussion would be. Our meeting lasted an hour and a half and convinced me that the entire disturbing affair had made some impression on him. He wished to know, from my point of view, what he could do to ensure that my very regrettable experience would not beset anyone else in the company. He revealed his deep concern and acute awareness that the rate of retention of black male hires was dismally poor. I supported this revelation with my story about the black Harvard MBA and proceeded to explain what I saw as problems and opportunities regarding the possible retention of black hires.

At the very outset it had to be understood that while we may find it distasteful to admit, the fact is that American and company tradition strongly and effortlessly supported *the good ol' white boys' club*. This club was far from color blind but would deny this failing onto death. This made the exercise of bias in our company invisible, automatic and self fulfilling in regard to blacks and women. But since the club found women less discomforting we could observe a few women in senior management positions in the company but no more than two black men. It is not without significance that the two black men were in staff positions. There certainly was not a single black VP in the technical-manufacturing area of the company. I pointed out that there was a black scientist in R&D who had over twenty patents to his name, had been with the company more than twenty years but was merely a director. In order to retain bright black hires, these hires must see people like themselves in senior management positions in order *to believe* that their own potential had a chance to be realized and recognized. The power of evidence and example is real.

To be fair, it was not only true that white men feel uncomfortable with black men. Black men were perhaps even more uncomfortable with white men – and for historically substantial reasons. The company had to find a way to bridge this comfort gap if it hoped to improve its chances of meeting its stated objective regarding diversity. One of the most perplexing aspects of this dilemma for the chairman of the company had to be the fact that his signature validated the company's Code of Conduct which was demonstrably failing in its commitment to equal opportunity and fair treatment of employees. Sadly, in my opinion, many affected employees will believe that even the chairman of the company did not believe in the very Code of Conduct bearing his signature. I expressed the view that Carl owed it as much to himself as to the company to ensure that his integrity was not sullied because the behavior of the company's officers and senior management remorselessly violated the Code of Conduct.

It could not be denied that he was in fact the guardian of the gate, so to speak. Ultimately, he was the person who would be judged by employees and history as accountable. It was clear to me that this disturbed him and he attempted to minimize his own accountability by explaining that he was only one man and could not do this alone. My response was that there was no need for him to do this alone. He simply needed to enforce commitment to the Code of Conduct among his direct reports. I would not let up and went on to quote a broadly distributed statement from the HR department:

"What we Recognize and Reward is what is Noticed and Valued."

I emphasized that there were no penalties attendant to the violation of the Code of Conduct by officers and senior managers of the company. They all continued to receive generous bonuses, raises and promotions in spite of demonstrable failings at one of their most critical responsibilities. There was no incentive for them to change their behavior. He did not disagree with this logic and asked how he could best change people's behavior in this regard, since ultimately disincentives alone will not change company culture and may only have short term impact at best. I explained to him that his most enduring effectiveness would be to improve the honesty and integrity of the mentoring system in the company, ensure that his direct reports were exposed to black senior executives at other companies, since we had none, and, as quickly as possible, promote qualified blacks to the position of Vice President. I expressed the view that because the situation was so bad in the latter respect there were ample opportunities to act quickly and make a difference. It was heartening to learn, less than a year later, that the multiple patent holder at R&D was named a VP.

Carl asked that I compile a one page list of recommendations for him before my departure to Africa. Among my recommendations was a reading list which included, *"The Rage of a Privileged Class"* by Ellis Cose and *"Invisible man"* by Ralph Ellison. It was very gratifying to me that my efforts at addressing one of the most vexing problems of all our lives in America were at least appearing to bear fruit. I left America for Africa once more. There was more bounce in my step, supported by a feeling of deep satisfaction that I had struck a blow against prejudice and bias in the company.

VII. ZIMBABWE, AFRICA SOUTH

The First Three Years:
On Arrival

Third World countries never fail to make multiple impressions all at once. Zimbabwe was no exception.

The city of Harare was modern in appearance and cleaner than most cities its size anywhere. The streets and avenues were without the blemish of pot holes and the sidewalks and medians were manicured with jacaranda and bougainvillea everywhere. It was impossible not to notice how wide the main avenues were. The explanation is that in old Zimbabwe the common means of transport was horse or oxen drawn buggy or carriage. These had to be able to make a full, three sixty degrees turn without having to back up. Noticeably, few cars on the street were of recent vintage. Most were small British models from the days of my youth in Jamaica. This was one of the mixed blessings of the former Rhodesia having been under an embargo by much of the morally sensitive world. It was fascinating to see the excellent condition of these old vehicles. In many respects, the country had become very self sufficient as a result of the embargo. As has often been said, "What doesn't kill you makes you stronger."

I had already done my personal due diligence on Zimbabwe. The exchange rate to the USD was about eight local dollars to one, but the cost of living in Zimbabwe was much more favorable than this rate of exchange indicated. For a country recently released from the shackles of apartheid, the life style was grand indeed for a surprisingly large number of those who previously bore the brunt of this indignity. But the hangover from sanctioned apartheid was evident everywhere: in the elaborate walls and electric fences securing residences; from the workplace and the shops to the ritzy residential neighborhoods and the people who were on foot on the streets. Personally, I was beginning to sense that I would become a witness to an unusual kind of redemption and reconciliation of an entire nation. There was no doubt in my mind that my sojourn would be as intellectually stimulating as it would be financially rewarding. In a number of respects Africa was a far better choice than Barbados. It will always remain pitiful that it took such an unpleasant and circuitous route to get there.

Settling in Once Again

The Zimbabwe operation was very diverse in its staffing. The GM was a teddy bear of an English man who came to Africa with his parents before he was ten years old and thought he was essentially African. His father had worked with the railways in Zambia. He was one of the most encyclopedic persons I have ever met. I thought he devoted far too much of his time and life to his work. He was a delightful raconteur, was always great company and had a hot, spicy temper. I cannot forget him telling an employee who upset him that the employee was an *oxygen thief*. The financial controller was Filipino. He was a reputable tenor, a devout Roman Catholic and choir master for his church. He was as affable as someone from *the islands*, as Caribbean islanders routinely describe the Caribbean in shorthand. The marketing director was a white Zimbabwean of British heritage who hailed from a small village, Gwanda, in rural Zimbabwe, grew up around native Zimbabweans and understood his country's culture very well. He was always teased about his village by being told that it was so barren that when traffic lights were installed, the very first time they went green the goats ate them. The plant manager was Pakistani, a citizen of Zimbabwe and a practicing Muslim. The purchasing manager was a white Zimbabwean of Dutch heritage and was an avid outdoorsman. The sales manager was native Zimbabwean of the Shona tribe. I found this diversity most interesting and very refreshing.

Within a few months of my arrival there was the usual business review. Much of what was required for the review was not at hand because of earlier manpower restraints. It took much effort to get all the necessary exhibits prepared for the review. This was a good thing. It forced me to learn much of the business history and operational details very quickly. As was the case in Kenya years earlier, my wife was left to perform the usual chores of finding a house and following up on progress with the shipment of our personal and household effects. This was not as difficult a task this time around as neither our children nor my mother-in-law accompanied us on this assignment. Both boys were of course out of college and working and my mother-in-law, who is hearing impaired, was very comfortably settled into an assisted living facility for the deaf in Toronto. But this would do nothing to reduce the wait time for our container or the challenge to find appropriate housing. In the meantime we would do as we normally did and make the best of our three months in the hotel.

We had become accustomed to finding Jamaicans wherever in the world we went. Not surprisingly there was a number of Jamaicans living in Zimbabwe. Most were women who had met and married Zimbabwean men while studying in England. Their husbands were all very important nationals who held highly influential positions in government, the judiciary and banking. Others were professors at the local university. The women themselves were professors, lawyers, doctors, nurses and entrepreneurs. It would require relatively little effort on our part to feel at home even this far away from North America and the Caribbean. In addition to the Jamaicans there was a number of folks from Guyana, Trinidad and Barbados. We were a very gregarious group and did a lot together. We often joked that attempts at forming a federation of our countries had failed miserably but whenever we met as a group abroad, the principles of federation worked very well indeed.

We became friends with a South Korean couple while in the hotel. The Koreans were in similar circumstances as we were, awaiting their personal and household effects and looking for a house. They had come from South Africa to help establish the first South Korean Embassy in Zimbabwe. Both men went to work while our wives house hunted together. It was a little more difficult than we expected to find a suitable house. Eventually we had to settle for an older house that was in need of some repair. I negotiated with the company to approve and pay for the repair in exchange for a significant reduction in rent.

The landlord was a white Zimbabwean who had migrated to South Africa but retained ownership of his house. This was not without some risk in Zimbabwe at the time, as the government looked askance at this kind of arrangement. It was a beautiful house on nearly four acres. Our neighbor was the Minister of National Security. On the one hand this was comforting; on the other, if things ever went awry this particular Minister would probably be among the first to be attacked, especially since he was of the Ndebele tribe and held office by virtue of an arrangement allowing the Ndebele to have a certain number of positions in the government. Essentially, the government was run by representatives of the major Shona tribe of which the president, Robert Mugabe, was the most notable.

Before long we were comfortably settled in our house and started to have visitors from North America. Africa remains a most fascinating place to most people regardless of their race or ethnicity. On average we had six to eight visitors per year. My wife basically worked much of the time as an honorary travel agent and tour guide. Apart from the well-known national parks like Hwange, Mana Pools and Gonorezhu, Great Zimbabwe (the stone ruins of a 12th to 15th century Shona kingdom), and the out-of-this-world Victoria Falls, the husband of one of the Jamaican women was a major banker and had routine access to his bank's chalet just outside of a quaint rural town called Nyanga. The chalet overlooked a large lake and was nestled half way up a picturesque mountainside which separated the chalet from the neighboring golf course. By association we also had free access and our visitors loved to spend time at the chalet which came with a butler, a maid and a gardener-handyman. This entire arrangement was a hangover from the colonial days. The natives happily hung on to this type of perk. This is understandable, of course. Among our visitors were our two sons whose visit I had negotiated as a part of my compensation package. I took time off from work and the family went on an extensive safari which included Victoria Falls, Hwange, Cape Town, Johannesburg and the Stellenbosch wine country.

Experience versus Youth and Faith

Work became more intense as I began to formulate a training and succession plan for Zimbabwe and to design a study to rationalize products and plant sites throughout East and Southern Africa. This would affect regional logistics and production and involve Kenya, Malawi, Botswana, Namibia, Zambia and South Africa. Simultaneously the company was negotiating the purchase of the largest native hair products manufacturer in South Africa. This latter exercise would prove to be very challenging for the company and truly instructive for me.

At the same time, integral to my succession planning program, I had to hire two engineers. I initially contracted with a search firm to provide candidates for interviews. I eventually abandoned this procedure when I discovered that all candidates, although experienced, exhibited a clear reluctance to accept responsibility for disciplining workers who violated the rules of attendance, for example. To a man they all indicated that this would be a matter for the HR manager to address. I knew then that I had a problem. This is not an unusual occupational deficiency in all the African countries with which I am familiar. There is a sense that the only person truly responsible and accountable is the *Chef* or highest person in the hierarchy. To be fair, there is some causal historical reason for this. Natives were traditionally never in positions which required that they be responsible and accountable. When an entire society is subjugated for an extended period of time all major matters affecting that society are the responsibility of others. It could take generations to overcome this insult and its attendant deficiencies.

I addressed the problem by deciding that the best thing to do was to hire young, inexperienced engineers and provide them with the training that would allow them to satisfy the needs of the company as I saw these at the time. Accordingly, I went to the local university and met with the dean of the school of engineering. I requested the résumés of the top twenty students of the current graduating class. What I discovered was truly revealing. On paper, these students were academically as good as, or superior to, any similarly qualified candidate I had ever interviewed.

The standards for gaining entry into the University of Zimbabwe were extremely high. This was true, in part, because competition for entry was so intense. As a result students would very often obtain two to three times the number of certificates required for entry. This would clearly improve their chances of acceptance into the school of engineering. I interviewed the best ten of these twenty students and selected two. They were put through an intensive and extensive training program which exposed them to the essentials of the most critical areas of the business: customer service, marketing, sales, accounting, logistics, operations, capital and operating budgets. They were then assigned to multiple areas in manufacturing under the direct supervision of the plant manager. At the end of their probation period they were sent separately for a month in the South African plant, the most complex company facility in Africa. The program was a resounding success. The challenge now was to retain them. They were now among the most attractive candidates for poaching by the largest and most highly regarded local companies.

I quickly promoted one to production manager and the other to plant engineer. Compensation became a matter of great concern and not just for them but for the plant manager as well. The compensation protocol in Zimbabwe was the same as it was in the Jamaica subsidiary early in my career. I understood the system perfectly. It took several months of negotiating with head office to obtain approval to move the compensation scales to where I believed they should be. A year later I successfully negotiated a company vehicle for each of the newly hired engineers and strongly supported payment of a portion of the Plant Manager's salary in USD. At a critical juncture during my negotiations with head office I was told that I had been co-opted by the natives. To my mind I had simply done what I was convinced was the right and sensible thing to do.

Y2K Scare

The infamous, globally anticipated Y2K debacle scared nearly everyone who either knew too much, or just enough, about computers inside and outside of the company. An extraordinary amount of contingency planning was done on a scale never before witnessed, by us as well as by every business organization with which our company had a relationship. In addition to my other responsibilities, I was assigned the responsibility of overseeing all related preparatory and contingency activities in East Africa and Southern Africa, internally and on the part of all our suppliers and customers. Universal compliance was the clear objective. It was an enjoyable challenge. As we now know Y2K came and went with little or no dislocations. I remain unsure whether this was owing to, or in spite of, all that was done in anticipation of what was supposedly the arrival of doomsday. Regardless, the company's efforts to prepare for Y2K did succeed in improving our image and our relationship with suppliers and customers.

First World Folly

The story of the native hair products company is a most fascinating one and demonstrates the hubris with which First World countries generally approach countries in the Third world. The owner of a very successful hair products company had become the first native and youngest millionaire in South Africa after the fall of apartheid in 1994. He was still a fairly young man, perhaps under forty years old. He had started his business the way most such businesses are started in Third World countries: compounding product at home and selling only to native hairdressers and barbers who most often provided their services in the open, under trees for shade. His products were formulated specifically for black natives. He also allowed extensive credit to nearly all of his customers. He eventually bought property in an industrial park and built a modern factory. While his processes and equipment were upgraded he did not change much else, especially his distribution network, credit policy and practice.

My company developed an intense interest in this hair products company which I shall call NHPC. This was in response to the attempts of a couple of major competitors to get into the South Africa market with a number of competitive hair care products. The purchase became a real challenge because my company had no experience with the products in question and was certainly ignorant of the sales and marketing strategy of the native company whose entire clientele was black. As we pursued the purchase I visited the facility to assess logistics, equipment and capability. Given what NHPC's objectives were, its manufacturing, sales and marketing strategies were very appropriate. I advised my company to proceed cautiously. The nature of the business we were pursuing was not at all compatible with any of our business models. I also cautioned against attempting to transform the company into a clone of our own.

It was clear to me that this company had to be allowed to retain as much of its natural character and identity as possible. This, to my mind, should apply especially to its sales and credit policies. If we eventually purchased the company this would allow a kind of uniquely attractive reverse technology and product transfer from the Third World to the First. I envisioned a Third World product being marketed in places like Brazil, the Caribbean, the rest of Africa and North America by one of the most reputable First World Personal Care Products marketers.

In short order the company ended up taking ownership of NHPC and just as quickly disposing of it again. The purchase was made with a combination of cash and company stocks. In real terms, the young native millionaire was even wealthier now, as it should be. He was retained after the transaction to ensure a seamless transition and effective continuity and loyalty to NHPC's clients. This appeared to work well initially. Regrettably, as I feared, the company began to tinker with three of NHPC's most crucial aspects: its credit, sales and marketing strategies. The unacknowledged intent was to make NHPC into a clone of its new owner.

The VP for Africa and the Far East was now a likeable Dutchman who had enumerated a number of highly unrealistic objectives for Africa, not the least of which was to double sales in two years. Under his direction the 100% native sales force of NHPC was disbanded and its functions folded into the responsibilities of the company's almost all-white South Africa sales force. This in theory would reduce duplication and cost. Next, we inflicted First World credit policies on NHPC: receivables would now not exceed twenty one days, just as was the case for the company at large. On paper this was an understandable decision; in practice, however, it was a predictable disaster. Finally, we reorganized NHPC's distribution system and would distribute products through our traditional wholesale network. When all was said and done, we had effectively destroyed NHPC and squandered all the very attractive opportunities it presented. In a tribute to poetic justice we cajoled the young native millionaire into buying back his company. I understand that the price he paid was much less than we had paid for NHPC in the first instance.

Third World Politics: A Heavy Hand

If all politics is local, as some believe, then Third World politics is strictly local and intensely intrusive and oppressive. Two most revealing examples will attest to this contention. While noticeably different in scale, they both reveal the boundless power of Robert Mugabe, the president of Zimbabwe. The first has to do with a brave young reporter who dared to report that the president had in effect remarried but was keeping this a secret. The president's Ghanaian first wife had died shortly before my arrival in the country. The second has to do with a native businessman being hounded by influential politicians into relinquishing contractual rights previously granted by the government.

In the first case, after a number of relatively mild rebuttals from the office of the President and the continued insistence of the reporter to the contrary the reporter and his newspaper were publicly castigated for spreading lies and in effect defaming the president. When neither the newspaper nor the reporter relented the reporter was quietly but very effectively banned from working anywhere in the country as a reporter. For as long as I remained in Zimbabwe he was unable to obtain employment as a reporter. Ultimately, it turned out that Mugabe had in fact committed to his new wife-to-be and her family that he would marry. This was somewhat embarrassing because the official period of mourning for his first wife had not ended. It should be noted that in local culture there is hardly any difference between committing to marry and actually marrying. Yet the young reporter's indiscretion was sufficient to warrant him being effectively banned from his profession by Mugabe.

In the second case, a local businessman had been granted government approval to start the first local cell phone service company. However, headline after headline in the major local newspapers revealed that he was being harassed and stymied by influential people in government. They were demanding, and were being refused, participation in the businessman's new company. Zimcel, as I shall call the company, took the government to court for breach of contract and undue interference. The case proceeded through the judicial system all the way to the High Court which is the equivalent of the U.S. Supreme Court. Up to this point Zimcel had lost at every step. The company hired a new lawyer. He argued that it was in fact unconstitutional for representatives of the government to interfere with his client's right to act on a legally binding agreement granted by the government that would ensure freedom of speech. At first this appeared to be an unjustifiable argument.

The new lawyer was ingenious. He argued that the constitution of Zimbabwe guaranteed freedom of speech. The actions of the government through its representatives violated this right. He indicated that the advent of his client's business would allow tens of thousands of Zimbabweans to exercise their right to their constitutionally protected freedom of speech which had been denied for more than ten years. The government owned post office was claiming, under the law suit, to have the sole right to provide telephone services in the country. This claim also meant that the Post Office was responsible for the interminable waiting list of Zimbabweans who had remained without telephone service for years. Zimcel's lawyer argued that this failure effectively robbed

Zimbabweans of the right to freedom of speech. To the surprise of many, the High Court agreed with Zimcel's lawyer.

Not surprisingly, the very next day Mugabe issued a statement over ruling the court. While this was shocking to many, it was not totally unexpected. Opposition by the local media as well as media elsewhere in Africa and Europe was relentless. It was very helpful that Zimcel had two foreign partners: one Swedish, I believe, and the other American. The embassies of both protested directly to the government. No formal retraction was ever made but Zimcel was allowed to proceed with its operations without further interference.

It is clear that at all levels of every society power has excessive privileges which are extremely difficult to curtail.

A Pain in the Neck

Mugabe's abusive use of power, while a real pain in the neck generally, did not affect me personally. But I would experience, soon enough, my own literal pain in the neck. One morning I sneezed while reaching for my toothbrush. I felt a very sharp pain in my neck and right shoulder. It was so intense it stopped me in my tracks. The pain quickly went away and I again reached for my toothbrush. Again I sneezed. This time the pain was like a red hot poker had been jammed into my back. My entire right side went numb. I was basically immobilized.

My wife was in bed asleep and I was in the bathroom some twenty feet away from our bedroom. I tried to call out but had difficulty speaking. I had to find a way to get to the bedroom. I limped and clawed my way against the bathroom wall until I was close enough to our bedroom and weakly launched myself with one leg onto the edge of our bed awakening my wife. Immediately she realized something was amiss. I managed to blurt out that I thought I was having a heart attack or stroke and needed to get to the hospital immediately. She called the emergency services then two very good friends. One was a native orthopedic surgeon who we knew would help to arrange for us to see the best cardiologist or any other appropriate specialist without delay. The other was a Jamaican lady who was the administrator for the best private hospital in the country. My wife alerted them both to my situation and they agreed to meet us at the hospital.

The private ambulance arrived within minutes of being called. The attendants were apprised of my situation and decided that the best course of action was to treat me for the worst likely problem: a heart attack. I was given nitroglycerine under the tongue and a drip was installed before I was moved to the ambulance and transported to the hospital. Our two friends were already at the hospital when we arrived. Our orthopedic friend had the best cardiologist in tow and the administrator had already completed all the required paper work. My wife simply needed to affix her signature. I was introduced to the cardiologist who examined me promptly and asserted that it appeared very unlikely that I had a cardiac issue. However, out of an abundance of caution he placed me in the ICU and hooked me up to all the usual heart monitoring equipment. In the meantime he alerted a neurosurgeon colleague to my problem. That evening the cardiologist returned to review all the data from the monitors. The results confirmed that my heart was fine.

The neurosurgeon came to see me the following morning and had me take an MRI and X-Rays. Both indicated that my spinal cord was pinched between my fifth and sixth vertebrae. This was the cause of my transient paralysis. He also indicated that the situation was very serious. If I sneezed, stubbed my toe or were bumped from behind there was a good chance that I could snap my spinal cord. This would paralyze me permanently and I would become a paraplegic. His prognosis was that I needed to have the problem addressed urgently. This meant surgery. He proceeded to tell me that he had done hundreds of this type of surgery successfully but he recognized that as an expatriate who obviously had alternatives, I may not wish to have such surgery done locally. In any event, he cautioned, I should not delay doing what was required. He appeared more resigned to the reality of my expatriate option than offended by it.

He was Congolese and had studied, trained and qualified in Switzerland. His qualifications and experience were never in question. His resignation that it was unlikely that my surgery would be done locally, accurately reflected my own position as well as that of my company which had a world wide emergency service for exactly this type of event. I was fitted with a soft neck brace, directed not to move about and to lay propped up in bed on my back after being released from the hospital.

The emergency service was provided by a Swiss company out of Geneva. It would take at least three to four days to get me to America. I was asked by head office whether I would wish the service activated on my behalf. Both my wife and I felt this was unnecessary as she had already researched on line the best hospitals in America for the procedure I would undergo as well as the fastest way to get to America from Harare under the current set of circumstances. We concluded that Colombia Presbyterian Hospital in New York and British Airways qualified on each count and convinced head office that these were the best choices.

Our friends rallied to our side. One such friend was the Speaker of the Zimbabwe House of Parliament. His wife was born in St. Kitts, went to university in Jamaica and unilaterally decided that she could legitimately claim Jamaican citizenship. None of the Jamaicans disapproved of this claim and accepted her as such. In any event, it was impossible to tell from her speech and behavior that she was not born in Jamaica. Her husband arranged for us to be chauffeured in his official Mercedes Benz to the airport and ensured our treatment as super VIP's. In spite of this, it was laughably out of place to be moved on board our British Airways flight in first class, my wheel chair on a regular wooden pallet, hoisted by common forklift, onto the entry way to the galley of the aircraft. Our friend's influence could not overcome the technological limitations of the local airport.

Our flight to America was uneventful. However, my status as a wheelchair bound passenger made all the difference in the world to how expeditiously we were whisked through immigration and customs at Kennedy Airport on arrival in New York. The company had two limousines and an HR representative awaiting us at the terminal. One limousine was to take me directly to the hospital; the other was to take my wife to the hotel to check in and subsequently to the hospital. It was an impressive display of planning and caring. Within an hour of being checked into the hospital and assigned a temporary room I received a telephone call from Carl, the chairman of the company. He wished to know how I was, how my wife and family were doing and whether there was anything else that he could do to make my situation more comfortable. I told him everything was going as well as I could possibly wish and expressed my deep appreciation for the very impressive manner in which the company was handling my situation.

I had taken all the relevant medical records with me from Harare. I had assumed that this would expedite action by my surgeon and the hospital in New York. To my surprise every MRI and X-Ray was repeated, apparently without a single reference to the records I had brought with me. By reputation, my surgeon was the very best in his field. He had invented a unique procedure for repairing or fusing vertebrae. The procedure required the use of sea coral in the process. He explained that he had reservations about the long term effects and reliability of metal implants or radiated bone from cadavers. Instead he would remove bone from my own hip to fuse my affected vertebrae and replace the bone from my hip with sea coral. He also warned that my hip would hurt intensely as a result but that the injury to my neck would be repaired without any discomfort or painful aftermath. He also repeated a long list of things that could go wrong during my surgery. None of his patients had ever suffered any of these mishaps. Despite this comforting fact, he was never the less obliged to reveal the possible pitfalls.

At the time my niece, who shared an apartment with our older son, was doing her medical internship at the hospital. Not surprisingly, my wife had consulted her medical books on my surgery and had gleaned from this that there was one possible consequence of my surgery that my surgeon had failed to highlight: there was a remote possibility that if a certain nerve were damaged I could become impotent. On her next meeting with the surgeon she took him to task on her discovery. He agreed with her but said he did not reveal this remote possibility because of the risk that on learning this I may have cancelled my surgery. This provoked a long, hearty laugh from all of us. The surgeon would subsequently meet my niece whom he invited to sit in on my surgery. If I had had any reservations about his skill and confidence they surely disappeared then.

My surgery went well. I awoke and asked for my surgeon and was told that he had gone. In response, I quipped that he was a strange one who simply cut and ran. Since I was oblivious to the occurrence, I continue to blame it on the anesthesia. I was required to remain in the New York area for three months for routine post-op procedures. After a couple weeks in a New York hotel we decided to relocate to a much more family friendly Embassy Suite across the Hudson River in New Jersey. This was one bus stop away from the train that would take us into Manhattan. Not only were we more comfortable here but this saved the company money. At the end of the period my surgeon confirmed my readiness to return to work but advised that I should limit my activities. I certainly should not jog or play any sports for the next nine months. My wife and I then left New York for Harare once again.

Subsidiary Culture:
Relevance and Discord

But for the discernable differences in culture and the manner in which conducting business differed one country from another, my job could have become less challenging and routine.

Our operations in South Africa were particularly interesting and challenging. Much of the cause for this was directly related to the effects of apartheid, the number of ethnic groups, the variety of languages, the palpable mistrust between whites of Dutch or Afrikaner heritage and whites of British heritage, as well as the visible impact of the dramatic socio-political changes that were occurring in South Africa. It is important to understand that, in many respects, the relationship between Afrikaners and their white, non-Afrikaner counterparts was as discomforting and complex as was the relationship among the various ethnic groups. This was also true in terms of the relationship between these groups and white South Africans generally.

The effects of all of this were clearly visible in the South African subsidiary. Apartheid had officially ended but its inevitable aftermath resulted in a seething anger, especially among the Zulus in the company. They comprised the largest, most hostile and outspoken group in the country as well as in the plants. The plants had the misfortune of having multiple union representation. This was of much greater significance to management than it was to the unions themselves, despite the multiplicity of ethnic languages spoken. The fact was that the Zulus controlled all aspects of labor relations at both the site in Johannesburg and the site in Durban.

To his great credit, the manufacturing director, who was German, recognized and understood the implications of the complexity of the culture in his facilities. He was very much aware and highly respectful of my experience with operations in America, especially in the facility in Burlington, New Jersey. He requested my assistance specifically in mitigating the effects of the obvious anxieties at his sites. Even among management there were many troubling issues quite similar to those of my own experience in our operations in America.

Although the subsidiary had spent significant sums of money to train and prepare natives for management positions, there was a pervasive reluctance to fulfill the promise this implied. There is the instance of a young Zulu HR manager who was ready for promotion to replace his white boss who was leaving the company. Senior management was unwilling to promote him even after a protracted period of discussions between corporate HR management and the subsidiary. The company lost the Zulu HR manager as a result. This was a senseless and completely avoidable loss that the subsidiary would regret given the obvious value of the Zulu's interface with the native workforce. The Zulu manager's competence was never in question. The same cannot be said of the company's judgment. It is very clear that just as the company propagates its best technical practices all over the world it also propagates many of its worst human resources deficiencies.

Thoughts of Retirement

    My wife and I had agreed in the mid1980's that I would retire at the earliest opportunity. We had calculated the asset base we would require to be able to do so comfortably. By my calculations we had arrived at this point by 1998 which, coincidentally, was the year in which my work permit for Zimbabwe expired. To me this was a happy coincidence. My wife, ever cautious, calculated at the time that if I were to leave the company then, I would lose 7% of my company retirement benefits. We realized that if I worked an additional two years I would avoid this loss. I was willing to accept this loss of benefits. My wife was not. She convinced me that working another two years would be child's play compared to what I had already endured. It was also her unrelenting conviction that the company could not possibly deserve such a donation from me. It was sheer serendipity that at the same time the division's VP of manufacturing approached me with the request that I work in Africa for an additional two years. I was more than willing to consider the request but was concerned about the role I would play over this period. Based on the responsibilities I had been assigned, I was of the opinion that I had done all that could reasonably have been expected. I asked directly for an explanation in regard to my extended role. His explanation surprised me and was not without some cause for skepticism.

I was told that my role over the period would be to implement the training and rationalization recommendations I had made for the region over the previous three years. I expressed serious concern since, to my knowledge, none of my recommendations had been formally accepted by head office. Certainly, none had been acted upon. I was incredulous that I would now be asked to implement these recommendations. He did his best to try to convince me that the company was now ready to act in earnest to rationalize and streamline operations throughout East and Southern Africa. I did not believe this and for effect asked if I would have carte blanche in deciding product shifts and plant closings in the region. I did not desire a response and interrupted him before he could provide one fully. I agreed to consider the proposal after being provided with more definitive details. In the ensuing months not many additional details were forthcoming. I therefore developed my own set of responsibilities for my final two years in Africa.

To my mind, the most critical of any set of responsibilities I could develop had to include training and succession planning. This would be the focus of my remaining time in Africa. I was, and remain, convinced that even a modicum of success in respect of these objectives would be the most lasting impact I could conceivably make. This was significant as much for my own sake as for the sake of the native Africans with whom I worked.

The Last Two Years
A Long Goodbye

These last two years were the years of a long goodbye. There is no comfortable way to say goodbye to Africa. The place is as amazing as it is bewildering: amazing because of its noticeable changelessness in so very many respects; bewildering because of its raw, inexplicable contradictions. While I certainly consider it my good fortune to have been there, I was not unhappy to depart when the time came. Inevitably, Africa forces thoughtful humans to contemplate our origins and our future. This, I suspect, is much more the case for people like me.

Whence Am I Who?

I am a tree
Sleek and tall,
Solid ebony.
I pray for night when it is day.
I, an impostor.
I sprout green leaves instead of black
No roots must show.
Thicken foliage, thicken.
Grow deeper roots, go deep.
Equally separate
In all save life

The one is twain
Yet disparate.
Weighty in camouflage
I grow taller yet.
In another's forest
I supplant myself.
As my own murderer I am best.
Present soil as well of ancient mix
Accommodates another root reluctantly.
We two alike and foreign grapple.
Enlightened by my underground
I too am loot.
Together we make the knot
Of roots of common strain.
A beginning
To look toward our history's heartland
A winning
But there is no getting there
No journey to arrival
No, none to life.
There are no seasons in the heartland
No strife.
Stout ebony is on common ground
With all its kind.
Rebirth.
History rectified unites
Turns the mind into itself
Hallowed earth
Earth of Africa.

The lasting impact of European adventure on sensitivities and language in Africa is demonstrated by an experience with my gardener. One weekday evening we were away from home when a friend stopped by. On our return Patrick, our gardener, told us we had had a visitor. This was relatively rare on a weekday evening. Since Patrick did not get the name of the visitor he attempted to describe the person to us. The person was male, tall, drove a white car and was a *warungu*. In Shona this word means European. We therefore concluded that our visitor was a white person. Still, we could not determine which of our white friends it was who would have visited at that unusual time of day.

Later that evening our visitor telephoned to tell us he had come by. The visitor was a black Guyanese. We accosted Patrick about this. He agreed that the visitor looked like us. We are certainly not white or European and therefore not warungu, we told Patrick. But Patrick insisted that we were. We later enquired of a native friend what the word was for foreigner in Shona. She indicated that she did not know of a word for foreigner. However, when she was growing up all foreigners were European. You may recall my experience with the Swahili word, *muzungu*, in Kenya. Historically, since all foreigners were white there was no need for a word to describe a black foreigner. It is quite remarkable that even when the European did not impose his brand by cohabiting with natives he effectively did so through the sheer power of his distinctive presence and its impact on the native language.

Shona Stone Carvings

It is inconceivable that anyone could visit or live in Zimbabwe and not be captivated by the ubiquitous and exquisite works in stone. Unlike our first encounter with Africa in Kenya, my wife and I were now much more sophisticated in our taste and appreciation for native art and artifacts. Zimbabwe was famously rich in the art of stone carving. Nearly all the major stone carvers were of the Shona tribe, the largest tribe in Zimbabwe. These carvers worked in various types of native stone. Some, like Verdite, were extremely hard, considered semi-precious, rare, difficult to carve and relatively expensive. Others, like Soap Stone, were soft, common, very easy to carve and quite inexpensive. There were entire communities in Zimbabwe whose main source of income was from stone carvings. Interestingly, very few natives collected these carvings as they consider them just stone. Expatriates and tourists consider them remarkable works of art whose value increases significantly once removed from Zimbabwe. Notably, galleries in America and Germany, especially, carry works by some of the most famous as well as the not so famous Zimbabwean stone carvers at astonishing prices.

There were relatively few stand alone galleries. All the major hotels carried some of the most exquisite pieces of stone carvings. Like the galleries, they were very expensive. But good work was also available from galleries on the street if the purchaser knew what to look for. We selectively purchased from all of these sources and took special care in advising friends, visitors and expatriate colleagues on what to look for when making purchases. It is astonishing that so many competent artists can be found in a single country working in the single medium of stone. While our collection of Shona stone carvings constantly reminds us of our time in Zimbabwe there are other memories that are equally persistent but far less pleasant.

A Blueprint for Disaster

Very shortly after my arrival in Zimbabwe I was taken to see one of the country's most impressive commercial operations: *The Tobacco Sales Floor*. This was literally the stock exchange for trading the country's tobacco. This trading floor was as well run as Wall Street. Traders had immediate access to up-to-the-minute information on bids, the latest foreign exchange rates and the volumes and product classifications sold. It was perhaps the most demonstrative example of a free market on the continent. The traders came from a number of countries including Japan, Germany, the U.S. and England. It was difficult to believe that I was in a Third World country. The level of sophistication was incredible. Tobacco is called the *Golden Leaf* in Zimbabwe. It was the country's main export and employed nearly a million Zimbabweans. The Tobacco Floor was such an impressive operation, I imagined that any country that could so effectively operate such an enterprise would surely be able to run the rest of its economy with much better than average success. My last two years in Zimbabwe would prove my assumption to be almost ridiculous.

First, Zimbabwe's president, Robert Mugabe, injected his armed forces into Joseph Kabila's intractable war in the Congo. Then he started to cultivate an army of veterans and pseudo-veterans to vilify and persecute white farmers in preparation for the confiscation of their farms. It appeared that Mugabe was purposely ravaging the very underpinnings of the country's economy - its agriculture.

When I first arrived in Zimbabwe, the country was considered the breadbasket of southern Africa. This was no longer the case. Zimbabwe was beginning to have difficulty feeding its own people. The signs of decline were all around: petrol was being rationed; the currency was being devalued rapidly; citizens who opposed government policies were being set upon by marauding Mugabe and party-in-power supporters; basic staples were fast becoming unaffordable to the masses; an entire retail industry was developing based on the resale of used clothing donated by foreign charities and expatriates for distribution to the poor for free; beggars, unseen or absent before, now assailed tourists and anyone who appeared able to spare a dollar; petty crime, all but non-existent earlier, was now on the rise.

Ian Smith, the villain of apartheid in Zimbabwe, was beginning to appear to far too many natives as the lesser of two evils. This was a shocking observation considering the history of the country. This sentiment was being expressed by a range of locals; from gardeners and maids to bankers and lawyers. None of this appeared to bother Mugabe or his minions. This state of indifference was understandable. In the main, Zimbabweans are by nature a very peaceful people because of proscriptions in their culture against inflicting unjustifiable harm. The common equivalent in our world is the concern that the sins of the fathers will be visited upon the children.

For example, a British educated Shona brand manager approached me once with a request that I speak with her boss, the white Zimbabwean marketing director, about allowing her a week off from work so that she could accompany her fiancé, a young medical doctor, to his village. I inquired of her why she would not speak with her boss herself. She felt that he would not understand. She revealed that her fiancé needed to go to his village to participate in a ceremony to placate the spirits

263

because of an evil deed by a paternal uncle. She would not tell me what this evil deed was but indicated that two uncles had so far died inexplicably after another had committed suicide. Suicide is forbidden among the Shona and is thought to occur only because of some unpardonable cultural infraction by the subject. If atonement is not made by the family, every paternal male will eventually die. I agreed to speak with her boss on condition that she commit to do so herself after I did. I was certain the he would understand. He did understand and she was allowed the time off from work.

Obviously we could assume a number of causes for both the suicide and the subsequent deaths. One convenient assumption would be that the suicide and deaths were all related to HIV Aids which was endemic in Zimbabwe. Regardless of what we may assume, the real lesson is that when an indigenous people are put under severe stress, in spite of exposure to the bounties of western civilization, including a first class western education, they revert to the comfort of their native culture for security. In other words, the more horrendous the assault on life, the more deficient and untrustworthy adopted western culture appears. We may consider this irrational and unacceptable but to deny not only the reality but its significance as well, would be disastrous in any attempt on our part to understand the culture in the midst of which we lived and conducted business.

Because of the cultural proscription against wanton violence I was unaware of a crime being committed with a firearm in Zimbabwe until I read of an incident in the local newspaper. Two young natives had held up a retired white couple. One pointed a gun at the elderly man who promptly slapped him in the face as he expressed his amazement that he was being held at gun point in his own home. The two intruders turned and ran away. Even more demonstrative of the peaceful nature of Zimbabweans is the fact that I witnessed Ian Smith strolling through downtown Harare without a single body guard. He clearly had no concern for his personal safety.

Still, as a community, the population in the city was being squeezed so badly by the failing economy that riots occurred from time to time. These had horrific consequences for the rioters who were beaten mercilessly by the police, ably assisted by Mugabe's goon squads. Not surprisingly, these incidents were never seen on local television but if one had a satellite dish one would see them on CNN. Riots could take place in the city and the population at large would be oblivious to the fact. Mugabe consistently claimed that these displays of public protest were fomented by the "disloyal," unrecognized, embryonic opposition political party. Even if this claim were true, it in no way mitigates Mugabe's despotic behavior.

Of course, the progression from bad to worse to unbearable continued. Many natives and white citizens with the connections and means to do so began to emigrate to places like South Africa, the U.K., New Zealand and Australia. Four years earlier, the rate of exchange was at eight local dollars to one USD. It was now at forty to one USD. Strangely, in neighboring Zambia the exchange rate situation was much worse at thirteen hundred to one USD. In spite of this, dislocations in the local economy were nowhere as pronounced or catastrophic as these were becoming in Zimbabwe. But as Zambians went to great lengths to explain to me, it would not be too long before Zimbabwe's exchange rate was identical to theirs or worse. The reasoning was simple and full of intended irony. Zimbabweans had always boasted of being able to outperform Zambians at everything. We now know that this was a most prescient observation as Zimbabwe has since endured unimaginable rates of hyper inflation and incomprehensible devaluations of its currency.

Succession: First Fruits

Several months prior to my final departure from Zimbabwe I recommended to head office that the plant manager be promoted to take over my responsibilities in the local subsidiary. In my estimation he was ready. As part of his preparation he had recently spent a month in the South Africa subsidiary on an intensive program of exposure and introduction to the inter-subsidiary relationship from a non-Zimbabwe perspective. His position as plant manager would not need to be filled as additional responsibilities would be given to the production manager as part of his ongoing development. I outlined in an elaborately detailed document, precisely why the time was right for this transition. I also elaborated on the positive impact this would have on site morale as well as on morale in the other subsidiaries in the region. The document even explained that at some point the company may be unable to obtain work permits for expatriates, making it imperative that locals be given the appropriate training, exposure and experience in being truly responsible and accountable for operations.

This was not a baseless concern given my earlier experience in Kenya. It occurred to me that the corporation literally had no memory; only certain people within the corporation did. Somewhat to my surprise the company did not agree that the plant manager was ready to take on my local responsibilities in the subsidiary. Instead,

I was asked whether I would be willing to remain in Africa a little while longer. I did not hesitate to turn down this request and to re-emphasize the validity of my recommendation. Head office was unyielding in its position.

It is quite expensive to travel business class back and forth between Harare and New York and to be put up in a five star hotel on each trip. In my last three months, however, I had to do exactly this once each month before head office was convinced that I would not extend my stay in Africa. The real problem was not that my succession plan was defective. I suspected that head office was willing to go to great lengths to keep me out of its operations in the U.S. or to stymie localization of senior manufacturing management. No one knew that my intention at this point was not just to leave Africa but to leave the corporation altogether. My wife and I agreed that I would relentlessly press the company to find me an appropriate position in the U.S. operations until it became obvious that only an offer of a golden handshake would resolve the impasse. My long goodbye ended up being capped by a most interesting game of cat and mouse.

My Mother

During this period of mild turbulence, my mother passed away in Jamaica. This was February of the year 2000 and only a few months before I would retire. The coincidence of her passing in the year of my retirement marked a new watershed in my life. It signaled the end of an era for me and the rest of my family. It also reinforced my commitment to ensure that I spend as much time as I am able to with my own children, siblings and close relatives and friends. Both my parents maintained very close relationships with family members and had many very good friends. As a result, our house was very often the gathering place for birthday celebrations and holiday get-togethers. I remain forever grateful for the lasting impression this made on me. It has certainly contributed to my own very strong commitment to stimulate and maintain intimate connections with family and friends throughout my life. Happily, my wife unreservedly shares this sentiment.

My mother more than compensated for the extent to which my father appeared to occupy merely the periphery of his children's lives. Even when she was away working in America during our teenage and early adult years, as so very many Jamaican parents did and still do, we never felt that her presence in our lives had taken a holiday. While she may not have personally initiated any action on our part in terms of what we would do with our lives after our teenage years, she never failed to remain directly and intimately involved with any decision any of us made to pursue higher education goals. Clearly, she was very limited in her exposure to the requirements of these aspects of our progress and the choices we would be required to make. In spite of this, mother never failed to provide very useful advice, support and guidance.

Unlike our father, she exhibited keen, ongoing interest, not merely in what we planned or did but in how we were coping as we went along. She certainly needed no encouragement to express publicly how proud she was of her children's plans and accomplishments. It is difficult to imagine that she and my father never discussed these things. Still, nothing in his behavior revealed that this was in fact the case. In very many respects it appears that my mother was the one who went the extra mile to make her marriage work and her children succeed. She certainly was the one who visibly monitored the progress of her children far into adulthood. At times, in observing my own life, it seems that in some critical respects I may have married my mother.

Two years before my mother passed away, my wife and I observed a serious decline in her mobility and a noticeable dullness in her ability to recall recent events and occurrences. We decided then that we should spend as much intimate time with her as we could. It is one of our fondest memories that we took her to spend a week with us at a hotel on the North Coast of Jamaica. Apart from the excessive curvature of her upper back she had aged most attractively. Her memorably radiant, attractive white hair sparkled and her bubbly laughter made us believe that she had much more time with us than was actually the case. She remained engaging and challenging company and was never reluctant to express her opinions, especially on the politics and politicians of the time in both America and Jamaica. Although we made this extra effort to spend time with her, it is one of the most painful of realizations that no amount of time spent with an aging, ailing parent is ever enough.

Wasted Wisdom

Once again, I was being courted by very senior officers in the company in an attempt to convince me that an extended stay in Africa, all things considered, would be a very wise move on my part. One of my counter moves was to present the company with a definitive job description of a created position which would have at its core the preparation of expatriates for potential assignments abroad and the assistance of minorities and women with developing career planning objectives within the corporation. The common response was that the corporation's HR function already did these things. My rebuttal was that, if indeed this were the case, then these were being done in the greatest of secrecy.

All but one of the senior officers in the company who devoted precious time to see me were men. It was revealing that only the single female officer thought that my proposition was very insightful and worthy of serious consideration. She indicated unequivocally that she could in fact make the idea work. After pointing out to her that she was unique in this regard, I indicated that I had crossed my own Rubicon in my relationship with the company and could see no way in which the matter could be resolved to our mutual satisfaction. She nevertheless indicated that if I should have a change of heart she would be more than willing to work on my proposal with me. She most certainly recognized the relevance and validity of my suggestion. The truth is, most of the employees who were sent abroad to work, especially in Third World countries, were totally unprepared in a socio-cultural sense, or were ill prepared where any attempt at preparation was made at all. It was also true that career path planning did not exist in the company in any meaningful or formal sense for minorities and women, the two most disadvantaged groups of employees in this regard.

Time and time again my experience confirmed the lack of socio-cultural preparedness on the part of expatriates regarding even relatively simple inter-personal relationships while abroad. In most Third World countries labor is alarmingly cheap. It was therefore not uncommon for expatriates to have several domestic employees, including cooks, maids, nannies, gardeners, chauffeurs and security guards. Many wealthy and not so wealthy natives enjoyed this bounty as well. There was a noticeable difference in how natives treated their domestic help and how most expatriates treated theirs, in terms of respect, compensation and compassion. Natives generally paid as little as possible to their domestic help, were indifferent, often disrespectful and at times downright abusive. Expatriates were often uncomfortable, excessively compassionate and overly indulgent. This indulgence prompted an unforgettable comment, from a long time Jamaican resident, that expatriates suffered from what locals call "compassionate syndrome". These tendencies on the part of expatriates had notable consequences.

In the case of natives, domestic helpers were always seeking opportunities to quit working for them to go to work for expatriates. Employees of expatriates seldom ever wanted to quit, enjoyed super status among their peers and sometimes abused their employers' naive understanding of the relationship that should exist between domestic help and their employers in Third World environments. The relationship, while simple on the face of it, is quite complex for a number of reasons. Not least among these is the fact that the vast majority of expatriates, especially Americans, were new to the world of having domestic help. In America, as in most industrialized countries, only the truly wealthy could afford the kind of help now available to expatriates for a pittance. They needed to acquire the skills necessary to manage the relationship well. On a cautionary note: white as well as black American expatriates' over indulgence, in my view, is not unrelated to a weighty communal guilt complex due to white society's historically racist behavior and black society's super-sensitivity to unfair and disrespectful treatment. Neither situation is particularly helpful in managing the social interface under discussion.

In most, if not all, Third World countries, having household help is a very common occurrence among a much larger cross section of the native population than is the case in America. In Jamaica, for example, it is not unusual for domestic help themselves to have domestic help, especially if pre-school-aged children are at home. My wife and I were therefore quite familiar and comfortable with the bountiful domestic help available in Kenya and Zimbabwe. It fell to our lot to assist our expatriate American friends in coming to grips with the exhilaration, discomforts and confusion of what was clearly a whole new world of social and cultural interaction.

A much more poignant and directly relevant story is that of a white plant manager in our Egyptian subsidiary just outside of Cairo. He was invited to attend the wedding of a male factory employee. With the best of intentions but in abysmal ignorance of local customs, he kissed the bride on the cheek at the end of the wedding ceremonies. While a very acceptably normal, congratulatory act in America this is among the gravest of insults to the husband and the family of the bride in Egypt. Subsequently, his safety and the image of the company became matters of such great concern that the husband had to be placated by payment of an undisclosed sum and the plant manager relocated to a subsidiary outside of Egypt.

Likewise, career planning for minorities and women in the company was so obviously deficient, if it existed at all, that my suggestion in this regard was a no brainer. Even so, I was not surprised that the idea only resonated with a single officer of the company who happened to be female. The club of good ol' white boys surely never saw any need for this kind of thing. After all, should things go awry on the people front they would always be blameless. In the words of some wise observer of corporate life, "It's not whether you win or lose but how you place the blame." And who is most blamable for failing to overcome obstacles placed in his murky path than the disadvantaged employee himself?

Coming Home

In the end, with some degree of trepidation, corporate HR made an offer for an amicable separation. I suspect that the offer was very hesitantly made because HR probably recalled my instantaneous refusal of a similar offer many years before. But, as I said to the HR representative, now was a different time and I was certainly in a different place in my life. I was therefore willing to consider the company's offer, provided that after reviewing and agreeing to all the details, the offer was put in writing for me and my wife to study. I requested a twenty four hour time delay after my review before I would make a decision. Of course, my decision had been made before the meeting. I was simply enjoying the game based on my own rules. It was wonderful to have had such control. I agreed to the amicable separation package, said my goodbyes and left for Zimbabwe a few days later. It would be several weeks after my final departure from Zimbabwe before I would receive the legally vetted documents for my signature. The legalese was amazing and explains why I do not identify my former company or name involved senior executive business associates anywhere in this work, except where specific permission has been granted by any of these associates to do so.

Someone once asked if I had any regrets about retiring early: just one. I should have done so earlier. But it is probably true that nothing happens before its time.

Within a couple months after my return from head office I left Zimbabwe and Africa for good. My wife and I were ecstatic in anticipation of our new life ahead. In spite of itself, the company had provided us with a good living which, against great odds, we had successfully turned into a wonderful life with absolutely no regrets. We had long ago decided that America would be our home. We had come home and had every confidence that America would make good on its promise to all who arrive at its shores. We had already commenced building our house in Florida. It was scheduled to be completed three months after our return from Zimbabwe. Until then, the company provided temporary accommodations and a rental car and covered our living expenses. Our long goodbye to Africa had melded into our long emotional embrace of our country of choice. We had come home to America.

VIII. AMERICA REPRISE

Comity, Fear and Reluctance

It is a truism that retirement is the beginning of the rest of our lives.

Our focus was now the completion of our house. Our temporary accommodations were a mile away from our residential community and house site. I would jog to and from the site each day and meet with the building superintendent as necessary. When completed, the community would comprise about five hundred houses and be recognized as one of the more ritzy neighborhoods in Central Florida. Its manicured lawns and twenty four hour manned entrance only enhanced its mystique. Each time I entered the community the white security guards and construction workers at our house expressed their curiosity about me by enquiring about my profession. I refused to confirm or deny their professed assumptive queries: A ball player? A musician? These were the most common queries. Finally, on one occasion the site superintendent who was aware that I had come to Florida from Africa, jokingly responded to the query of a tile layer that I had been a lion tamer in Africa. The tile layer thought this was perfectly reasonable. He in turn tried to confirm this with me one morning. I went along with the charade. The tile layer then expressed the opinion that my job was obviously very dangerous and explained why I earned enough money to be able to afford a house in this exclusive neighborhood. It is clear that although I successfully evaded the usual stereotypical professions I was still confined to the realm of the arcane and highly unusual. This was not at all surprising to me. Speaking generally, America still has a long way to go, as much in its perceptions and expectations of black people as in its awareness and understanding of itself.

We took occupancy of our house in October of 2000, shortly before our container of personal and household effects arrived. Our community was in its final stages of completion. It is a gorgeous community. Of the five hundred households fewer than ten are black with four of this number being of Jamaican heritage. There is something curious about this. Why is it that more black people, in particular black Americans, do not live in our community? Perhaps the question was answered by my black American physician friend in Kentucky, or by my workmate at the plant in Jeffersonville who could not imagine any way in which he could comfortably work with a good ol' Indiana boy, or by the young, black Harvard MBA who left the company in frustration, or by the vacuity of Proctor Masters, the Australian corporate VP who knew me better than anyone else: the implication being that he knew what no one else did – that I really did not want to be promoted. Paradoxically, part of the answer to the question clearly lies in the fact that the question itself is asked. Until we achieve clarity and balance in our expectations and perceptions of one another such a question will continue to be asked. The answer will perhaps remain the same: we do not know one another and are quite fearful and reluctant to want to know one another.

This is clearly visible in our own beautiful community. We recently attended the funeral services of two white Americans: one, a former resident, wife and mother, in her late forties; the other, the octogenarian mother of a resident. I estimate that the first funeral was attended by nearly three hundred people. I observed just three black mourners. My wife and I were two of these. In the second case there were perhaps six black attendees of about a hundred mourners. With extremely rare exceptions, whenever we attend parties in our community we are the only black people. Surely this is a sign that white Americans know very few black Americans beyond the level of casual acquaintanceship.

Of course, the reverse is also true. Yet, whenever we have gatherings our neighbors constantly marvel at the diversity of our company. Our relationships are not contrived but happen naturally. They are based on a certain compatibility with those with whom we interact, regardless of color or status. This requires very little effort but much willingness to be open to those around you. We are always amazed at how little our neighbors appear to interact with one another without elaborate preparation and planning. In spite of this, relationships continue to appear cordial but mostly casual.

Undoubtedly, the reality of the distance between white Americans and their black fellow citizens contributed directly to our reluctance to believe that Barack Obama could win the presidential nomination of his party and go on to win the presidential election itself. As we watched the political process unfold, we frequently thought that it was such a great pity that someone so obviously brilliant and qualified would never be seen as a viable candidate because of the color of his skin. The historic irony is that only after the viability of his candidacy was validated by the white people of Iowa, did we suddenly realize that white America could actually refuse to continue to be held hostage by its misplaced, paranoid commitment to race. Some continue to misconstrue the meaning of the miracle of Iowa. It is not that black people in America needed to have permission from white America to consider Barack Obama a viable candidate. Instead, it is that black people, realistically, needed confirmation of their hope. American history is replete with stories of black people's hopes being dashed because of unrealistic, not invalid, expectations.

We have now come full circle to the motivational place from which this story started. We will proceed to contemplate the meaning and significance of recent seminal events in America.

President Obama:
Meaning and
Significance

It is very difficult to imagine anyone being able to say anything on this subject that has not already been said. This may prove to be the case here as well. Never the less, I feel compelled to say my piece, if only because of my perception of many of the commentaries and observations from a number of my own friends and acquaintances, the vast majority of whom happens to be white.

At the very outset there are a few observations I wish to make:

First, it is not without significance that other black candidates have run for the Office of President. Most notable among these are Shirley Chisholm, Jesse Jackson and Al Sharpton. No one believed at any time that any one of these could have received their political party's nomination, let alone win the Office. It would have been unrealistic to expect otherwise. Realistically, none of these candidates, individually or collectively, could have expected differently. In every case, these candidates were simply making a statement, fully aware of the historical significance of their action. Apart from all else that may have doomed their candidacy, they had no chance of escape from the weighty burden of the largest human organ: their skin.

Second, all of these earlier candidates, intentionally or by implication, appeared to be more focused on righting past wrongs rather than on creating a new future within the confines of the political party to which they belonged. It is hard to imagine a more frightening prospect to white America than that of retribution or reparations for the sins of slavery and racism.

Third, in Obama's case he was all about a future that would be different. It is no accident that he continues to say that he is more interested in looking forward not back. This is a far less threatening or discomforting a position to take in courting the confidence of white America. From this perspective Obama created an environment which moved his chances of becoming president from the realm of the possible to that of the probable.

Finally, consider the crucial realities of Obama's parentage: a white mother from Kansas and a father from Kenya; his upbringing with his white grandparents and his schooling at Columbia and Harvard Universities. These realities set him apart from the average black American and make him more akin to someone like Colin Powell than to a Jackson or a Sharpton. Both Powell and Obama had to seriously consider, if not overcome, the skepticism and distrust of their "own people" in the critical initial period leading up to their decision to run or not to run for the presidency. In a number of respects their realities are similar. They are both of the people but are not one of the people.

In most cases there seems to be a very visceral response to Obama as the first black president. I continue to have the greatest of difficulty understanding the rationale behind far too many of the commentaries about Obama. I get the sense that many commentators are on purpose irrationally disrespectful of facts or truth and feel not the slightest need to second guess the absurd claims they make or the positions they support or take. Not surprisingly therefore, the Obama presidency has varied meaning and significance, depending on one's perspective, expectations and view of a shared or personal future. Some few but vocal Americans even refuse to accept that he is in fact American. Accordingly, he cannot be President of The United States of America legitimately.

There are four clear positions I observe being taken on the Obama presidency: First, the position of the Irreconcilables; Second, the position of the Redemptionists; Third, the position of the Partisans; Fourth, the position of the Pragmatists.

The Irreconcilables

These are people who consider America already in decline because of its inability or unwillingness to control the world and its own borders and to expel illegal immigrants. They see the Obama presidency as an acceleration of this decline. The fact that Obama is black is itself justification and vindication of their position. To these people the righteousness of their position is so palpably clear that they are utterly amazed that the rest of America does not accept and support their view. In the age of electronic media they constantly unleash a barrage of hate mail without compunction. I will not dignify their indefensible position by reproducing any of their most repugnant statements or claims but will provide a couple examples of some less offensive correspondence forwarded by some of my more intolerant friends and acquaintances.

As a guise for some of the claims they make they first state categorically that Obama is not American and that his real objective is to make America socialist or communist. They then set about creating stories to show the effect of such a calamity. Below is one example of this:

Change You Better Believe
John

U. A. S. R.

UNION OF AMERICAN SOCIALIST REPUBLICS

Aka: The American Union

An economics professor at Texas Tech said he had never failed a single student before but had, once, failed an entire class. That class had insisted that socialism worked and that no one would be poor and no one would be rich, a great equalizer. The professor then said ok, we will have an experiment in this class on socialism.

All grades would be averaged and everyone would receive the same grade so no one would fail and no one would receive an A. After the first test the grades were averaged and everyone got a B. The students who studied hard were upset and the students who studied little were happy. But, as the second test rolled around, the students who studied little had studied even less and the ones who studied hard decided they wanted a free ride too; so they studied little. The second test average was a D. No one was happy. When the 3rd test rolled around the average was an F.

The scores never increased as bickering, blame, name calling all resulted in hard feelings and no one would study for the benefit of anyone else. All failed, to their great surprise, and the professor told them that socialism would also ultimately fail because when the reward is great, the effort to succeed is great; but when government takes all the reward away, no one will try or want to succeed.

This appears to be more indicative of what is hoped for rather than of what is likely. I seriously doubt that the story is authentic but it is none the less a story an acquaintance is willing to accept as true and to shamelessly circulate. But if I assume the story to be true then my conclusion is that the professor and his students are equally dumb and all deserve an "F".

It is basically impossible to have a discussion with ir-reconcilables. They tolerate no dissent and are perfectly content in their self inflicted misery. They go to great lengths to express their views, totally convinced their views and positions are unquestionably right. At the same time they are sickeningly bewildered by the fact that the majority of Americans do not share or support these views and positions. Their mental agony is severe and leads to behavior that is, in my view, paranoid. They continue to find it intolerable that a black man is the president of the United States of America. Stripped to the core their views and positions are fundamentally inspired by racism. They comb the foreign press for articles and commentary which support their views because to their mind there is not enough insightful criticism of Obama in the American press. The article below forwarded to me by a friend demonstrates this diligence:

Subject: Obama in the British Media

Interesting article from a British columnist about our "President Pantywaist." Perhaps we need to replace our media with the Brit media so that we at least get the other viewpoint which is no longer forthcoming here in the U.S.
Trevor
Ex Telegraph.co.uk
By Gerald Warner

If al-Qaeda, the Taliban and the rest of the Looney Tunes brigade want to kick America to death, they had better move in quickly and grab a piece of the action before Barack Obama finishes the job himself. Never in the history of the United States has a president worked so actively against the interests of his own people - not even Jimmy Carter.

Obama's problem is that he does not know who the enemy is. To him, the enemy does not squat in caves in Waziristan, clutching automatic weapons and reciting the more militant verses from the Koran: instead, it sits around at tea parties in Kentucky quoting from the US Constitution. Obama is not at war with terrorists, but with his Republican fellow citizens. He has never abandoned the campaign trail.

That is why he opened Pandora's Box by publishing the Justice Department's legal opinions on water boarding and other hard-line interrogation techniques. He cynically subordinated the national interest to his partisan desire to embarrass the Republicans. Then he had to rush to Langley, Virginia to try to reassure a demoralized CIA that had just discovered the President of the United States was an even more formidable foe than al-Qaeda.

"Don't be discouraged by what's happened the last few weeks," he told intelligence officers. Is he kidding? Thanks to him, al-Qaeda knows the private interrogation techniques available to the US intelligence agencies and can train its operatives to withstand them - or would do so, if they had not already been outlawed.

So, next time a senior al-Qaeda hood is captured, all the CIA can do is ask him nicely if he would care to reveal when a major population centre is due to be hit by a terror spectacular, or which American city is about to be irradiated by a dirty bomb. Your view of this situation will be dictated by one simple criterion: whether or not you watched the people jumping from the twin towers...

President Pantywaist's recent world tour, cozying up to all the bad guys, excited the ambitions of America's enemies. Here, they realized, is a sucker they can really take to the cleaners. His only enemies are fellow Americans. Which prompts the question: why does President Pantywaist hate America so badly?

In spite of the impossibility of having a dialogue with the Irreconcilables I felt obliged to respond to this mail. The sender obviously supports the view that the president of the United States of America hates Americans.

Dear Trevor,

As you know I hate to respond to gibberish but as usual one has to make exceptions now and then.

First, it is truly symptomatic of the paranoia of the irrational right that in spite of the rife anti-Obama sentiments which dominate talk radio, opposition TV and print, not to mention the Congress, "we need to replace our media with the Brit media so that we at least get the other viewpoint which is no longer forthcoming here in the US". Imagine that! I am sure there is a number of other things in this country we would like to replace with things British. I am certain many of us are having serious regrets about the success of the Mayflower enterprise. After all we love the Brits and their politics and governance so much our forefathers had to flee the grand isle. How conveniently we forget.

I know nothing of Gerald Warner and suspect that I don't need to, but I can reasonably surmise from his photograph that he is far more likely to be a "pantywaist" (whatever this means!) than the president. But I understand. Paranoia often makes strange bedfellows. I am sure that by now you are more than a little familiar with my own position regarding extremes. Nowhere in nature or politics do extremes work - except in a unique way among the irrational right. Incomprehensibly, the more their numbers dwindle the more irrational they become. The more irrational they become the more certain they are of their position on everything. There is a medical term for this malady - lunacy. Unfortunately there is no effective medication and even time does not help for the reasons mentioned earlier. So there is no cure. But reasonable people do visit the asylum from time to time just to make sure that the lunatics do not hurt themselves. This is the best that we can do. Regrettably it is not enough.

Yet there is hope. In spite of the overwhelmingly predominant irrational view in the asylum, Democracy does work. Even the irrational are allowed a vote in deciding which party runs the country. Yet, even though the majority of the total population voted in the current president and continues to support him overwhelmingly, the irrational right which never ceases to tout the virtues of Democracy appears to question the wisdom of the electorate. Naturally, the irrational right sees no contradiction here. Of course not. After all the irrational right are the only members of our population with the wisdom and knowledge to govern. In the end, I must reluctantly admit, it may be that lunacy is more acceptable than a president who happens to be not merely different but unique in many ways.

Although it will mean absolutely nothing to the irrational right, Obama and the Democrats did in fact win the last election. On the basis of their pathetic logic this means that the majority of Americans are stupid. Maybe we should dump Democracy in favor of rule by the irrational right. There is a name for this too - fascism. But those self-confined to the asylum need to remember: there will be another presidential election in which they will assuredly be allowed to vote. They have a very simple task: convince the majority of reasonable Americans to move to the side of the irrational right. This is simple enough. Unless, of course, they choose to remain incarcerated in their secure asylum fearing that to venture out is far less effective in attaining the suspect end they seek.

Almost finally, there is always the possibility of reversing the Mayflower story so we can all return to the preferred safety and security of the "motherland". Surely Mr. Warner will welcome all with open arms. He may even have sufficient panties for all so we too may join the "pantywaist" brigade and be assured of taxation at last with representation. But we may have another problem here, alas. Is England socialist? I hope not. Yet I fear I can just detect a weather beaten sign at immigration saying, "Abandon hope all ye who enter here". But there is an upside to being on the irrational right: the sign is meaningless as they have already abandoned hope. I am not attempting to force any sympathizer of the irrational right to think, as I would feel extremely guilty were this to *happen. The last thing I want is to make any sympathizer try to escape from the asylum because I am desperately afraid he would be set upon by his mates with dire consequences for which I would feel severely guilty forever.*

Finally, if you have read this far, do not ponder too long on any of the foregoing. The last thing I want is the irrational right thinking. Things could really get worse, after all.

Owen

I am unaware of any other president who has been taken to task for hating his own countrymen. In summary, to the Irreconcilables the meaning of Barack Obama's presidency is clear: he is the destroyer of America. The real significance of this irrationality is that there are intelligent Americans who are willing to believe this and shameless enough to freely express this belief. These people are impervious to embarrassment or shame.

The Redemptionists

These are the people who believe that America needs to, or should, atone for the sins of slavery and racism and the tolerance of gay people. To them the election of Barack Obama must have a reason beyond the mere political. It is inexplicable that a black man can be president without some kind of divine intervention meant to punish America for its gross transgressions. Many of these people are professed Christians.

Once again, America's hypnotic fascination with race drives the sentiments of a significant segment of the population. It is an inescapable paradox that while Redemptionists see divine intervention as a viable explanation many also see Obama as a representative of Satan, as a Muslim foisted on America, as an interloper not born in America. In this respect they have something in common with the Irreconcilables. But at least they have not taken the leap into the abyss of irrationality without a parachute. Rather, they are resigned to the reality that Obama is in fact the president. They simply must find a way to ensure his failure even if this means risking their own well being or that of the country.

Both Irreconcilables and Redemptionists take great comfort in the supportive rants of right wing media whose doctrinaire thrust is, in all respects, anti-Obama, even if at times this means being anti-America in the process.

They are driven by fear which is strongly supported by ignorance and malice. The intensity of intolerance in America as I write is frightening. Otherwise normal looking citizens carry side arms and assault weapons to locations at which the president is meeting with interested citizens to discuss the vexing topic of Health Care. While the law in some states does allow citizens to bear arms in public, I am unable to find evidence of this disturbing and irrational behavior occurring in the case of any other president. The explanation given by these patriotic bearers of arms is that they have the right to do so. One gun toting patriot carried a sign alluding to Thomas Jefferson's statement that the tree of liberty must from time to time be watered with the blood of tyrants and patriots. Incendiary speech has now graduated to incendiary behavior without the slightest hint of embarrassment or remorse. Regrettably, I must conclude that there can be no doubting the trigger for this intolerance and outlandishly irresponsible behavior: the race of the president. Hopefully we will be spared the worst possible price of such obscene, irrational intolerance.

Intolerance

Residence of the feeble minded
More convinced others wrong
Than they are right.
How clear, how simple our lives
Outlined in stark black and white?
No need to question or to wonder
Simply silence reason's thunder.

Still lightening strikes
In thunder's absence
Whether we choose to hear or see
'Tis of no moment in the asylum
But for rotten claims of victory.
A doctor murdered in his church
A guard killed at holocaust's perch.

Denying your reality
In time denies my own
Though not to those of feeble mind
Whose disagreeable right
In lofty document as mine enshrined
Must bend others to superior views
Compassionate savior from Satan's pews.

Any means is justified coercing
Non-believers to convert
There is and can only be the one
True incontrovertible truth. Mine.
There is none other to summon.
Save yourself the painful useless chore
Rely on my solemn truth to be secure.

No need to pursue knowledge
Itself a maze of false promises.
Rescued, safe in my sacred cul-de-sac
I pity others, regret their sorry lot
My truth their only turning back.
Tolerance intolerable facing undeniable fact
Demands you accept my truth or die by my act.

Yet your dying disappoints
Dramatizing the failure of my faith
To convert the sinner to the saint
Why am I not happy? Why so sad?
In fact the power of my truth is faint
But my complicity holds me hostage
In the crucible of my self righteous rage.

Buried deep in my mind's morass
Are locked treasure chests
Of questions I and others dare not ask.
Why sully certainty, upset God's plot?
There is no doubting my sacred task
Until too late, too far, too dear the cost.
Uncertain in my certainty I too am lost.

Behold the sun and moon
The days and nights
The universe in all its glory
The birds, the bees, the flowers, the trees
None demand we ascribe a common story
To their existence, to their synchronized journeys
As we devise and fight mind's mock tourneys.

Decry murder but murder in defense
Of views supporting life as sacred
Abuse those who are different
To defend the sanctity of our own difference.
The past is prologue the future current.
Such is the endless turmoil of our existence
Unless comity and balance inform insistence.

We live in chosen purgatories
Condemning others to our hell or heaven
Even as they assign us to their own
If all are right we end up where we are,
No matter our ceaseless efforts to disown
Where we have always been
Between purgatory's two ghastly mirrors
Eyes impaled on shared reflected horrors.

The Partisans

These are the incidental antagonists of the Irreconcilables and the Redemptionists. They do not set out to be such. Their fundamental purpose is to be for Obama not against the irrational right. But like all partisans they will steadfastly defend that which they support. It is not without meaning that the Irreconcilables and Redemptionists are clearly against Obama. It is equally unclear what it is they are for. The partisans will always see the Obama glass as half full never half empty.

To the Partisans Obama's presidency needs no justification or defense. Its existence is no less valid and authentic than that of any other presidency; none of which needed special justification or defense. At the same time they recognize its psychological fragility in the face of alarmist, irrational far right demagoguery which could conceivably demoralize supporters and raise doubts as to the effectiveness of the president and his policies. They worry less about the historical import of the Obama presidency than about the blatant intolerance and vitriol which accompany criticisms of the president. They do not openly or often express their concern for the president's safety but worry about it.

The Partisans are an amalgam of the far left, the progressives and the left of center liberals and independents. Their homogeneity is never permanent but always purposeful. This is a function of the group's willingness to question its partisanship when the objective sought is at odds with the actions being taken to achieve it. They will disagree with some positions taken by Obama and publicly oppose these but in the end will support the Obama positions most of the time because there are no attractive alternatives. The current debate on Obama's Health Care Plan exemplifies this. While Obama is apparently prepared to compromise on the public option portion of the plan, for example, the Partisans, by and large, are not. Partisans are doctrinaire but rational and even pragmatic at times. It would appear that at least 90% of black Americans, for example, fall into this category.

To the Partisans the meaning of the Obama presidency is very clear: America has taken a step away from its history of bigotry but it has not abandoned this history and could very easily revert. In short, Partisans are not indifferent to the possibility of a backlash but believe that having come this far, America, generally speaking, is unlikely to have what some termed buyer's remorse during the run up to the election for the presidency. Of great significance to the Partisans is a sense of honest inclusion of many who felt marginalized, especially minorities. It is simply impossible to minimize the power of the possibilities which Obama has made clear to many Americans. If the faith and hope of minorities in America were waning or lost, Obama's achievements will go a long way toward their recovery. It is perhaps not an unfounded assumption on the part of Partisans that many Americans, including some who are irretrievably opposed to Obama, are proud that America has demonstrated to itself and the world that it is capable of making and embracing difficult, even unlikely choices, in the hope of a different and better future for all its citizens.

The Pragmatists

Obama himself belongs in this category. These are the people whose support is almost entirely dependent on the outcomes they seek from the candidate and the political process. Accordingly, their support is fluid but always with purpose. Independents will comprise a significant portion of this category. Supporters here are less sensitive to the hypnotic influence of race and, like Obama, may on occasion make compromises in the belief that half a loaf is better than none. To them, sensible compromise is not weakness but the exercise of reasonable, responsible judgment. They are sometimes seen as incrementalists on this account.

Pragmatists see Obama as the future. Many are between the ages of thirty and fifty with a keen sense of what their children's America will be like. They are visibly more hopeful than afraid. This group moves freely between itself and the Partisans. Fortunately, along with the Partisans they overwhelm the Irreconcilables and the Redemptionists. Like Obama, Pragmatists are future oriented and will visit the past to better understand the future they seek, not to reorder it or to use the past as a club with which to chastise those they oppose.

Pragmatists find much comfort in Obama's positive view of the future and his hopefulness about America's place in the new world order which they correctly see as inevitable.

In Summary

While it is undeniable that race is a pivotal issue in how much of America perceives the election of Obama and his ensuing presidency, race is not the only catalyst for the fear, intolerance and sheer irrationality of the disturbing reactions being witnessed. There are black Americans who for reasons not quite clear to me appear to have as sharp a response to Obama as any Irreconcilable or Redemptionist. To set the record straight: I am absolutely opposed to the view that "If you are black you must support Barack". We should never ever support any political candidate or cause solely on the basis of race. This is an irrational position to take. But when blacks oppose the Obama presidency on the simple premise that the Irreconcilables are correct in their views, I am confused. While race must not determine the political choices blacks make, blacks should certainly take into account the fundamental thinking and beliefs of Irreconcilables and the part racial animus clearly plays in the socio-cultural positions taken and cultivated by Irreconcilables. Blacks whose views align with the views of the Irrational Right or Irreconcilables are quickly embraced by them as exhibit one in the marketing of their misguided philosophy.

The Irreconcilables overwhelmingly reside in the dark, far right wing corner of the Republican Party. The party will never disown them no matter how outrageous they become. The Republicans have traditionally had very few elected black representatives in Congress and currently have none. Yet, the chairman of their party is a black man, Michael Steele. This irony should not be lost on the reader. Is it a simple coincidence that America elects a black president and the Republican Party elects a black man as its chairman? Perhaps. But I seriously doubt this. Just as the country is torn over the election of Barack Obama, the supporters of the Republican Party are demonstrably more torn over Michael Steele. The huge difference between the two circumstances is that there is no Machiavellian plot in the election of Obama.

Then there is the position of Star Parker, syndicated columnist and author. Ms. Parker is black and clearly a remarkable person. Ms. Parker's self-powered, God-assisted redemption from a life of debauchery, which is said to include welfare fraud, drug abuse and multiple abortions, is exemplary. Quite remarkably, she has become a family advocate. Like the Irreconcilables, her opposition is based on her love of God and being against the evils of Socialism. Of course, Obama is a socialist in Ms. Parker's mind as, apparently, are the Democrats generally. In her commentary, *"Back on Uncle Sam's Plantation,"* Ms. Parker makes a number of noteworthy claims. Not least among these is her belief that America's salvation lies in God and Capitalism. Other claims include:

The legacy of American socialism is our blighted inner cities, dysfunctional inner city schools, and broken black families.

Through God's grace, I found my way out. It was then that I understood what freedom meant and how great this country is.

Instead of poor America on socialism becoming more like rich America on capitalism, rich America on capitalism is becoming like poor America on socialism.

The endless, acrimonious debate regarding the direction in which the new president is moving the nation is driven by paranoia and a camouflaged desire that he fails. These are the bedrock of the Irrational Right which is basically in the camp of the Irreconcilables. I have read a little of Ms. Parker's biography and wonder what was the springboard for her former life. On the face of it, this would appear to have to be some socialist dogma or deception. After all, capitalism naturally inoculates us against all human failings and, in combination with God, makes us *right*. The most remarkable thing about this view is that it is the capitalist system that itself created and supported the conditions that led to the very programs Ms. Parker derides and likens to being back on the proverbial plantation. Indeed, slavery is the quintessential exercise of capitalism in its purest form.

In addition, although I am not a psychologist, I have come to recognize and understand certain diabolical aspects of addiction. The most diabolical of all is the likelihood that the addict's addiction is merely a part of a much larger and more tragic and sinister disability: a profound and easily overlooked predisposition to addiction itself. In other words, an addict will escape one addiction but quickly be seduced by another which may be totally unrelated to the original, abandoned addiction. It is therefore not surprising to me that Ms. Parker's life is one of polar extremes.

The truth is, there is no perfect social, political or economic system. Reasonable persons must be willing to embrace a mix of options for addressing our social, political and economic ills and be very wary of the labels they ascribe to these options, as many labels are inflammatory and tend naturally to hold reason hostage. I caution the *redeemed* among us: never forget that you live among a variety of people who overcome or fail to some degree, the many challenges living relentlessly provides; your own testimony of redemption is legitimate cause for celebration not justification for supporting irrational, insensitive positions; extremes, like addiction, are untenable and hold no promise of success in addressing life's problems; do not credit any single political or social device for your own liberation (uncertain as this may be) as this is never truly the case; compassion and empathy are useful virtues that should always be applied the minute we attempt to judge our fellow citizens; above all "to thine own self be true". Of course, this last piece of advice requires that we not merely find ourselves but understand what we have found.

In general, as I explained to one of my friends, America realized that, in many important ways, the Bush years had contributed significantly to a shrinking of America's image in the world with no compensatory domestic achievements and an abominable, indefensible war. In its collective wisdom the electorate determined the need for a dramatic change. Barack Obama was seen as the embodiment of this change. Before the presidential election I expressed the view that were Obama to be elected president our image abroad would instantly improve measurably.

I remember being in Germany before the presidential elections and being accosted by a German gentleman who recognized that I am American. He expressed the view that the rest of the world should be allowed to vote for the American president. When asked why, he replied that America's influence in the world is so great, the election of the American president should not be left to Americans alone. He was very afraid that Americans would not vote for Barack Obama. In his opinion Obama was exactly what America and the world needed.

There is no doubt that America is viewed by the rest of the world in a much more positive light since Obama became president. It is also true that if he succeeds in turning the faltering American economy around and implements health care reform, his impact on the nation will equal or exceed his impact on the image of America in the world. Perhaps the most enduring reflection I have read on what the election of Barack Obama means to America is by American author Judith Warner. Ms. Warner's reflections are reproduced in full below, not so much for the general reader as for my grand daughters for whom this work is written.

November 6, 2008, 9:03 pm
Tears to Remember

On Wednesday, Nov. 5, 1980, my 10th-grade American history teacher started class by unfurling *The New York Times*. She pointed to its triple banner headline: "Reagan Easily Beats Carter; Republicans Gain in Congress; D'Amato and Dodd are Victors."

"Save this paper," she told us. "This is the start of a whole new era."

And it was. An era of unbridled deregulation, wealth-enhancing perks for the already well-off and miserly indifference to the poor and middle class; of the recasting of greed as goodness, the equation of bellicose provincialism with patriotism, the reframing of bigotry as small-town decency.

In short, it was the start of our current era. The Reagan Revolution was the formative political experience of my generation's lifetime, like the Great Depression, the Second World War or Vietnam for those before us. And in its intellectual and moral paucity, in its eventual hegemony, these years shut down, for some of us, the ability to fully imagine another way.

I will admit that back in January, when Barack Obama, in his post-Iowa victory speech, spoke about the "cynics," the "they" who said "this country was too divided, too disillusioned to ever come together around a common purpose," he was talking about me.

I will admit that the call of "change" did not speak to me as an achievable goal.

Until it actually came.

On Wednesday, there was a run on newspapers, as voters rushed to grab a tangible piece of the history they'd made. My husband Max and I, unable to find extra copies brought our own worn papers home to 8- and 11-year-old Emilie and Julia.

Sept. 11, the seismic event that we'd feared would forever form their political consciousness, shaping their world and constricting the boundaries of the possible, had actually been eclipsed, light blotting out darkness, the best of America at long last driving away the demons of fear. We wanted them to see that it was the end of an era.

"Look," we said, pointing to the headline "Racial Barrier Falls." "This is huge."

We labored to make them understand that their world — art that day, and orchestra, and Baked Potato Bar at lunch — had irrevocably changed.

But how can you understand change when you've only known one way of being?

They were happy because we were happy. They rose to the occasion in that bemused way children do when adults tell them what they should feel. They were glad to be rid of George W. Bush and to be saved – for now – from the specter of Sarah Palin. ("It is not O.K. to say she's an 'idiot,'" I had snapped when they came home from school stoked by the mob. "Prove your case. Show, don't tell.")

They'd had, like many D.C. children, more than their share of politics. After first following the country into battle against the all-purpose boogeyman Saddam Hussein, they'd become antiwar. They had opinions on tax policy and spoke angrily about the "wealth gap." In the past election year, they'd been fired up about the woman thing, in all its pretty girl versus smart girl iterations; in fact, they and their friends had remained hard-core Hillaryites long after their moms had moved on.

But the race thing? The groundbreaking immensity of the election of our country's first African-American president?

"You're being racist," Emilie had said when I made a comment about how particularly earth-moving this election was for black voters. "Why should it matter if people are black or white?"

Theirs has often looked to me like a world drained of meaning. Girl power put to the service of selling Hannah Montana. Feel-good inclusiveness that occulted the very real conflicts, crimes and hatreds of history.

It isn't easy to let go of the past to embrace something new, to risk heartbreak on the chance of the world's actually having changed.

Or at least, it hasn't been easy for me. But it comes naturally to some. Like the hundreds of <u>George Washington University students who gathered in front of the White House on Tuesday night</u>, cheering and screaming and shouting their goodbyes to the political era of their youth.

"Bliss it was to be alive, but to be young was very heaven," Max emailed me, paraphrasing William Wordsworth on the French Revolution, at 11:30 p.m. on election night, after leaving his desk to walk among the revelers downtown. I, home with the kids, was in bed, sleeping the drugged sleep of an alcohol-abstaining migraineuse after drinking half a glass of celebratory champagne.

Colin Powell did not dance for joy over Obama's victory; he wept.

"Look what we did. Look what we did," he said, puffy-faced, red-eyed, fighting back more tears on CNN. "He's won. It's over."

David Dinkins was similarly solemn. "Things do change. There is a God. They do get better," said the mayor who presided over New York City at a time of toxic racial tensions.

Obama, too, resisted giddy gladness on Tuesday night. But he did proclaim an end to the world as we've known it for far too long.

"To those who would tear the world down: we will defeat you," he promised. "This is our moment. This is our time."

The glory of Barack Obama is that there are so many different kinds of us who can claim a piece of that "our." African-Americans, Democrats, post-boomers, progressives, people who rose from essentially nowhere and through hard work and determination succeeded beyond their parents' wildest dreams are the most obvious.

But there are also people who respect intelligence and good grammar. People who see their spouse as their "best friend," as Barack called Michelle on Tuesday night. People whose children have the same knowing look as Sasha and Malia, who are probably more excited about their puppy than about their father's presidency.

Two images will forever stay in my mind to mark this epoch-breaking Election Day. One is that of Jesse Jackson's face, drenched in tears, in Chicago's Grant Park on Tuesday evening.

And the other is a photo that ran in The Times on Wednesday. In it, a black mother and daughter sit on the floor of a church in Harlem. The mother, Latrice Barnes, having heard of Obama's victory, is doubled up in tears; her daughter, Jasmine, is reaching a tentative hand up to soothe her. To me, she looks like the future, reaching out to heal the past.

It is, I suppose, in part a matter of temperament, whether one shouts or weeps at happy transformative moments. But I also think it's a matter of what has come before. The young people joyfully frolicking in front of the Bush White House never knew the universe whose passing was marked by Obama's victory and Jackson's tears.

This moment of triumph marks the end of such a long period of pain, of indignity and injustice for African-

Americans. And for so many others of us, of the trampling and debasing of our most basic ideals, beliefs that we cherished every bit as deeply and passionately as those of the "values voters" around whose sensibilities we've had to tiptoe for the past 28 years.

The election brought the return of a country we'd lost for so long that it was almost forgotten under the accumulated scar tissue of accommodation and acceptance.

For me, this will be the enduring memory of election night 2008: One generation released its grief. The next looked up confusedly, eager to please and yet unable to comprehend just what the tears were about.

McCain-Palin: Meaning and Significance

Power has many currencies. These are freely exchanged at home and abroad among the powerful and influential. Among the most common of these currencies are armaments, race, religion, wealth, and heritage. Power is a blessing and a curse. In its pursuit the pursuer often ends up intoxicated or addicted, as power becomes an end in itself rather than a means for doing good. Even as he promises that his pursuit is purely selfless his behavior belies his promise. I can find no satisfactory explanation in my own mind for the choice of Sarah Palin by John McCain to be his vice presidential running mate during the last presidential elections. His was a monstrous miscalculation based on a faulty and disturbing assumption: the Irreconcilables and Redemptionists, along with a smattering of the uncommitted, to which a black candidate might be basically unacceptable, would win him and the Republican Party the Presidency. Sarah Palin was his trump card to attract and hold the Irrational Right who instinctively viewed McCain as a pseudo-conservative. Some of my Republican friends even dub him a liberal.

This ploy becomes very meaningful in a couple of respects. First, McCain and his party anticipated a significant backlash against Obama's candidacy, and for sound, historical reasons. The lessons of the history of race in America made this expectation quite a realistic one. Second, the Democrats would remain split between those who were more committed to Bill and Hilary Clinton than to the Democratic Party itself. These people, it was thought, would eventually seek refuge in the McCain camp but not in the Republican Party as such. Surprisingly, America responded favorably to the message and personality of Obama. Neither McCain nor the Republicans expected this.

The Irrational Right did not fully trust McCain and the reasonable, independent, white American found Sarah Palin not merely vacuous but downright dangerous as the person who would be just a heart beat away from the presidency. I doubt there is a Republican who will admit to the strategy outlined above. McCain certainly does not. But anyone who understands race and its everlasting influence in American culture cannot fail to appreciate the practical wisdom of the strategy. This appreciation is the only way to understand the current ongoing racially tinged and, at times, outright racist attacks on Obama. It is not unreasonable to think that after being elected president, regardless of affiliation, the vast majority of citizens would respect and support the new president. This, after all, has been the tradition in America. How do we rationally explain the shameless discourtesy shown the new president by an outspoken, disrespectful, irrational fringe of the Republican Party?

I believe that the average American is only now beginning to appreciate and understand fully the nature and significance of the rejection of the McCain-Palin partnership of convenience. The fact that this rejection occurred in spite of the unquestionable, historic relevance and impact of race in America, is without a doubt one of the most marvelous occurrences in America's history. If I needed additional reasons to choose America as my home this would trump them all. Never the less, we continue to be haunted by the twin ghosts of bigotry and anti-intellectualism. British best selling author, news paper columnist and social activist, George Monbiot, attempts to explain this predicament in the commentary below. While I find some of Monbiot's comments rather unnecessarily caustic, the thrust of his argument should be seen as more revealing and instructive than offensive.

Why morons succeed in US politics

By George Monbiot. Published in the Guardian 28th October 2008.

How was it allowed to happen? How did politics in the US come to be dominated by people who make a virtue out of ignorance? Was it charity that has permitted mankind's closest living relative to spend two terms as president? How did Sarah Palin, Dan Quayle and other such gibbering numbskulls get to where they are? How could Republican rallies in 2008 be drowned out by screaming ignoramuses insisting that Barack Obama is a Muslim and a terrorist? (1)

Like most people on this side of the Atlantic I have spent my adult life mystified by American politics. The US has the world's best universities and attracts the world's finest minds. It dominates discoveries in science and medicine. Its wealth and power depend on the application of knowledge. Yet, uniquely among the developed nations (with the possible exception of Australia), learning is a grave political disadvantage.

There have been exceptions over the past century: Franklin Roosevelt, Kennedy and Clinton tempered their intellectualism with the common touch and survived; but Adlai Stevenson, Al Gore and John Kerry were successfully tarred by their opponents as members of cerebral elite (as if this were not a qualification for the presidency). Perhaps the defining moment in the collapse of intelligent politics was Ronald Reagan's response to

Jimmy Carter during the 1980 presidential debate. Carter - stumbling a little, using long words - carefully enumerated the benefits of national health insurance. Reagan smiled and said "there you go again" (2). His own health programme would have appalled most Americans, had he explained it as carefully as Carter had done, but he had found a formula for avoiding tough political issues and making his opponents look like wonks.

It wasn't always like this. The founding fathers of the republic - men like Benjamin Franklin, Thomas Jefferson, James Madison, John Adams and Alexander Hamilton - were among the greatest thinkers of their age. They felt no need to make a secret of it. How did the project they launched degenerate into George W Bush and Sarah Palin?

On one level this is easy to answer. Ignorant politicians are elected by ignorant people. US education, like the US health system, is notorious for its failures. In the most powerful nation on earth, one adult in five believes the sun revolves around the earth; only 26% accept that evolution takes place by means of natural selection; two-thirds of young adults are unable to find Iraq on a map; two-thirds of US voters cannot name the three branches of government; the maths skills of 15 year-olds in the US are ranked 24th out of the 29 countries of the OECD (3).

*But this merely extends the mystery: how did so many US citizens become so dumb, and so suspicious of intelligence? Susan Jacoby's book **The Age of American Unreason** provides the fullest explanation I have read so far. She shows that the degradation of US politics results from a series of interlocking tragedies.*

One theme is both familiar and clear: religion - in particular fundamentalist religion - makes you stupid. The US is the only rich country in which Christian fundamentalism is vast and growing.

*Jacoby shows that there was once a certain logic to its anti-rationalism. During the first few decades after the publication of **The Origin of Species**, for example,*

Americans had good reason to reject the theory of natural selection and to treat public intellectuals with suspicion. From the beginning, Darwin's theory was mixed up in the US with the brutal philosophy - now known as Social Darwinism - of the British writer Herbert Spencer. Spencer's doctrine, promoted in the popular press with the help of funding from Andrew Carnegie, John D. Rockefeller and Thomas Edison, suggested that millionaires stood at the top of a scala natura established by evolution. By preventing unfit people from being weeded out, government intervention weakened the nation. Gross economic inequalities were both justifiable and necessary (4).

Darwinism, in other words, became indistinguishable to the public from the most bestial form of laissez-faire economics. Many Christians responded with revulsion. It is profoundly ironic that the doctrine rejected a century ago by such prominent fundamentalists as William Jennings Bryan is now central to the economic thinking of the Christian right. Modern fundamentalists reject the science of Darwinian evolution and accept the pseudo-science of Social Darwinism.

But there were other, more powerful, reasons for the intellectual isolation of the fundamentalists. The US is peculiar in devolving the control of education to local authorities. Teaching in the southern states was dominated by the views of an ignorant aristocracy of planters, and a great educational gulf opened up. "In the South", Jacoby writes, "what can only be described as an intellectual blockade was imposed in order to keep out any ideas that might threaten the social order."(5)

The Southern Baptist Convention, now the biggest Protestant denomination in the US, was to slavery and segregation what the Dutch Reformed Church was to apartheid in South Africa. It has done more than any other force to keep the South stupid. In the 1960s it tried to stave off desegregation by establishing a system of private Christian schools and universities. A student can

now progress from kindergarten to a higher degree without any exposure to secular teaching. Southern Baptist
beliefs pass intact through the public school system as
well. A survey by researchers at the University of Texas in
1998 found that one in four of the state's public school
biology teachers believed that humans and dinosaurs
lived on earth at the same time(6).

This tragedy has been assisted by the American fet-
ishisation of self-education. Though he greatly regretted
his lack of formal teaching, Abraham Lincoln's career
is repeatedly cited as evidence that good education,
provided by the state, is unnecessary: all that is required
to succeed is determination and rugged individualism.
This might have served people well when genuine self-
education movements, like the one built around the
Little Blue Books in the first half of the 20th century, were
in vogue. In the age of infotainment it is a recipe for
confusion.

Besides fundamentalist religion, perhaps the most potent reason why intellectuals struggle in elections is that
intellectualism has been equated with subversion. The
brief flirtation of some thinkers with communism a long
time ago has been used to create an impression in the
public mind that all intellectuals are communists. Almost
every day men like Rush Limbaugh and Bill O'Reilly rage
against the "liberal elites" destroying America.

The spectre of pointy-headed alien subversives was
crucial to the election of Reagan and Bush. A genuine intellectual elite - like the neocons (some of them
former communists) surrounding Bush - has managed to
pitch the political conflict as a battle between ordinary
Americans and an over-educated pinko establishment.
Any attempt to challenge the ideas of the rightwing elite
has been successfully branded as elitism.

Obama has a good deal to offer America, but none
of this will come to an end if he wins. Until the great
failures of the US education system are reversed or religious fundamentalism withers there will be political

*opportunities for people, like Bush and Palin, who flaunt
their ignorance.*
www.monbiot.com

References:
1. *For a staggering display of ignorance
   and bigotry, see: http://uk.youtube.com/
   watch?v=IPg0VCg4AEQ*
2. *You can see this exchange at http://uk.youtube.
   com/watch?v=px7aRlhUkHY&feature=related*
3. *All these facts are contained in Susan Jacoby,
   2008. The Age of American Unreason: dumbing
   down and the future of democracy. Old Street
   Publishing, London.*
4. *Susan Jacoby, ibid. Chapter 3.*
5. *Susan Jacoby, ibid. Page 57.*
6. *Susan Jacoby, ibid. Page 25.*

So powerful is the bigotry and anti-intellectual tan-
dem, some intellectuals choose to abandon their intellect in favor of the irrationality of racism. I am forever
grateful to the ever scowling Patrick J. Buchanan and
the grumpy William Bennett, respected, erudite but not
so wise commentators on politics, history and culture in
America, for helping to confirm a suspicion I have always
had but very much doubted and resisted. If we are not
careful our intellect is often used to protect and defend
deep feelings which on the face of it our intellect ought
to find indefensible and repulsive.

Buchannan, advisor to presidents Nixon and Ford,
a former presidential candidate himself, unapologetic
apologist for the far right wing of the Republican Party
and author, volubly opposes affirmative action, for example, as pure and simple reverse discrimination against
white men. It is noteworthy and quite telling that he does
not say *white people* just *white men*. He is incensed that
white men built this country and all its institutions and now
are being persecuted by reverse discrimination. Clearly,

the implication of the phrase *reverse discrimination* is lost on most that use the term. One may only reverse a biased process that was already in effect to the benefit of one group versus another.

To Buchannan's way of thinking there is no justification whatsoever for affirmative action. The white man is owed everything he thinks he deserves because, all by himself, he developed this country. The white man is, of course, naturally intellectually superior to all other groups. So much so that Buchannan shamelessly posits, without a shred of supporting evidence, that he certainly received better grades in university than Sonia Sotomayor, the new associate justice to the U.S Supreme Court who graduated with highest honors from Princeton University. Only because of affirmative action, in his view, did Sotomayor get into Princeton and only because of affirmative action is Sotomayor being elevated to the highest court in the land. This is repulsively and reflexively unfair to the white man. Buchannan may be strong in intellect but displays an unforgiving poverty of spirit that belies his erudition.

If white men are so superior why are they so instinctively afraid of competition from those whom they have steadfastly discriminated against and purposely disadvantaged in America and who, by their own admission, are intellectually inferior? To my mind, giving the disadvantaged, inferior minorities compensatory opportunities should never engender fear, hate or anger among the superior white man. In fact, as a comparison they should feel like the world's greatest sprinter, Ussain Bolt, competing over two hundred meters against a twelve year old whose parents are too impoverished to provide the youngster with a pair of running shoes. Certainly, Bolt would gladly and fearlessly give the youngster a head start. I conclude that it is not fear per se that drives the deep revulsion that white men like Buchannan have for affirmative action. It is a very specific and quite rational concern. In a word, it is fear of retribution that the formerly disadvantaged may legitimately seek against the former oppressor were the disadvantaged ever to be in positions of power.

This is not an irrational fear. In the white man's mind such retribution is deserved. He has developed a conscience. He appreciates this conundrum very well when he stops to consider how he would react were the tables turned. But, understandably, this does not make providing compensatory opportunity more acceptable. Just because he is guilty does not mean he has to be punished. After all there is another option: forgiveness. Yet it appears that in a strange, twisted way, white men like Buchannan do not believe that their tribe has done anything for which forgiveness is necessary. After centuries of affirmative action in favor of the white man it must be painful in the extreme to contemplate losing this distinctly decisive advantage.

The following description of William Bennett comes from a write up on the World Wide Web: *"William Bennett is an American teacher and scholar and was chairman of the National Endowment for the Humanities (1981–85), secretary of the Department of Education (1985–88), and director of the Office of National Drug Control Policy (1989–90). He continues his efforts to improve education and fight drugs, and he is an active voice for traditional values."* I believe you can see from this description why Bennett's views regarding Palin and Obama would be fascinating to me. Bennett is convinced that Sarah Palin, the Republican Party's Vice Presidential nominee during the presidential election campaign of 2008, is a far more qualified candidate for the presidency of the United States than Barack Obama. This is not only surprising but mystifying. It may be that *traditional values* direct him to this conclusion.

Bennett who was Education Secretary under Ronald Reagan, and like Obama attended Harvard, has to be far from ignorant or unaware of the basic floor of knowledge, mental discipline and exposure to pivotal ideas and culture that should be required of anyone seeking such high office. He himself is a respected scholar and intellectual. He writes books, is a respected commentator on radio and television, is something of an ethicist and gets paid to speak. Yet, Bennett is not at all uncomfortable stating unequivocally how much less qualified Obama is for high office than Sarah Palin. Understand that Palin is pitifully ignorant, has the severest of difficulty being coherent on the simplest of matters and does not exhibit any but the shallowest capacity to be analytical. But Palin is not only white. She happens to be good looking as well.

Should we believe for a minute that were the tables turned Bennett or any one else of his stature would find it defensible that such a deficient Obama could be considered more qualified than such a remarkably qualified Palin? Visceral feelings and fear overwhelm us when guilt and potential for retribution are contemplated.

People like Buchannan and Bennett, in a perverse way, substantiate the greatness of a Nelson Mandela, and, as I am willing to predict, that of a Barack Obama as well. While we doubtlessly copied much from the white man, we appear not to have copied his mean spiritedness. Thankfully, the likes of Buchanan and Bennett are unlikely to hold sway in the America I have come to know and have unreservedly accepted as home.

Associate Supreme Court Justice Sotomayor: Meaning and Significance

Xenophobia is unbecoming of America.

I have often wondered how things would have turned out had the Pilgrim Fathers been the indigenous inhabitants of America and the indigenous Indians the ones who arrived on America's shores uninvited. There is no doubting the bravery and faith of the first uninvited, illegal immigrants to come to America. There can be no doubt as well that not all the natives were friendly or accommodating. Yet accommodations were made by all and the survival of the immigrants was assured. And here we are today. In a very real sense, the tables have turned and Hispanics are the new pilgrims, many of them uninvited and illegal. The times and the circumstances are certainly different but the moral equivalent of the accommodations made in 1620 need to be contemplated in a manner compatible with current time and circumstance and certainly not without some empathy on the part of today's white America. But paranoia, and, maybe, even a sense of terror, stand firmly in the way.

The unhappy truth is that a significant and vocal section of white America feels threatened by the number of Hispanics already in their midst. The forecast of accelerated growth rates among Hispanics even were immigration curtailed today only sharpens the perceived threat. While I understand the anxiety, I do not accept this as a valid reason for intolerance and hate mongering. Some relevant data from the U.S. Census Bureau should put things in perspective. In 2006 Hispanics accounted for almost 15% or 44 million, or 1 in 7 of our total population and one half of the nation's recent total population growth. Their growth rate of just over 24% was more than three times the rate of total population growth and clearly outstrips that of non-Hispanic blacks and whites. The birth rate for whites is a mere 0.8%.

It is projected that by 2050 whites and minority groups overall will be equal in size. This is the reality. The face of America is changing. This is not unusual and, in fact, has always been the case. The uncomfortable difference is that the change is being made by a population group that is visibly non-European in origin and appearance. This change I term the "browning of America." Since white America has historically had serious problems with skin color, the anxiety mentioned earlier is understandable. Still, if we intend to maintain a viable, vibrant civil society, accommodations will have to be made. Corporate America in particular, must take this into account in every long term plan it makes.

The foregoing should help to explain the great anguish among those who so insensitively and sometimes viciously attacked the nomination of Sonia Sotomayor for a place on the bench of the U.S. Supreme Court. It also puts into perspective the endless critical recycling of Sotomayor's expression about the judgment of a wise Latina woman being more informed than that of a white man. During her confirmation hearings, being the wise Latina woman she is in fact, she attempted first to explain the expression away then later apologized for it.

Whether the white man accepts it or not, the truth is that his judgment is no less informed by his own *white experience* than Sotomayor's is by her *Latina experience*. No judge is an empty sack waiting to be filled with the essence of the law as he sits in judgment. The law guides his thinking and subsequent judgment. A good judge will hew as strictly as he can to the generally accepted understanding or interpretation of the law. This is the only explanation for why there are often dissenting views to nearly every judgment. This also explains the need for courts of appeal. We may justifiably argue about the extent to which "non-law" influences should be allowed to impinge on judgment but there should be reasonable agreement that a judge's decisions are inevitably and legitimately influenced by his or her life experience.

Ironically, this influence is most often brought to bear at critical moments when the law, taken on its face, may only be able to address a matter partially or inadequately. At this point law is applied but justice is not done. If this were not in fact the case, racial discrimination, for example, would continue to be enshrined in law today. How, for example, do we explain the gross unfavorable differential in sentencing between white offenders and black offenders who commit similar crimes? How do we explain the overturning of a law by the Supreme Court, especially when such a law has no visibly direct link to the Constitution? At some future time, should the law protecting a woman's right to choose be overturned, on what basis will this be done, if not on the basis of a majority of the judges of the Supreme Court bringing their own personal beliefs to bear on the matter? These beliefs, it is fair to say, have no basis in existing law and certainly grow out of the life experience of these judges.

The fundamental significance of this reality clearly explains why Republicans as well as Democrats fight divisive, partisan battles during both the nomination and confirmation stages for placing a judge on the Supreme

Court. On what basis is a Justice Roberts or Alito preferred by one party but opposed by the other? In the end Sotomayor's wise Latina comment is honest and not without merit. It was just offensive to some vocal, powerful white men and their fearful constituents.

President Obama, a black man. Justice Sotomayor, a Latina. Where will this end? This must be the question haunting many who see diversity as threatening. Why would a Supreme Court on its way to reflecting the diversity of America be seen as suspect to some? Why is it that an all-white or all-male Supreme Court is a greater comfort to many? It must be that, as a matter of inescapable logic, there is a fundamental belief that race and gender significantly affect judgment. The purists who are so discomforted by a Latina on the Supreme Court as well as by a black citizen in the White House see no contradiction here.

Regardless of our views the *browning of America* is inevitable. Our shared challenge lies in the manner in which we approach this inevitability. It is this very diversity that will, in the long run, hold the greatest promise for our survival as a free, respected society and a leader in the world. In fact, as we face the ongoing threat of terrorism within and without, this diversity so many seem to fear may yet be our strongest offsetting advantage.

There is no doubt that the Hispanic community in America and elsewhere for that matter, see the historic elevation of a Latina to the highest court in the land as a signal of positive change in a manner similar to how all minorities see the rise of Barack Obama to the highest office in America. Unclear possibilities are now clear probabilities. This bodes well, not just for Hispanics and other minorities, but for America as a whole. In a very real and crucial sense we are all dependent on one another for our communal as well as individual survival. The changing order does allow us to begin anew to strive toward a more perfect union.

Beginning Anew

In tin can
In the hand of a black man
In soft hat
In the hand of a white man

In a wedge of stone
In beaten metal sword and armor
Atom assembled, disassembled
Light arrayed, disarrayed
By land, by sea, by air
At distance far or near

In armies large and small
Egypt, China, Rome,
Ethiopia, Byzantium, Spain
England, France, America, Israel
Power graphed in shifting sand
Briefly certain, permanent in memory

Regret, regret
Again, again, regret, forget
Punish others, punish ourselves
Awaiting justice from elsewhere
Feigning powerlessness to deceive
The complicit, the meek, the hopeful

Still we wait
Nothing lasts even what is past
We choose are chosen as we choose
But one will come or few
Toussaint, Gandhi, Garvey, Malcolm, King
To burnish justice, truth, the law, the prophets.

Time moves
In digits single, double, matched
How deny our own salvation

On basis base as shadow's shade
For fear of colors we brought aboard
In hearty evidence painted hands.

Amorphous beginning's promise
Arrives with blinding clarity, like the sun,
Survival's womb. Birth. Rebirth. Rebirth.
Diaspora's drama takes the stage
Needs no plan, no guide, no script.
Change, its own time, own place, own mirror's glass.

Time travels
Through us all ourselves despite
Unwitting, unwilling conduits, vessels none the less
Confused places, distant, current nightmares
From, to, in, out, lost, found, lost again and found.
At crucial junctures found.

In finding some are lost
Retrieving pain from paid storage
Devalued currencies, ignorance, vile wishes.
None can help. Least themselves. Few can save.
Hopeless, the less they know the more certain.
Hopeful, the more we know the less certain.

Yet we arrive
At places safe but not so
The deliverer oaths to waiting millions
A nation celebrates, the world as well
Anticipates beginning anew from firmer ground
Uncertain but secure in the Luo pilgrim's ship.

In tin can
In the hand of a black man
In soft hat
In the hand of a white man
Beggars both in silence or in sound
From each other. Givers both. Brothers.

The Professor Gates Affair: Incident and Incidentals

This incident is of value in our discussion because it demonstrates clearly how easily the divisive, unresolved issue of race can inject itself into discourse and behavior among individuals. The unfortunate reality here is that, as the facts will reveal, bias is exercised unconsciously by many white people. They do not intend to be biased since they are truly unaware that they are in fact acting out of bias. Ironically, this is where the gravest danger lies in addressing bias. Confronting someone on an indiscretion he commits but of which he is unaware, more often than not will first elicit denial then subsequently anger. My own experience confirms that bias is exercised automatically and unconsciously because of the extent to which it has enjoyed institutional support throughout the history of our country. The duration and intensity of this support have had an almost DNA-like effect in our lives. In other words, in a Darwinian sense, bias has survived because it has traditionally provided significant advantage to those who exercise it. At first it was seen as *necessary*. Over time, such bias came to be considered *right*. Subsequently it became *natural* behavior. At this point there is no need *to think about it*, it simply happens. Pretty much like breathing. This is the great difficulty in addressing bias effectively.

Let us recount the essential facts surrounding the Gates Affair.

1. A resident reports by telephone, what appears to be a burglary in a predominantly white, residential neighborhood.
2. The resident describes the men she thinks may be burglars without any racial reference in her narrative. A fact confirmed by the police's own taped recording of the report.
3. The responding police officer, Sgt. James Crowley, who happens to be white, assumes that the burglars are black and so records this assumption as fact in his report.
4. On arrival at the residence in question the officer discovers that there is indeed a black man inside the residence.
5. The white police officer asks the black man for identification.
6. The identification is provided and establishes the identity of the black man as Henry Louis Gates, a Harvard professor, who had just returned from a trip to China that very day.
7. Apparently an argument ensues and intemperate words are exchanged between the officer and Gates, including an accusation by Gates that the officer, Crowley, is racist.
8. Gates asks Crowley to provide his name and police badge number.
9. Crowley refuses but tells Gates that he will do so if Gates steps outside the residence.
10. Gates follows Crowley outside the front door of the residence and at this point is handcuffed and arrested by Crowley.

These are the indisputable facts.

The subsequent occurrences and commentaries on the Affair are very interesting. Gates is released by the police without charge; citizens take sides, mostly along racial lines. In response to a query by a news reporter, the President of the United States, who happens to be black and is a friend of Prof. Gates, expresses the opinion that the action of the police, under the circumstances, was stupid. The latter opinion was then mangled and repeated by the police and much of the media as the President saying the police officer, James Crowley, was stupid. No one likes to be called stupid even if one's actions may in fact be stupid. In what it considered righteous anger, the union of police demanded an apology from the President of the United States. Thankfully no apology was given and the President subsequently invited Gates and Crowley to meet with him at the White House over beers.

Now, I pose the question: What do we suppose the response from the community would have been were Crowley the professor and Gates the arresting officer and the situation handled in exactly the manner detailed above? Even so, the much larger question remains: Why did James Crowley assume that the possible burglars were black? I conclude that this is the DNA-like effect alluded to earlier. I can find no other reasonable explanation, especially when it is taken into account that James Crowley actually teaches a course at the local police academy on "Community Race Relations". If only we were able to walk in another's shoes easily.

Many articles have been written on the Affair but to my mind one stands out above all the others I have read. It is very instructive and so powerful in its implications that it is repeated here in its entirety. The writer, Raj Jayadev, is the director of Silicon Valley in California.

What if Henry Louis Gates Were Not an Acclaimed Professor?

New America Media, Commentary, Raj Jayadev, Posted: Jul 29, 2009 Review it on

NewsTrusthttp://news.newamericamedia.org/news/view_article.html?article_id=0e04e004de044e2a27a019 53c3f5a74d

SAN JOSE, Calif. – Professor Henry Louis Gates, recently arrested, gets to share a beer with the man who arrested him, Sgt. James Crowley, at the White House with the President of the United States. It is a highly uncommon ending to an unfortunately very common occurrence – a man of color citing racial profiling after an arrest. If this incident is really to be the "teachable moment" President Obama hopes for, the real question to explore is this: What would have happened to Dr. Gates if he were not an acclaimed scholar and author, friend to the President, and someone whose stardom could greatly embarrass a city and county justice system? First things first, charges for his disorderly conduct would not be dropped shortly after his arrest, and Dr. Gates, a few weeks after the incident, would just be starting his journey in the criminal justice system, rather then reflecting on it in hindsight, while throwing back a beer with the leader of the free world. Let's start from there. Since every city in the country is different in arresting practice, the way to approach this is not to examine Cambridge, but to ask what would happen if the arrest happened in your own town. Let me roll out what would have happened if Dr. Gates, were he not a noted scholar, was arrested in my city, San Jose, California with the same fact pattern, even as described by the police report. Starting from arrest, Dr. Gates would have been charged with more then disturbing the peace, (penal code 415 in California). From the narrative of what happened at his home,

Mr. Gates would have also picked up a 148 resisting arrest, a misdemeanor.

California Department of Justice numbers show San Jose has much higher arrest rates for these charges than cities of comparable size, in a racially disproportionate fashion. For resisting arrest in 2007, for example, 54.2 percent were Latino, although Latinos only represent roughly 30 percent of the city's population. Blacks, who represent only 3.5 percent of San Jose residents, accounted for 15.4 percent of these arrests. Communities of color in San Jose claim the discrepancy is due to a practice some call "attitude arresting," where police are using these particular charges that rely heavily on officer discretion to arrest someone when they don't like their attitude, rather than for an actual criminal act. As for the comment, "You don't know who you are messing with," Dr. Gates would have also likely picked up a penal code 69 (felony in this case), for making a criminal threat to a police officer.

Dr. Gates would not know of all these charges until he was arraigned at court. It is here that police abuse can take a more subtle, yet problematic direction – the well known practice of over-charging. Sometimes, it is not the gun or taser, which is the weapon of concern: it is the pen used for a police report. In all likelihood, someone less well known and well connected than Mr. Gates would be represented by the Public Defender's office, which represents over 90 percent of all defendants in California. His attorney, over-worked, with an over-whelming caseload, would read the police report and speak with Dr. Gates, likely on the day of his first court appearance. He or she would tell Dr. Gates of his maximum exposure – what he would receive if convicted on all charges – which may be a year, given the felony. The attorney would tell Dr. Gates "it doesn't look good" since it is his word versus the police officer, and juries trust police officers. The Public Defender and the District Attorney would be anxious to resolve the case, since they are seeing their average case loads steadily increasing, as their offices budgets are shrinking. Across the country, plea bargains resolve roughly 95 percent of all felony cases.

The Public Defender would tell Dr. Gates that he or she met with the District Attorney's office, and that the prosecutor is offering a deal if he pleads guilty just to the two misdemeanor charges. He would do only ten days in county jail, and have a three-year probation, but the heavier charge would be dismissed. Dr. Gates would feel conflicted. Every fiber in him would say that he is innocent of any crime, but he would also feel he could not risk loosing a jury trial and going to jail for an extended period of time. He would know he would be facing a mainly white jury, who he fears would carry their own bias into the courtroom when they hear of an erratic acting black man. Demoralized and worn down from the process, Dr. Gates would plead guilty to the 415 and 148 charge, and do a week in jail, after time served is subtracted.

After his release, and back into the normal motions of his life, he would feel haunted by the injustice. He will be stigmatized by every interaction he has with a law enforcement officer when they run his name, even in innocuous driving stops. Motivated to right a wrong, he might approach a civil rights attorney to file a claim against the police department for false arrest and racial profiling. Although sympathetic and believing, the attorney would tell Dr. Gates that he has no case because he took a plea deal. As a last resort, if only to prevent such an episode from happening to another person down the road, Dr. Gates could file a claim against the arresting officer with the police department's internal affairs unit. He would meet with an internal affairs investigator, who would listen to Dr. Gates' story of the officer abusing his authority, and tell him he will report back on his findings. Months later, Dr. Gates would receive a form letter from the Internal Affairs office informing him that they reviewed his case and found no wrong doing by the involved officers.

Throughout the course of his process, which started with a jammed door to his own home, Dr. Gates would have interacted with all these many aspects of the criminal justice system, and would have felt betrayed by all of them. The less well-known Dr. Gates would not be making a documentary after all this, would not be sipping cold beers with the president of the United States and the man who arrested him. No, he would simply be trying to restore normalcy back to his permanently altered life.

The above is the sad reality of the impact of racial bias in our society. On a personal level, I have attempted to respond to queries and comments from some of my white acquaintances and friends on the Gates Affair. In all cases they see Gates as a troublemaker. One suggests that were Gates to call 911 in the future the police should not respond on his behalf. In other words he wants retribution against Gates. He is clearly not immune to the DNA-like effect of his history regarding race. My response to one of his notes to me is below.

Dear John:
I am flattered that you ask me to comment on this very troubling matter. I also respect very much your initiative and willingness to discuss the issue.
Let me say at the outset that my perspective on the matter cannot be given without a critical point of reference. I was born in Jamaica, had my early schooling there, studied in the U.S. and Europe and lived and worked in several countries including the U.S., Canada and Africa for a Fortune 500 American multi-national company. This set of circumstances informs my views on race and politics in a country I happily call my own by choice. I am familiar with the history of the U.S. and the part played by slavery and race in its development. This history casts a long and sometimes painful shadow. The pain, in my view, is shared by both whites and blacks. I believe, however, that black people in America have

suffered the brunt of this insult and in many respects this continues to be the case. Having said that let me now turn to the case at hand.

I am of the opinion that Prof. Gates over-reacted in his response to the police. While I do not believe his over-reaction was wise or helpful I do understand why he would over-react. Prof. Gates has yet to escape fully from the long shadow of history referred to earlier. In some respects neither has the police officer. I am of the opinion that Prof. Gates stoked in the police officer the latent fire of residual discomfort with "upper class" black people. Note that I use the word **"discomfort"** purposely. I do not believe, given the evidence I have read about the arresting officer, that he is **consciously racist**. If, as is reported in some places, Gates did say, "Don't you know who I am?" then Gates himself added fuel to the fire. This is definitely among the poorest ways to respond to nearly any situation involving confrontation with authority. Even a black police officer in this situation is likely to be offended by such a statement and what it in fact implies. My friends in Jamaica relate a story about an important person who demanded special treatment at the airport. When denied this deference, he asked the attendant if she knew who he was. She in turn announced over the PA system that there was a gentleman at the counter who did not know who he was. She then proceeded to ask if anyone present could assist the pompous traveler in determining who he was. Instructive and priceless.

I am also of the view that the officer over-reacted. Under the circumstances the officer is the person in a superior position of power, with the greatest opportunity and potential to diffuse what was obviously a very uncomfortable situation. This view is reinforced by the fact that this particular officer teaches **"Community Race Relations"** at the Police Academy. What a wonderful teaching opportunity presented itself here! Imagine the officer successfully defusing the situation and using the entire episode as an example of "best behavior" under very trying conditions in lecturing to his students! I think *he missed a marvelous opportunity. I do not think it was necessary for the officer to hand cuff and arrest Gates. Yet all is not lost. I do believe that much good may yet be gained from the incident provided cooler heads prevail. Your engaging me on the incident is one such good outcome, in my opinion. Already the incident is bearing fruit.*

The question of whether the Cambridge police should in the future respond promptly to a 911 call from Prof. Gates really has no place in the discourse. It merely raises other disturbing issues, not least of which is the idea of retribution, which has no validity. It is one of the most admirable things about this country that even the common criminal has rights even after conviction. I am familiar with countries in which, even when innocent, citizens have no such rights. The fact that the Prof.'s behavior may be questionable in no way diminishes his right to the protection afforded all citizens by the police.

It is very true that we generally shy away from discussing race among ourselves. Certainly between black Americans and their white fellow citizens. The greatest reason in my mind is the inevitable discomfort any such discussion will engender. Yet it is a subject that we must eventually be willing to address honestly and respectfully on an individual to individual basis.

In closing let me relate an experience of mine here in our own neighborhood a couple years ago. I stupidly locked myself out of the house after setting the alarm. I compounded my error by opening the pedestrian door from my garage. This door is the only door in the house that has no time delay and so immediately set off the alarm. As expected, and as has been my experience, the police arrived within minutes. I was sitting on a bench by my front doorway. Fortunately, although I had locked myself out I did have my bill fold on my person. This meant that I had access to appropriate personal identification documents. The officer parked his car in the driveway by my garage and approached me. I stood up and waited. He asked me if I had a problem. I responded by referring to the still active alarm and confessed that I had locked myself out of the house. His next question was, "Do you live here?" I confirmed this. He next requested identification which I provided. He expressed sympathy with my plight and asked whether he could assist in any way in helping me gain access into the house. I thanked him but declined the help and indicated I would wait until my wife returned from church. He humorously suggested I not get into any further trouble before my wife's return.

The lesson I wish to share here is that my response to the police could have gone awry from the question, "Do you live here?" Why didn't it? Sadly, I have to conclude, because I had the good fortune, by share circumstances of birth, of avoiding the long shadow of American history regarding race. I do not carry the weighty baggage of the psychologically destabilizing hangover from the racial turbulence that most Americans carry, black as well as white, by virtue of a shared, continuing, painful experience. I always have positive expectations of all people regardless of their race and I certainly never assume that the police are intent on committing some insult against me as a black person because I happen to be black. Regrettably, it is a fact that not so recent, recent and current history reveals that people of color do suffer unfair treatment disproportionately at the hands of the police. This engenders suspicion and ill will on both sides and completes the disruptive circuit of negative expectations by the police as well as those they confront.

Again I thank you for seeking my views on a very complex cultural matter. I sincerely hope that I have been helpful.

My white acquaintance did admit that my perspective is in fact different and shared this with a friend of his in North Carolina who responded as below.

Dear John,
Your friend Owen is very articulate and apparently willing, and able, to at least address this problem intel-

ligently, unlike most others of his race, color, or whatever, one wishes to term it.

I would love to have both of you on my NC mountain deck for about 10 hours to thoroughly discuss this issue. Owen can communicate without getting an attitude. I love it!

Vernon.

Sadly, in spite of the unusual willingness of my acquaintance and his friend to discuss the subject, neither appears willing or able to understand why it is I am able to discuss the matter *without attitude*. Neither do they appear to understand that they seem unable to discuss the issue *without attitude*. They remain blind to their own injury by the pervasive impact of racism in America. Yet, I believe that the fact that the discussion is taking place augurs well for improvement in race relations in America. Some optimism is warranted.

White Fear, Black Despond or Quiet Rage?

As an American by choice who was born in Jamaica and spent his early years there, I am able to observe and understand the difficulties, problems and opportunities of a changing society, especially as these issues relate to race. As related earlier, Jamaica did itself go through and survive a period of racial anxiety. The majority group in the Jamaica population was and continues to be black but recognized early enough the value of diversity and social harmony. It is very clear that not to allow equal opportunity for success to any segment of a society is harmful to that society. We only have to imagine the number of citizens like Barack Obama and Sonia Sotomayor, Bill Gates and Steve Jobs, that has been lost to our society on this account, to realize how absurd a failing this is.

The fear and paranoia being displayed by a highly visible, vocal and frighteningly demonstrative segment of white America are alarming. They are never the less quite understandable. But this in no way makes them acceptable, especially when whites comprise such a large proportion of the population and generally control the levers of power in American society. The fear and paranoia are clearly baseless and irrational. Unfortunately, this observation does nothing to diminish the reality or its effects.

The DNA-like tenacity of prejudice and bias will not be easily or speedily addressed effectively. But it must be. I believe that, like Obama himself, those who support his presidency realize the urgent need for this. We have entered a crucial period in American history. Perhaps the rest of the world recognizes this more than Americans do. We surely need to approach ourselves and the world with greater balance, respect and genuine concern for our common welfare. Still, charity should begin at home. This requires no more, and certainly no less, than our willingness to endure the discomfort of open dialogue about race and our feelings about race in our culture.

Obama's response to the effect of his former pastor's views provided a bright spark for such a dialogue. However, the spark failed to ignite any fires, partly because of its suffocation by the hot, humid air of politics during a contentious political campaign and the cynicism with which many, black and white, came to see Obama's comments subsequently. But once again, less for the general reader than for my two grand daughters, I will reproduce Barack Obama's response to what many dubbed his *Jeremiah Wright Problem*. I implore my fellow Americans not simply to read but to study Obama's response. I will make sure that my grandchildren do.

Remarks of Senator Barack Obama: 'A More Perfect Union'

Philadelphia, PA | March 18, 2008

As Prepared for Delivery

"We the people, in order to form a more perfect union."

Two hundred and twenty one years ago, in a hall that still stands across the street, a group of men gathered and, with these simple words, launched America's improbable experiment in democracy. Farmers and scholars; statesmen and patriots who had traveled across an ocean to escape tyranny and persecution finally made real their declaration of independence at a Philadelphia convention that lasted through the spring of 1787.

The document they produced was eventually signed but ultimately unfinished. It was stained by this nation's original sin of slavery, a question that divided the colonies and brought the convention to a stalemate until the founders chose to allow the slave trade to continue for at least twenty more years, and to leave any final resolution to future generations.

Of course, the answer to the slavery question was already embedded within our Constitution - a Constitution that had at its very core the ideal of equal citizenship under the law; a Constitution that promised its people liberty, and justice, and a union that could be and should be perfected over time.

And yet words on a parchment would not be enough to deliver slaves from bondage, or provide men and women of every color and creed their full rights and obligations as citizens of the United States. What would be needed were Americans in successive generations who were willing to do their part - through protests and struggle, on the streets and in the courts, through a civil war and civil disobedience and always at great risk - to narrow that gap between the promise of our ideals and the reality of their time.

This was one of the tasks we set forth at the beginning of this campaign - to continue the long march of those who came before us, a march for a more just, more equal, more free, more caring and more prosperous America. I chose to run for the presidency at this moment in history because I believe deeply that we cannot solve the challenges of our time unless we solve them together - unless we perfect our union by understanding that we may have different stories, but we hold common hopes; that we may not look the same and we may not have come from the same place, but we all want to move in the same direction - towards a better future for our children and our grandchildren.

This belief comes from my unyielding faith in the decency and generosity of the American people. But it also comes from my own American story.

I am the son of a black man from Kenya and a white woman from Kansas. I was raised with the help of a white grandfather who survived a Depression to serve in Patton's Army during World War II and a white grandmother who worked on a bomber assembly line at Fort Leavenworth while he was overseas. I've gone to some of the best schools in America and lived in one of the world's poorest nations. I am married to a black American who carries within her the blood of slaves and slave owners - an inheritance we pass on to our two precious daughters. I have brothers, sisters, nieces, nephews, uncles and cousins, of every race and every hue, scattered across three continents, and for as long as I live, I will never forget that in no other country on Earth is my story even possible.

It's a story that hasn't made me the most conventional candidate. But it is a story that has seared into my genetic makeup the idea that this nation is more than the sum of its parts - that out of many, we are truly one.

Throughout the first year of this campaign, against all predictions to the contrary, we saw how hungry the American people were for this message of unity. Despite the temptation to view my candidacy through a purely racial lens, we won commanding victories in states with some of the whitest populations in the country. In South Carolina, where the Confederate Flag still flies, we built a powerful coalition of African Americans and white Americans.

This is not to say that race has not been an issue in the campaign. At various stages in the campaign, some commentators have deemed me either "too black" or "not black enough." We saw racial tensions bubble to the surface during the week before the South Carolina primary. The press has scoured every exit poll for the latest evidence of racial polarization, not just in terms of white and black, but black and brown as well.

And yet, it has only been in the last couple of weeks that the discussion of race in this campaign has taken a particularly divisive turn.

On one end of the spectrum, we've heard the implication that my candidacy is somehow an exercise in affirmative action; that it's based solely on the desire of wide-eyed liberals to purchase racial reconciliation on the cheap. On the other end, we've heard my former pastor, Reverend Jeremiah Wright, use incendiary language to express views that have the potential not only to widen the racial divide, but views that denigrate both the greatness and the goodness of our nation; that rightly offend white and black alike.

I have already condemned, in unequivocal terms, the statements of Reverend Wright that have caused such controversy. For some, nagging questions remain. Did I know him to be an occasionally fierce critic of American domestic and foreign policy? Of course. Did I ever hear him make remarks that could be considered controversial while I sat in church? Yes. Did I strongly disagree with many of his political views? Absolutely - just as I'm sure many of you have heard remarks from your pastors, priests, or rabbis with which you strongly disagreed.

But the remarks that have caused this recent firestorm weren't simply controversial. They weren't simply a religious leader's effort to speak out against perceived injustice. Instead, they expressed a profoundly distorted view of this country - a view that sees white racism as endemic, and that elevates what is wrong with America above all that we know is right with America; a view that sees the conflicts in the Middle East as rooted primarily in the actions of stalwart allies like Israel, instead of emanating from the perverse and hateful ideologies of radical Islam.

As such, Reverend Wright's comments were not only wrong but divisive, divisive at a time when we need unity; racially charged at a time when we need to come together to solve a set of monumental problems - two wars, a terrorist threat, a falling economy, a chronic health care crisis and potentially devastating climate change; problems that are neither black or white or Latino or Asian, but rather problems that confront us all.

Given my background, my politics, and my professed values and ideals, there will no doubt be those for whom my statements of condemnation are not enough. Why associate myself with Reverend Wright in the first place, they may ask? Why not join another church? And I confess that if all that I knew of Reverend Wright were the *snippets of those sermons that have run in an endless loop on the television and You Tube, or if Trinity United Church of Christ conformed to the caricatures being peddled by some commentators, there is no doubt that I would react in much the same way*

But the truth is, that isn't all that I know of the man. The man I met more than twenty years ago is a man who helped introduce me to my Christian faith, a man who spoke to me about our obligations to love one another; to care for the sick and lift up the poor. He is a man who served his country as a U.S. Marine; who has studied and lectured at some of the finest universities and seminaries in the country, and who for over thirty years led a church that serves the community by doing God's work here on Earth - by housing the homeless, ministering to the needy, providing day care services and scholarships and prison ministries, and reaching out to those suffering from HIV/ AIDS.

In my first book, Dreams From My Father, I described the experience of my first service at Trinity:

"People began to shout, to rise from their seats and clap and cry out, a forceful wind carrying the reverend's voice up into the rafters....And in that single note - hope! - I heard something else; at the foot of that cross, inside the thousands of churches across the city, I imagined the stories of ordinary black people merging with the stories of David and Goliath, Moses and Pharaoh, the Christians in the lion's den, Ezekiel's field of dry bones. Those stories - of survival, and freedom, and hope - became our story, my story; the blood that had spilled was our blood, the tears our tears; until this black church, on this bright day, seemed once more a vessel carrying the story of a people into future generations and into a larger world. Our trials and triumphs became at once unique and universal, black and more than black; in chronicling our journey, the stories and songs gave us a means to reclaim memories that we didn't need to feel shame about... memories that all people might study and cherish - and with which we could start to rebuild."

That has been my experience at Trinity. Like other predominantly black churches across the country, Trinity embodies the black community in its entirety - the doctor and the welfare mom, the model student and the former gang-banger. Like other black churches, Trinity's services are full of raucous laughter and sometimes bawdy humor. They are full of dancing, clapping, screaming and shouting that may seem jarring to the untrained ear. The church contains in full the kindness and cruelty, the fierce intelligence and the shocking ignorance, the struggles and successes, the love and yes, the bitterness and bias that make up the black experience in America.

And this helps explain, perhaps, my relationship with Reverend Wright. As imperfect as he may be, he has been like family to me. He strengthened my faith, officiated my wedding, and baptized my children. Not once in my conversations with him have I heard him talk about any ethnic group in derogatory terms, or treat whites with whom he interacted with anything but courtesy and respect. He contains within him the contradictions - the good and the bad - of the community that he has served diligently for so many years.

I can no more disown him than I can disown the black community. I can no more disown him than I can my white grandmother - a woman who helped raise me, a woman who sacrificed again and again for me, a woman who loves me as much as she loves anything in this world, but a woman who once confessed her fear of black men who passed by her on the street, and who on more than one occasion has uttered racial or ethnic stereotypes that made me cringe.

These people are a part of me. And they are a part of America, this country that I love.

Some will see this as an attempt to justify or excuse comments that are simply inexcusable. I can assure you it is not. I suppose the politically safe thing would be to move on from this episode and just hope that it fades into the woodwork. We can dismiss Reverend Wright as a crank or a demagogue, just as some have dismissed

Geraldine Ferraro, in the aftermath of her recent statements, as harboring some deep-seated racial bias.

But race is an issue that I believe this nation cannot afford to ignore right now. We would be making the same mistake that Reverend Wright made in his offending sermons about America - to simplify and stereotype and amplify the negative to the point that it distorts reality.

The fact is that the comments that have been made and the issues that have surfaced over the last few weeks reflect the complexities of race in this country that we've never really worked through - a part of our union that we have yet to perfect. And if we walk away now, if we simply retreat into our respective corners, we will never be able to come together and solve challenges like health care, or education, or the need to find good jobs for every American.

Understanding this reality requires a reminder of how we arrived at this point. As William Faulkner once wrote, "The past isn't dead and buried. In fact, it isn't even past." We do not need to recite here the history of racial injustice in this country. But we do need to remind ourselves that so many of the disparities that exist in the African-American community today can be directly traced to inequalities passed on from an earlier generation that suffered under the brutal legacy of slavery and Jim Crow.

Segregated schools were, and are, inferior schools; we still haven't fixed them, fifty years after Brown v. Board of Education, and the inferior education they provided, then and now, helps explain the pervasive achievement gap between today's black and white students.

Legalized discrimination - where blacks were prevented, often through violence, from owning property, or loans were not granted to African-American business owners, or black homeowners could not access FHA mortgages, or blacks were excluded from unions, or the police force, or fire departments - meant that black families could not amass any meaningful wealth to bequeath to future generations. That history helps explain *the wealth and income gap between black and white, and the concentrated pockets of poverty that persists in so many of today's urban and rural communities.*

A lack of economic opportunity among black men, and the shame and frustration that came from not being able to provide for one's family, contributed to the erosion of black families - a problem that welfare policies for many years may have worsened. And the lack of basic services in so many urban black neighborhoods - parks for kids to play in, police walking the beat, regular garbage pick-up and building code enforcement - all helped create a cycle of violence, blight and neglect that continue to haunt us.

This is the reality in which Reverend Wright and other African-Americans of his generation grew up. They came of age in the late fifties and early sixties, a time when segregation was still the law of the land and opportunity was systematically constricted. What's remarkable is not how many failed in the face of discrimination, but rather how many men and women overcame the odds; how many were able to make a way out of no way for those like me who would come after them.

But for all those who scratched and clawed their way to get a piece of the American Dream, there were many who didn't make it - those who were ultimately defeated, in one way or another, by discrimination. That legacy of defeat was passed on to future generations - those young men and increasingly young women who we see standing on street corners or languishing in our prisons, without hope or prospects for the future. Even for those blacks who did make it, questions of race, and racism, continue to define their worldview in fundamental ways. For the men and women of Reverend Wright's generation, the memories of humiliation and doubt and fear have not gone away; nor has the anger and the bitterness of those years. That anger may not get expressed in public, in front of white co-workers or white friends. But it does find voice in the barbershop or around the kitchen table. At times, that anger is exploited by politicians, to gin up votes along racial lines, or to make up for a politician's own failings.

And occasionally it finds voice in the church on Sunday morning, in the pulpit and in the pews. The fact that so many people are surprised to hear that anger in some of Reverend Wright's sermons simply reminds us of the old truism that the most segregated hour in American life occurs on Sunday morning. That anger is not always productive; indeed, all too often it distracts attention from solving real problems; it keeps us from squarely facing our own complicity in our condition, and prevents the African-American community from forging the alliances it needs to bring about real change. But the anger is real; it is powerful; and to simply wish it away, to condemn it without understanding its roots, only serves to widen the chasm of misunderstanding that exists between the races.

In fact, a similar anger exists within segments of the white community. Most working- and middle-class white Americans don't feel that they have been particularly privileged by their race. Their experience is the immigrant experience - as far as they're concerned, no one's handed them anything, they've built it from scratch. They've worked hard all their lives, many times only to see their jobs shipped overseas or their pension dumped after a lifetime of labor. They are anxious about their futures, and feel their dreams slipping away; in an era of stagnant wages and global competition, opportunity comes to be seen as a zero sum game, in which your dreams come at my expense. So when they are told to bus their children to a school across town; when they hear that an African American is getting an advantage in landing a good job or a spot in a good college because of an injustice that they themselves never committed; when they're told that their fears about crime in urban neighborhoods are somehow prejudiced, resentment builds over time.

Like the anger within the black community, these resentments aren't always expressed in polite company.

But they have helped shape the political landscape for at least a generation. Anger over welfare and affirmative action helped forge the Reagan Coalition. Politicians routinely exploited fears of crime for their own electoral ends. Talk show hosts and conservative commentators built entire careers unmasking bogus claims of racism while dismissing legitimate discussions of racial injustice and inequality as mere political correctness or reverse racism.

Just as black anger often proved counterproductive, so have these white resentments distracted attention from the real culprits of the middle class squeeze - a corporate culture rife with inside dealing, questionable accounting practices, and short-term greed; a Washington dominated by lobbyists and special interests; economic policies that favor the few over the many. And yet, to wish away the resentments of white Americans, to label them as misguided or even racist, without recognizing they are grounded in legitimate concerns - this too widens the racial divide, and blocks the path to understanding.

This is where we are right now. It's a racial stalemate we've been stuck in for years. Contrary to the claims of some of my critics, black and white, I have never been so naive as to believe that we can get beyond our racial divisions in a single election cycle, or with a single candidacy - particularly a candidacy as imperfect as my own.

But I have asserted a firm conviction - a conviction rooted in my faith in God and my faith in the American people - that working together we can move beyond some of our old racial wounds, and that in fact we have no choice if we are to continue on the path of a more perfect union.

For the African-American community, that path means embracing the burdens of our past without becoming victims of our past. It means continuing to insist on a full measure of justice in every aspect of American life. But it also means binding our particular grievances - for better health care, and better schools, and better jobs - to the larger aspirations of all Americans – the white woman struggling to break the glass ceiling, the white man whose been laid off, the immigrant trying to feed his family. And it means taking full responsibility for own lives - by demanding more from our fathers, and spending more time with our children, and reading to them, and teaching them that while they may face challenges and discrimination in their own lives, they must never succumb to despair or cynicism; they must always believe that they can write their own destiny.

Ironically, this quintessentially American - and yes, conservative - notion of self-help found frequent expression in Reverend Wright's sermons. But what my former pastor too often failed to understand is that embarking on a program of self-help also requires a belief that society can change.

The profound mistake of Reverend Wright's sermons is not that he spoke about racism in our society. It's that he spoke as if our society was static; as if no progress has been made; as if this country - a country that has made it possible for one of his own members to run for the highest office in the land and build a coalition of white and black; Latino and Asian, rich and poor, young and old – is still irrevocably bound to a tragic past. But what we know – what we have seen - is that America can change. That is the true genius of this nation. What we have already achieved gives us hope - the audacity to hope - for what we can and must achieve tomorrow.

In the white community, the path to a more perfect union means acknowledging that what ails the African-American community does not just exist in the minds of black people; that the legacy of discrimination - and current incidents of discrimination, while less overt than in the past - are real and must be addressed. Not just with words, but with deeds - by investing in our schools and our communities; by enforcing our civil rights laws and ensuring fairness in our criminal justice system; by providing this generation with ladders of opportunity that were unavailable for previous generations. It requires all

Americans to realize that your dreams do not have to come at the expense of my dreams; that investing in the health, welfare, and education of black and brown and white children will ultimately help all of America prosper.

In the end, then, what is called for is nothing more, and nothing less, than what all the world's great religions demand - that we do unto others as we would have them do unto us. Let us be our brother's keeper, Scripture tells us. Let us be our sister's keeper. Let us find that common stake we all have in one another, and let our politics reflect that spirit as well.

For we have a choice in this country. We can accept a politics that breeds division, and conflict, and cynicism. We can tackle race only as spectacle - as we did in the OJ trial - or in the wake of tragedy, as we did in the aftermath of Katrina - or as fodder for the nightly news. We can play Reverend Wright's sermons on every channel, every day and talk about them from now until the election, and make the only question in this campaign whether or not the American people think that I somehow believe or sympathize with his most offensive words. We can pounce on some gaffe by a Hillary supporter as evidence that she's playing the race card, or we can speculate on whether white men will all flock to John McCain in the general election regardless of his policies.

We can do that.

But if we do, I can tell you that in the next election, we'll be talking about some other distraction. And then another one. And then another one. And nothing will change.

That is one option. Or, at this moment, in this election, we can come together and say, "Not this time." This time we want to talk about the crumbling schools that are stealing the future of black children and white children and Asian children and Hispanic children and Native American children. This time we want to reject the cynicism that tells us that these kids can't learn; that those kids who don't look like us are somebody else's problem. The children of America are not those kids, they are our kids, and we will not let them fall behind in a 21st century economy. Not this time.

This time we want to talk about how the lines in the Emergency Room are filled with whites and blacks and Hispanics who do not have health care; who don't have the power on their own to overcome the special interests in Washington, but who can take them on if we do it together.

This time we want to talk about the shuttered mills that once provided a decent life for men and women of every race, and the homes for sale that once belonged to Americans from every religion, every region, every walk of life. This time we want to talk about the fact that the real problem is not that someone who doesn't look like you might take your job; it's that the corporation you work for will ship it overseas for nothing more than a profit.

This time we want to talk about the men and women of every color and creed who serve together, and fight together, and bleed together under the same proud flag. We want to talk about how to bring them home from a war that never should've been authorized and never should've been waged, and we want to talk about how we'll show our patriotism by caring for them, and their families, and giving them the benefits they have earned.

I would not be running for President if I didn't believe with all my heart that this is what the vast majority of Americans want for this country. This union may never be perfect, but generation after generation has shown that it can always be perfected. And today, whenever I find myself feeling doubtful or cynical about this possibility, what gives me the most hope is the next generation - the young people whose attitudes and beliefs and openness to change have already made history in this election.

There is one story in particularly that I'd like to leave you with today - a story I told when I had the great honor of speaking on Dr. King's birthday at his home church, Ebenezer Baptist, in Atlanta.

There is a young, twenty-three year old white woman named Ashley Baia who organized for our campaign in Florence, South Carolina. She had been working to organize a mostly African-American community since the beginning of this campaign, and one day she was at a roundtable discussion where everyone went around telling their story and why they were there.

And Ashley said that when she was nine years old, her mother got cancer. And because she had to miss days of work, she was let go and lost her health care. They had to file for bankruptcy, and that's when Ashley decided that she had to do something to help her mom.

She knew that food was one of their most expensive costs, and so Ashley convinced her mother that what she really liked and really wanted to eat more than anything else was mustard and relish sandwiches. Because that was the cheapest way to eat.

She did this for a year until her mom got better, and she told everyone at the roundtable that the reason she joined our campaign was so that she could help the millions of other children in the country who want and need to help their parents too.

Now Ashley might have made a different choice. Perhaps somebody told her along the way that the source of her mother's problems were blacks who were on welfare and too lazy to work, or Hispanics who were coming into the country illegally. But she didn't. She sought out allies in her fight against injustice.

Anyway, Ashley finishes her story and then goes around the room and asks everyone else why they're supporting the campaign. They all have different stories and reasons. Many bring up a specific issue. And finally they come to this elderly black man who's been sitting there quietly the entire time. And Ashley asks him why he's there. And he does not bring up a specific issue. He does not say health care or the economy. He does not say education or the war. He does not say that he was there because of Barack Obama. He simply says to everyone in the room, "I am here because of Ashley."

351

"I'm here because of Ashley." By itself, that single moment of recognition between that young white girl and that old black man is not enough. It is not enough to give health care to the sick, or jobs to the jobless, or education to our children.

But it is where we start. It is where our union grows stronger. And as so many generations have come to realize over the course of the two-hundred and twenty one years since a band of patriots signed that document in Philadelphia, that is where the perfection begins.

If these words do not persuade us of the immense possibilities of our America, they should at least stir in us a deep sense of the need to understand and strive to bridge the racial divide in the greatest country on earth. There is absolutely no upside to racism, whatever the source. Those who continue to use this deformed morality as a deep wedge in our society deserve to be shunned; those who profit from its maintenance deserve to be abandoned. But we must not lose sight of the fact that the election of Barack Obama would have been impossible but for the large number of white Americans who are clearly willing and able to see beyond race. Even so, many supporters, white as well as black, will become impatient and disillusioned with Obama along the way. I caution greater patience, partly because our first black president, like America at this time, is navigating unique, uncharted waters at one of the most difficult times in America's history.

One of the wonders of my America is that at every critical juncture in our history America has been able to summon the visionary and courageous among us to make the difficult, often unpopular, but necessary choices to move America forward: think Abraham Lincoln and the *Civil War*, Franklin D. Roosevelt and *The New Deal*, John F. Kennedy and *The Space Program*, Lyndon B. Johnson and *The Civil Rights Act*. To quote William Shakespeare: *"There is a tide in the affairs of men, which taken at the flood, leads on to fortune. Omitted, all the voyage of their life is bound in shallows and in miseries. On such a full sea are we now afloat. And we must take the current when it serves, or lose our ventures." I urge us all to see this time as a time of great and unique opportunity, not a time of fear, discord and disunity.*

There is every reason to be hopeful. Below is a letter written by a white American, Dr. Andrew M. Manis. Dr. Manis is associate professor of history at Macon State College in Georgia and wrote this for an editorial in the Macon Telegraph in December of 2008.

When Are WE Going to Get Over It?

For much of the last forty years, ever since America "fixed" its race problem in the Civil Rights and Voting Rights Acts, we white people have been impatient with African Americans who continued to blame race for their difficulties. Often we have heard whites ask, "When are African Americans finally going to get over it?" Now I want to ask "When are we White Americans going to get over our ridiculous obsession with skin color?"

Recent reports that "Election Spurs 'Hundreds' of Race Threats, Crimes" should frighten and infuriate every one of us. Having grown up in "Bombingham," Alabama in the 1960s, I remember overhearing an avalanche of comments about what many white classmates and their parents wanted to do to John and Bobby Kennedy and Martin Luther King. Eventually, as you may recall, in all three cases, someone decided to do more than "talk the talk." Since our recent presidential election, to our eternal disgrace, we are once again hearing the same reprehensible talk I remember from my boyhood.

We white people have controlled political life in the disunited colonies and United States for some 400 years on this continent. Conservative whites have been in power 28 of the last 40 years. Even during the eight Clinton years, conservatives in Congress blocked most of his agenda and pulled him to the right. Yet never in that period did I read any headlines suggesting that any-

one was calling for the assassinations of presidents Nixon, Ford, Reagan, or either of the Bushes. Criticize them, yes. Call for their impeachment, perhaps. But there were no bounties on their heads. And even when someone did try to kill Ronald Reagan, the perpetrator was (sic) non-political mental case who wanted merely to impress Jody Foster.

But elect a liberal who happens to be black and we're back in the sixties again. At this point in our history, we should be proud that we've proven what conservatives are always saying—that in America anything is possible, EVEN electing a black man as president. But instead we now hear that schoolchildren from Maine to California are talking about wanting to "assassinate Obama."

Fighting the urge to throw up, I can only ask, "How long?" How long before we white people realize we can't make our nation, much less the whole world, look like us? How long until we white people can—once and for all—get over this hell-conceived preoccupation with skin color? How long until we white people get over the demonic conviction that white skin makes us superior? How long before we white people get over our bitter resentments about being demoted to the status of equality with non-whites? How long before we get over our expectations that we should be at the head of the line merely because of our white skin? How long until we white people end our silence and call out our peers when they share the latest racist jokes in the privacy of our white-only conversations? I believe in free speech, but how long until we white people start making racist loudmouths as socially uncomfortable as we do flag burners? How long until we white people will stop insisting that blacks exercise personal responsibility, build strong families, educate themselves enough to edit the Harvard Law Review, and work hard enough to become President of the United States, only to threaten to assassinate them when they do? How long before we start "living out the true meaning" of our creeds, both civil and religious, that all men *and women are created equal and that "red and yellow, black and white" all are precious in God's sight?*

Until this past November 4, I didn't believe this country would ever elect an African American to the presidency. I still don't believe I'll live long enough to see us white people get over our racism problem. But here's my three-point plan: First, everyday that Barack Obama lives in the White House that Black Slaves Built I'm going to pray that God (and the Secret Service) will protect him and his family from us white people. Second, I'm going to report to the FBI anyone I overhear saying, in seriousness or in jest, anything of a threatening nature about President Obama. Third, I'm going to pray to live long enough to see America surprise the world once again, when white people can sing of our damnable color prejudice, "We HAVE overcome."

Black America is not yet despondent in the face of the vocal, Irrational Right's onslaught against Obama but they are quietly outraged. For all our sakes I hope black America is never given cause to become despondent and demonstrably angry. One of the most disappointing and reprehensible things to observe, is the steadfast refusal of the leadership of the Republican Party to rebuke its irrational fringe for its extremely explicit racist and threatening statements about the President of The United States. The Party's silence and the open support of this fringe by some Republican members of Congress should not be seen as a political issue but as a national one. There will be no doubt who will be culpable should our worst fears ever materialize. Now is certainly not the time to support the irrational fringe with a wink and a nod. This is a very cynical and dangerous game to play at any time but more so at this time in our history.

At the same time, Black America must exercise patience and restraint and not make the mistake of assuming that Barack Obama is the president of Black America or that he can walk on water. And Black America must be willing to renew its faith in the goodness, conscience and justice that America has always promised, and at times exercised, for all its citizens. Black America must be willing to trust its white neighbors in spite of the offensive behavior of the Irrational Right. Black America must not devalue the contributions and sacrifices of heroes like *Sojourner Truth, Booker T Washington, George Washington Carver, Harriet Tubman, Malcolm X and Martin Luther King,* by failing to acknowledge kinship with White America and recognizing that there is more that unites Black America with White America than divides them. Our country belongs to all of us and none of us has the right to deny any of us full, unbridled, responsible ownership.

America is a constant work in progress. This is clearly demonstrated by the amendments to the Constitution of the United States. If anyone needed any proof that America is constantly working toward a more perfect union, the series of amendments must surely be evidence enough. Consider the first ten amendments to the Constitution which essentially enshrines *The Bill of Rights*. I am particularly fond of Amendments I and IV which I list below:

Amendment I

Congress shall make no law respecting an establishment of religion, or prohibiting the free exercise thereof; or abridging the freedom of speech, or of the press; or the right of the people peaceably to assemble, and to petition the Government for a redress of grievances.

Amendment IV

The right of the people to be secure in their persons, houses, papers, and effects, against unreasonable searches and seizures, shall not be violated, and no Warrants shall issue, but upon probable cause, supported by Oath or affirmation, and particularly describing the place to be searched, and the persons or things to be seized.

Still, like any other clearly identifiable sub-group in our society, blacks are themselves a house divided in a number of ways. These divisions are based on class, shades of color, education and heritage. There is nothing unnatural about this, as long as we recognize these divisions for what they are: islands of pride, comfort and convenience in a rolling social sea. There are blacks who see Obama in a similar way as most Republicans do. The black leader of the Republican National Committee certainly does. There are *Native* American blacks who view black immigrants in a less than friendly light; and there are blacks who see black society in terms of a hierarchy based on shades of white. Still, none of this cutting and dicing should get in the way of having a common view of the problems faced by black Americans generally.

Regrettably, these problems are traceable, in the main, to race. And here the traditional 1% rule applies. This nonsensical contrivance fascinates me, especially when an unexpected number of white Americans now observe that, if Obama is half black, there is equal reason to consider him white as there is to consider him black. Based on the psychology of the color code this should not be acceptable. Still, one must admit that the logic is irrefutable. In some ways this logic may be a blessing no one anticipated. It is no doubt a unique difference between Obama and any other black candidate who vied for the presidency. Both blacks and whites should see this as indicative of the bridge we need to build to accommodate one another in our quest for a more perfect union. This quest is worthy of our very best efforts, regardless of heritage, race or complexion.

IX. THE FUTURE: EXPECTATIONS AND PERSPECTIVE

America's Place in the World & Individual Responsibility

America, rightly or wrongly, is the standard against which much of the world judges itself. This has been the case for my entire lifetime. It is therefore very difficult to contemplate this not being the case at anytime over the remainder of my life. But both history and common sense tell me that this will not be the case forever. Currently, it appears that this is less a decline in America's pre-eminence than rapid progress on the part of countries such as Brazil, China and India, for example. However, this does not make the prospect any less daunting for most Americans. While America may lose its overall pre-eminence, I believe that some of the most wholesome aspects of American culture will be especially difficult to surpass or even equal in many cases. Most notable among these are our *Bill of Rights* which guarantees specific freedoms under our remarkable Constitution and *The Separation of Powers* doctrine and practice which allow the checks and balances relationship among the branches of government: Executive, Legislative and Judiciary. It is all but unimaginable that either of these devices which basically protects the rights of the people could ever be adopted in China, for example.

While I do not expect America to maintain its singular role of leadership in the world indefinitely, I do not anticipate that America will ever be diminished in influence or respect to a point of being marginal in the world. The pace and degree of acceleration by which others approach or even surpass America in some respects, will depend on the will and cohesiveness of Americans. This is why it is vital that, as a nation, we address and resolve the issue of race and its destabilizing effect on the social fabric of America. At the start of this writing, while I was very aware of this fact, I never thought that in 2009 after the election of a black president, race as an inflammable, divisive issue would ever be as strident, distressing and pervasive as it has turned out to be. My personal experience in America, in spite of my clear exposure to bias in the workplace, never led me to believe that I should infer that America beyond my professional life was the same as, or worse than, my professional experience. It is therefore somewhat shocking to me to witness the resurgence of the remorselessly fearless exhibition of racist behavior which was rampant in the 50's, 60's and 70's in America.

My older son, Gordon, agrees with me that the driving force behind the fear that stokes racist behavior is a very deep, perhaps even subliminal, concern on the part of white Americans about retribution. His view is that those who are concerned on this account should consider the fact that the energy required just to achieve equality, let alone maintain it, on the part of black Americans, leaves no energy or desire for retribution or vengeance. I also happen to believe that there is the not unrelated fear of *extinction* due to the *browning of America*. In any event, the lesson learned from introspection by the subdued and disadvantaged is that vengeance is a very poor substitute for justice. In fact, seeking vengeance is a debilitating vice while seeking justice is an uplifting virtue. In a sense, as I will argue later, this is a difference we failed to recognize as a nation in the aftermath of the terrorist attack of September 11, 2001.

It appears to me that the canker of racism had simply grown a scab. This scab was ripped away by the election of the first black American to the Office of the President of The United States. Fortunately for America the majority of Americans, black as well as white, is able to view the canker and the scab as the growing pains of a nation which continues to refine and find itself. Put in perspective, in the history of civilizations America is a mere embryo. We are still within the boundaries of our most formative years. This is why, as I indicated earlier, what we are witnessing is no longer an institutional dilemma but a problem whose solution rests squarely on the shoulders of individuals in our society: in our schools, colleges, neighborhoods, and public services like our police. No longer can we hide behind any badge of institutional authority, any claims of poor schools and curriculum, and any belief in superiority or inferiority based on race or other such transparent deceptions. With the election of our first black president we have, in a sense, bared our best souls to humanity. It is unimaginable that a society that took such a bold, historic, exemplary and unexpected step would then choose to reverse itself through needless, unproductive recklessness to become a pariah in the world. This is the danger facing America as we contemplate the future of our children and grand children and their children. It is no small task but we had better be up to it. We must break the back of the times, if not for ourselves certainly for our children.

Break the Back of the Times

Come,
Let us break the back of the times
So our children are not old
At sixteen.
Come,
Break the back of the times
On the treadmill of today
Save our children grey hairs

And carious minds
From never wishing
At sixteen.
Youth is old age
For little ones born already old.
Sixteen telescoped steps
From cradle to old age.
There is nothing to awe
Nothing to surprise.
Youth is an injected memory.

Come,
Break the back of the times
Before the owl stops hooting
Before babies are born to death
Before we are less substantial
Than our own shadows
Before it is afterwards.
Come,
Help me drag a homemade plough
Through my years
Deepen the furrows
Bury much of what is there
Sow new seeds
But gently.
Who will do the reaping?
Life grabs me by the shoulders
Bats me round and round.
I am dizzy.

Come,
Who will drag a plough
Through the years of the world?
Who will go beyond mere fallowing?
The children are dizzy.
Who will sow new seeds?
But gently,
Who will do the reaping?
Something has the world by the shoulders

The world is dizzy
I am dizzy
The children are dizzy
The world is dizzy.
The mind tumbles down
Down, down, down, down
From too much up
Up, up, up, up
It tumbles into the dust again

Come,
Let's rise from the dust ourselves
To rescue all our children
Buried before their death.
With no evidence for its effort
The heart falters
Jumps its tracks
Derails without destruction quite.
It needs time to find new rhythm
But time itself is out of joint
Things crumble into new disorder
As novelty destroys itself.
There is apostasy in the kingdom
Where chaos is the piper
And rebellion is the tune.
The children face the mirror
But we are their reflection.
Still, the mirror does not lie.

On Marriage

    More than at any other time in its history, America is embroiled in a debate about marriage. This debate dramatizes the predictably unyielding positions taken on the subject in respect of the Constitution and the Law, the Church and Tradition, Civil Rights and Human Rights as well as the very definition of marriage itself. It must not be forgotten or ignored that it is not so long ago that inter-racial marriage was illegal in America. This debate highlights the anger, confusion and pain that predictably accompany direct challenges to conventional wisdom or tradition.

    The national rancor over marriage among homosexuals is as divisive and gut wrenching as is the debate over abortion and a woman's right to choose. Nowhere in The Constitution is either marriage or abortion referenced directly, let alone defined, but the weight of law has been brought to bear on both never the less. And there are those who would change the Constitution to ensure their view of marriage and abortion is constitutionally and legally sanctioned. Currently, in the case of marriage, tradition appears to be winning the battle, even though, strictly speaking, tradition should yield in the face of both the Constitution and the Law on the basis of what I understand to be Civil Rights in America. It is not at all surprising that this confrontation exists. After all, marriage is one of the most sacrosanct culture symbols in our society. Yet, while marriage does have some public import, it is essentially a very private matter between two members of society. Ultimately, I feel obliged to address the subject on this basis. Indeed much of my story is profoundly influenced by the fact of my own marriage and the contributions of my wife.

While a wonderful and quite remarkable social contrivance, marriage, as we know it, survives in part because of religious beliefs and its fervently implied promise of our orderly survival as families and communities. There is nothing inevitable or natural about marriage itself. Yet, for those who choose to marry this may as well be the case. There is no doubt that communities can and do survive effectively without marriage as we know it. In any event, for me marriage is the much preferred choice and one that harbors not the slightest regret.

I met my wife's voice on the telephone before I met my wife in person or even knew her name. I was at university in Washington D.C. and she was a young overseas telephone operator with the Jamaica Telephone Company in Jamaica. She remained a mystery to me for several weeks. During this time she refused to reveal much about herself or to even provide her name. As a result, I thought of her wistfully as *Alice in Wonderland* (my own contrived Wonderland, of course) and wrote her an appropriately titled poem.

Alice

I found you in the summer
And shall love you for all seasons.
When water birds replace the sky
In winged ceremony
Above giant trumpet trees
When the torrents come to flood the ponds
And muddy the country side
When in lazy days
The sun cremates all things
And city streets lay buried

'Neath a million shifting mirages
When fleet crab grass grows crisp and thin
And little rain falls in odd places
But never near the dam
When long days and short nights are turned around
And blood red Poinsettia is everywhere
As arrogant as Poinciana
When the tall willow weeps
In fleeting marriage with cool December winds
I shall love you
And in loving you so love all the world.

I have been fortunate. By any measure I have had a very successful and exemplary marriage. I readily give most of the credit for this to my wife. In many respects, were it not for her I would certainly not have grown into the effective citizen of the world I have become. I have often remarked that in all likelihood, left to my own devices, I would have remained in our first, modest house in Jamaica, contentedly embracing my relatives and friends, lost among my books, spending endless hours listening to music and writing. I most certainly would never have approached the travails of my work experience in America in the manner that I have. In fact, but for her, I may never have returned to America at all. In particular, she has taught me to trust her instincts and to respect the instinctiveness of women generally, especially that of my mother in retrospect. She is the quintessential Jamaican woman: amazingly intuitive, frighteningly smart and sharply defensive of her family and friends. She is the alpha lioness of the pride. We complement each other in ways that make us a formidable couple in terms of our influence as the nucleus of our extended family among our generation and in some respects beyond.

I tell our friends, our children and their friends, many of whom we consider our adopted children, that love is necessary for a successful marriage but it is not sufficient. Only love in concert with deep commitment can make a marriage work and last. After more than forty years of marriage I am more convinced than ever of this. As we approach our sundown years we have come to grips with the tests occasioned by spending more time together than at any other period in our marriage and our lives. A retired friend sent me an e-mail recently to confirm this. The mail indicated that, among other troubling things, retirement offers twice as much husband and half as much money. I do not believe that anything in our pre-retirement years prepared us for this. Neither am I aware of any fool proof advice that anyone can provide on this account.

I have learned that only good communication can overcome the inevitable challenges presented by individual life changes, many of which are brought about by personal aging, children becoming unique and often testy adults, the life changing arrival of grand children and later life views that are sometimes at odds on some social and economic matters. Love, commitment, communication: these are strings on a single guitar. The strings of love and commitment are constantly fine tuned for harmony. The harmony is lost without communication. This too I have learned from my wife.

This is the lesson I hope others learn from observing our marriage. More than any other single factor, it is this lesson that has made it such a delight in being Jamaican by birth and American by choice. Clearly, this duality could not have been sensibly chosen unilaterally by either my wife or me. As with many other critical aspects of our lives, however, the journey to this duality was initiated by my wife. Generally, I tend to see our world in a constant state of flux. She not only expects a high degree of certainty in our world but, where certainty becomes doubtful, she does her best to impose it. This tension works for us in the manner in which woof and warp work to strengthen fabric. We respect each other's strengths and strengthen each other's weaknesses. There are no areas in which we compete; there are only areas in which we cooperate. To me this is the distillation of one of life's most profound lessons: how to thrive instead of just survive; how to be happy instead of being simply joyful. It is a lesson we hope we have effectively exemplified for our children and grand children.

Twin Maladies

Earlier I remarked that vengeance is not justice. I believe that in our pain and disgust after 9/11 we allowed our deep desire for vengeance to hijack our judgment. We suborned ourselves as a nation and initiated a war with Iraq that would turn out to be a millstone around our nation's neck. We are about to make a similar mistake in principle with our commitment to the war in Afghanistan. In some respects, the latter war is certainly more justifiable but the nation of Afghanistan did not attack America. The Taliban and/or Al Qaeda terrorists did. It may be very difficult to accept that there is a difference between the terrorist interlopers and the Afghan people who either succored or supported them freely or by force.

We have a very tough decision to make that needs to be made very shortly. This decision has short term as well as longer term implications. In the overall scheme of things, is it wise to expend more of America's blood and treasure to pursue the supporters and/or protectors of Osama bin Laden whose whereabouts and existence are at best uncertain? Or does it make more sense in the long run to contain the Taliban through cooperation with allies like Pakistan and Saudi Arabia? Simultaneously we would continue to search for the master mind of 9/11 and those closest to him, not with an entire army but with a highly skilled and prepared tactical force. This would get us away from the track of vengeance and closer to the track of justice. It should also contribute to the reordering of our economic priorities in a manner more in keeping with our current and longer term needs. This will not be simple or easy as there is a large number of Americans whose thinking remains focused on *getting even* rather than learning from the experience of 9/11 and ensuring that such an assault is never repeated.

But there is another scourge America must address in order to move our nation to a better place: the scourge of greed. Greed, like racial bias, divides our country. In respect of greed, however, there are clearly two groups only: the haves and the have nots. Its malignancy is as harmful but far more pervasive and egalitarian than racism. Racial bias almost exclusively affects minorities of color. Greed affects the entire population indiscriminately. An excerpt from a Wharton School publication of May 2, 2007, *Knowledge@Wharton*, makes the point: *"........critics saw executives getting richer while pay for lower level workers remained relatively stagnant. Studies by* Business Week *and other publications show that compensation for big company CEOs was more than 400 times the pay for average workers last year, up from a 42-to-1 ratio in 1980. If the minimum wage had gone up at the same rate, it would have been more than $22 an hour in 2006 instead of $5.15."*

I suspect that this insensitive, excessive display of greed raises concern among those whose consciences allow them to consider equity and fairness important social and even moral issues. I have always been amazed at the hue and cry whenever attempts are made to increase the minimum wage. The argument is that any such increase will inevitably lead to a loss of jobs and a harmful rise in the cost of living. No such concern is displayed when CEO's earn outrageous sums even when the companies for which they are responsible fail or are on the brink of collapse. Of course, this type of excess contributed in no small measure to the current recession. I cannot imagine any two communal malignancies which are even remotely as harmful to our long term, national well being, as racial bias and corporate greed. The ongoing Health Care debate exemplifies this on both counts. Like the issues of fairness and equity in compensation, Health Care has an even greater moral component which many appear to overlook. In a sense we are creating our own perfect storm for a disheveled society in which neither the *Haves* nor the *Have-nots* may be at peace. But we should not despair. There is reason to be generally hopeful.

Saving Grace: The 'SG' Generation

My hopefulness is based on exchanges I have had with younger Americans, those born between the mid 1960's and the early 1980's, i.e. they are between the ages of 28 and 50. They have been labeled generation 'X' and generation 'Y'. I simply call them the 'SG' generation, meaning the 'Saving Grace' generation. They include my own children and children of my friends and neighbors as well as the friends of these young adults. By and large they recognize profligacy, fear mongering, and the gross income inequities between corporate barons and employees. On a broader scale, they also recognize the indifference and recklessness with which we, as a nation, generally view our environment and our relationships with the poorer countries of the world and the poor and working poor among us. They are very wary of the traditional power structure and often coalesce electronically around a profound belief in the need for change. I do not call them the SG generation without good reason. In my view they tend to pull us back to a sense of community which appears to require that we once again recognize that we are our brother's keeper. As I said earlier, they see their world more from a perspective of hope than of fear.

I share the note below which is from the son of a friend after a somewhat intemperate on line debate between his dad and me. It exemplifies the stark difference in how he sees America versus how America is seen by his father.

Dear Owen,

Thank you for the very kind note. I would truly be honored to read anything you've written/contemplate writing or just hear your thoughts. I completely agree with your assessment that you probably view America differently than many. Most people born into America (and I include myself sadly to say too often in this group) take all that you have noted for granted and have of-ten lost perspective on how the ideals and principles of America's many founders are so uncommon across the world. It is easy to focus on all the negative stories and forget some pretty amazing social/cultural transforma-tions are happening in front of us.

America is changing rapidly and, as you say, will be comprised of dramatically different population mixes in-creasingly over the next decades. We all will be chal-lenged to live and govern from a different perspective as minorities become majorities and vice versa. Over time, we will hopefully begin to identify more with our status as Americans than whites, blacks, Hispanics, Asians, etc. I've often thought that there is a strong, unfortunate hu-man instinct to fear those whom are different from us (perhaps, I think to myself, it's an animal instinct related to survival....fear different animals until you know they do no harm). But then I think of my own children growing up in school with a multitude of races, religions, and abili-ties/disabilities....I don't think young children fear a child who is darker skinned or lighter skinned than they are or of a different religion– they just play with him/her. It's as we get older that we seem to project our stereotypes of various groups (Muslims, Asians, overweight people, etc.) onto people in these categories whom we have never known or spoken to and just assume or fear they fit the worst of our stereotypes.

I'm rambling, I know, but I thought of one other interesting perspective (..... about how I viewed events) that shows how little we truly "know" about our world and how our view is like (looking through) a soda straw. As the certainty of Obama's election became clear last November, I certainly understood the historic nature of the event, but had no idea of how life altering it was for nearly all black Americans. I felt silly, quite honestly, that I didn't see how phenomenal an event it was to them because, in my mind, I always thought it was possible/probable and didn't even consider America not voting for an African American man because of skin color. What hit me in the face with it, oddly enough, was watching Hank Aaron weep like a baby and I just stepped back and realized how, in his lifetime, the plight of African Americans had gone from being unable to vote to being the President–now that's amazing....yet the awesome magnitude of it had escaped me on that November day.

Scott

My response is reproduced below.

Scott:
I thank you so very much. My eyes well with tears reading your comments. They are so honest, real and, above all, moving and wise. Thank you. I must confess that there are moments when I fear for our country but you confirm my belief that even if I fear I should never despair. The future of this Democracy is safe because of young people like you, my own children and others. You are all the true guardians at the gate. America not only needs all of you but truly deserves you.

In a similar vein my younger son, Gregory, made a remark during an exchange between myself and some friends. It is so profoundly wise that I could not get it out of my mind and had to let him know how impressed I was with his observation. He observed that *the powerful has to be extra diligent to do good because power makes it so personally painless and easy for the powerful to do bad things.* This is profoundly true in our society today and a cause of much coarseness in discourse and indifference to the plight of the less fortunate among us. This observation is directly related to the triumph of greed in our society.

Hispanic Heritage, American Pride

One of my friends is of Puerto Rican heritage and a physician. He is not reluctant to claim his heritage even as he acknowledges his unabashed pride in being an American. Like me he sees no conflict or contradiction here. He is not unaware of the quite common stereotypical views of many white Americans about Puerto Ricans in particular and Hispanics in general. As a Puerto Rican he gushes with pride at the achievement of Sonia Sotomayor. He also views her confirmation as a justice of the Supreme Court of the United States as a clear sign that America continues to march toward the admirable goal of becoming a more inclusive society. In his view this amounts to a promise that his children will become adults in an America that is much less focused on what one looks like than on what and how much one may contribute. He feels compelled to facilitate the process of inclusion in any way he can. On this account he relocated from Georgia to Florida, primarily to minimize the potential exposure of his son to negative stereotypes by his schoolmates and others. His relocation was also influenced by a strong desire not to be constantly recognized as the *Hispanic Doctor*. He just wants to be another guy in the neighborhood.

He is convinced that the more Obamas and Sotomayors we have, the less meaningful and influential negative stereotypes will become. I share this view as well as his conviction that children naturally learn by example and, by and large, tend to emulate the influential adults around them. In other words, children from successful families and communities tend to succeed while those from failed families and failed communities tend to fail. American society is replete with examples that confirm this contention. In spite of this, however, there appears to be remarkable reluctance to mount an aggressive attack on the root causes of this nationally debilitating problem: prejudice and poverty. Instead, we fight wars, give tax breaks to the wealthiest among us and fail to implement and maintain high national standards for our schools. Even so, like me, he is quite hopeful. His own experience tells him that America continually gets better. It is patently obvious that his commitment to his heritage in no way diminishes or threatens his pride or faith in America. He speaks passionately of his love and respect for America, its wonderful institutions and the great opportunities America offers but he will never abandon or apologize for his unyielding attachment to his heritage.

This is as it should be and serves much more than individual integrity and peace of mind. This dual pride provides invaluable support for America's national bridge to the rest of the world. It also supports my view that there is good reason to be optimistic about America's future, especially its place in the changing world order.

From Africa with Love

Another of my friends is Nigerian by birth and came to America with his family after residing in the United Kingdom from his teenage years. He is a computer programming expert and author of a text in his area of expertise. Don Asumu is self employed as a consultant, advisor and trouble shooter. The Asumu family has immense respect and admiration for their adopted country. As is the case with my physician friend mentioned earlier, this does not lessen the family's affection for its country of birth. He quickly acknowledges the remarkable differences between Nigeria and America, especially in terms of his own upbringing in a society in which he was always a member of the majority group and was never subjected to the marginalizing effect of racism. While tribal differences do have some disruptive impact in Nigeria from time to time, the matter of race is of no moment. The issues of greed and corruption are of much greater concern. The significance of these circumstances is not lost on him and helps him put his view of America and black Americans in particular, in perspective.

Don Asumu was attracted to this country after a visit on vacation with his family. The primary cause of this attraction was the apparent friendliness of Americans as well as the visibly immense range of opportunities America offers. Having arrived in America in 1995 he is a relative new comer. Yet, his personal success over just fourteen years authenticates his view of what America promises. The fact that his twin daughters are both attending university and doing very well, further advances his positive expectations. One daughter has already decided that she wants to be a neurosurgeon. There is no doubt in the minds of the Asumus that their daughter's objective will be realized. They believe unreservedly in America's promise of opportunity. They also believe that commensurate effort has to be made to capitalize on this promise. Never the less, it is very clear to them that there are cultural nuances, engendered mostly by considerations of race, which should not be ignored.

Don's approach to this reality is most unusual and very instructive. He has determined that more minorities need to actively pursue careers in technical areas. His reasoning has immense merit: in these areas measurement or assessment of one's performance is significantly less, if at all, susceptible to subjective judgment. A computer program either works or it doesn't work. This is almost as clear as the zeros and ones comprising the programming code. In other words, Don has detected a maneuver to thwart intentional bias in assessing individual performance in the workplace. This in turn minimizes the chances of being put at a disadvantage which will often unfavorably impact professional progress. If Don's philosophy is acted upon by more minorities, inevitably more minorities will move into the upper ranks of workplace hierarchy and benefit automatically from all that this progression implies.

The Asumu strategy is ingenious and worthy of widespread recognition among minorities. It is yet another way to overcome roadblocks on the road minorities must travel to capitalize on opportunities that are clearly available in America.

Unusual Circumstances, Effective Equality

It is quite fascinating to realize that there is a small but influential group of black Americans who grew up in the most instructive, if improbable, circumstances: this group had grandparents and or parents who owned property or business or were exceptional professionals at a time when such a thing was all but impossible. Some in this group witnessed white people working as sharecroppers for black land owners, for example. So far my only validating evidence is anecdotal. However, the fact that documentation is extremely difficult or impossible to find should not be surprising in the least.

A friend of ours is a descendant of a family that is representative of this unusual group of black Americans. Her family has its origins in Alabama. She recalls being instructed by her grand father and father not to be disrespectful or indifferent to the white sharecroppers her family hired to work their relatively large farm of several hundred acres. This is such an extraordinary occurrence that in an interview for a professorial position at a leading university her interviewers automatically presumed that her family was among the sharecroppers after learning that she grew up on a farm with sharecroppers. They were incredulous that her family not only owned such a large farm but employed white sharecroppers.

She was also instructed to be equally civil to the German prisoners of war interned in the vicinity of her family's homestead. These circumstantial realities allow people like her to relate to white people from a position of natural, active equality and compassion as well as superior social standing. When necessary, this reality also allows our friend to relate to white people in a more actively aggressive, purposeful or confrontational manner. She also recalls her dad relating a startling story: a white man slapped her grand father in the face after feeling disrespected by what he obviously considered an "uppity nigger". Her grand father instinctively returned the assault with no resulting personal peril. This clearly demonstrates that absence of fear along with at least equivalent power permits mutually beneficial stalemate as well as teaches critical lessons about social relationships.

Expectations

At the outset I made reference to what I term the "progressive energy of example". The family above surely demonstrates the validity of this reference and emphasizes the point that it is clearly criminal and manifestly immoral to use malicious social constraints to prevent equality of opportunity among citizens. At whatever level one may consider this malady, it obviously makes no sense whatsoever and is demonstrably harmful to the well being of society at large. It is not at all surprising that the family's unshakable sense of self worth and unassailable self confidence are among the invaluable, success supporting characteristics passed down from generation to generation. It is probably not an unreasonable assumption that these are now as integral to the family's traits as to be a part of its DNA.

Black American families like the one above may be few in number and their history may be largely unknown, but neither fact interrupts the flow of the beneficial effects of their unusual history down through the generations of these families. I imagine the effect of the extraordinary circumstances referenced being like that of dropping a stone in a pond: how do we tell where the ripples end?

In conclusion, the cumulative effects of the thinking and behavior of the SG generation, Americans like my Puerto Rican and Nigerian friends and the black family with roots in Alabama, strongly reinforce my deep conviction that America's glass is always half full, never half empty. Concern about the future is understandable and even necessary but despair is baseless and harmful. America not only needs these groups but truly deserves them. They will certainly help to ensure not just America's survival but its continued progress as a unique world leader whose influence, waxing or waning, will warrant deference and respect; whose tolerance and respect for cultural diversity will always be seen as worthy of ad-miration and even envy.

X. IN THE END

Even those who criticize America most, find much about America that is admirable. Immigrants flock to our shores for many good reasons, not least of which is the radiant, implied promise America makes: if you dream it you can achieve it here. Hope is eternal in America. America is a place of high expectations, thinkers and doers whose freedom to think and do is unparalleled anywhere else on earth. Perhaps because of this, freedom and responsibility often confront each other aggressively in the world of ideas as well as in every day life. Americans, by and large, rely almost exclusively on the rule of law to settle such ardent confrontations. This, more than any other single aspect of American culture, sets America apart from all those countries that criticize America most. The rule of law is the final barricade against tyranny and social chaos. I have lived in countries where the rule of law is simply the mercurial dictates of one man. I am convinced that America is a most wonderful and satisfying place to live, hope and raise a family.

It is obvious from aggressively expressed anti-Obama bias, that many Americans do not trust their democracy and the rule of law. It is no small paradox that these Americans selectively distrust the very system and process which guarantee them the right to so crassly express their distrust. This is remarkably puzzling but makes America almost magical. This monumental yin and yang keeps America a vibrant, non-monolithic place, capable of absorbing and accommodating even its most alarming critics. Nothing moves me more than this about America. Still, immigrants who become citizens of this country find it useful and comforting to retain and nurture the things they value most in their native cultures.

Generally, this does not alarm America. And it should not. Like me and my story and millions of immigrants and their stories, America is a work in progress. Those who wish to freeze this progress in a unilaterally chosen, arbitrary place and time to support their dubious comfort, clearly do not understand or appreciate the wonder that is America. It is all but incomprehensible that these people do not realize that the very progress they would stop is the essence of America. But I understand. The combination of paranoia and fear is a most potent anesthesia. It is a blessing that the effects of anesthesia are temporary as long as one does not overdose.

On a more personal level, I want my grand daughters to understand that they must pursue their education fearlessly and with the greatest passion. There is no darkness that cannot be pierced by the illuminating light of knowledge informed by common sense and the accumulated wisdom of those who have gone before us. As a friend so eloquently put it, my grand daughters will enter the American highway and, I surmise, the Jamaican as well, from a different, newer on ramp. The on ramp may be new and different but the highway will undoubtedly be the same except for the traffic and maybe one or two pot holes.

I want my grand daughters to understand and appreciate the unique, extraordinary value and reliable refuge afforded us by family ties and friendship. If family is the hallmark of our lives, friendship is life's great halo. I want my grand daughters to know that they are forever angels, with the power to make a difference in their world and the world of others. I want them to know that in some ways they are indeed unique but in many ways they are not at all unlike their peers. This difference is not to be ignored but neither should it be considered a throne from which to judge others. I salute my grand daughters and wish for them the serenity which comes from an understanding of self and an appreciation of the value of human relationships best exemplified in family and friendship. I salute my angels in verse.

Angels

Grand daughters are angels in disguise
That grandparents know this is no surprise
They need make no effort or much fuss
To convince angels live among us

They laugh and smile they scream and cry
No comes early and often, later as often why.
They come in different shapes and sizes
In shades of brown with honey scented voices.

They naturally attract bright halos
Something every grandparent knows.
Sometimes a crown sits atop the noggin
Evidence they and princesses are kin.

At three and seven we ponder twenty one
What will they be, who will they become?
How will they fare the journey in between
Especially the testy confusing years called teen?

The dual perplexity of college and dating
Regardless the order the anxiety and debating
Late arrivals, stressful departures, career choosing
Expectations exceeded, not met, control losing.

Parents marvel at their own parents' tolerance
For departures from protocol they dared not chance
In time angel power parents come to understand
When their own hoped for angels touch their hand.

Grandparents wish with all their hearts
To see angels through life's testiest starts
There can be no greater ending to a life's story
Than grandparents witnessing grand children's glory.

So too I salute friendship, the best of all chosen human relationships.

Friendship

Friendship is life's great halo
Indifferent to heaven above, hell below
Illuminating all our tenses
Mending regrets and broken fences.

Regardless language, race or country
There is no greater more lasting bounty
From life's constant sowing and reaping
Than friendship's embrace laughing, weeping.

Friendship is choice reciprocated
Among souls from the mundane liberated
To soar beyond the different and extreme
To hold fast a self fulfilling dream.

Friends are more than personal mirrors
They inhabit our secret halls and corridors
Offer no threat of pain or rank illusion
Touch heart and mind, allay confusion.

If there is a single blessing to be wished
Strike all others from life's short list
Wish for a friend who will stay to the end
Who feels no need to see past every bend.

Then wish for every friend that he secures
Friends steadfast, sure and certain as yours
There is no more meaningful gift that this
With so much awry and so many remiss.

Finally, and most importantly, my grand daughters must come to know that the acknowledged, often ignored, but inevitable aim of our lives is happiness: their own and that of others. Even so they must understand that, as is said about luck, we make our own happiness. Never make the mistake to think that something or some other can make you happy. Not too late in my journey

I discovered that happiness is contagious. I strongly support getting infected. When we find our own happiness we actually facilitate the finding of happiness by others.

There are, of course, innumerable pathways to happiness but just a single doorway: contentment. This explains why some are happy with too little while many are unhappy with too much. Eventually all of us must determine at what point in our lives we are content with ourselves and with what we possess. There is no happiness without contentment and no contentment without finding ourselves and actively deciding to embrace our chosen place in our world. Happiness is a more public word for serenity and peace.

I caution my grand daughters to be wary of the divisiveness of all religions and the malicious duplicity and selfishness of their innumerable false prophets. They must never forget that, essentially, we are significantly more our actions than our words.

These things I wish for my two little angels.

I wish no less for all the world's children.

XI. GLOSSARY

Asians: East Indians or Indians as used in this text. Specifically, natives of India as well as their off springs whether or not born in India.

Bauxite: Perhaps the most commonly occurring mineral on earth and the primary ore for the manufacture of aluminum.

Brer 'Nancy: A staple of traditional Jamaican mythology. Brer is "brother;" 'Nancy is Anancy or Anansi and represents the spider - the archetypal trickster or conman in Jamaican folklore. Its origin is perhaps from Twi-speaking West African tribes.

Brer Tukuma: Also integral to traditional Jamaican mythology. Tukuma is usually the son, but sometimes the brother, of Anancy. He is Anancy's relentless adversary. Anancy is always the villain; Tukuma is always the hero.

Browning: A viscous commercial darkening agent which is commonly added to cake or pudding mix to darken the mix prior to baking.

CEO: Chief Executive Officer.

COO: Chief Operating Officer

Cricket: A game played with a bat and a ball between two teams of eleven players each. One team is at bat with two players always representing the side that is "in" (at bat) and eleven players representing the side that is "out" (bowling and fielding). The game originated in England during the 16th century and spread throughout the British Empire, now known as the British Commonwealth, during and after the colonial era. After soccer, cricket is perhaps the most watched sport in the world.

Crown Colony: A type of government administration typical of the British Empire in which a Governor was appointed by the Crown to represent the King or Queen of England during the period when the British owned colonies. This Governor literally "ran" these colonies although from time to time the Crown would cede some aspects of its executive powers to counsels whose members were all nominated by the Crown in the person of the Governor.

DNA: The standard abbreviation for *Deoxyribonucleic acid*, a nucleic acid that contains the genetic instructions used in the development and functioning of all known living organisms and some viruses.

EEOC: Equal Employment Opportunity Commission. The Commission is responsible for enforcing federal laws that make it illegal to discriminate against a job applicant or an employee because of the person's race, color, religion, sex (including pregnancy), national origin, age (40 or older), disability or genetic information.

HR: Human Resources

ICU: Intensive Care Unit.

IE: Industrial Engineer or Industrial Engineering.

ILO: International Labor Organization; an agency of the United Nations.

Jamaican Beef Patties: This is a turnover that contains various spiced fillings, most commonly beef, and in a flaky shell usually tinted golden yellow with an egg yolk mixture or turmeric.

Hand carts: Relatively large, man powered carts made of wood and salvaged motor vehicle parts like steering wheels, wheel bearings and pieces of rubber tires. A cart is basically a large deep rectangular box fixed onto a substantial, hand made wooden chassis with four wheels and an ample piece of rubber tire fixed appropriately to the back running board and touching the ground. The operator or hand cart man applies pressure with his foot to this piece of rubber to slow or stop the cart. Carts are usually owner made and operated and used to be perhaps the most common and affordable means of moving smaller sized goods around any large town in Jamaica where paved streets existed.

Mau Mau: An anti-British, anti-European nationalist group in Kenya in the 1950's. Its objective was to drive out these foreigners and win Kenya's Independence. The first president of Kenya, Jomo Kenyatta was arrested and tried by the British who claimed he was a leader of this group.

MHR: Member House of Representatives.

Rastafari: Used interchangeably with Rasta and Rastafarian. It is a movement and religion which originated in Jamaica in the 1930's. Haile Selassie I, emperor of Ethiopia is worshiped as the reincarnation of Jesus.

See-well-lash: A game, played mostly by boys, involving the skillful use of one foot or both feet to constantly bounce a relatively small object six to eighteen inches without allowing the object to fall to the ground. Objects could include small balls, gut and skin of partly eaten fruit, e.g. an orange, or even a small bunch of flowers or keys. A somewhat offensive rhyme was usually recited during play. The game is perhaps unique to Jamaica and may have become extinct.

Tram Car: British term for streetcar or trolley. Functions like a train car but much lighter in weight and usually smaller. Runs on tracks embedded in the common roadway shared by regular vehicular traffic.

INDEX

XII. SUGGESTED READING

Ashe, Arthur, & Arnold Rampersad, *Days of Grace*

Ball, Edward, *Slaves In The Family*

Clarke, Edith, *My Mother Who Fathered Me: A Study of the Families in Three Selected Communities of Jamaica*

Cose, Ellis, *The Rage of a Privileged Class*

Ellison, Ralph, *Invisible Man*

Gates, Henry Louis, Jr. & Cornell West, *The African American Century*

Gunst, Laurie, *Born Fi Dead: A Journey Through The Jamaican Posse Underworld*

Hill. Jason D., *Becoming Cosmopolitan*

James, C.L.R., *The Black Jacobins*

Kennedy, Kerry, *Speak Truth to Power*

Lee, Easton, *From Behind The Counter*

Manley, Michael, *The Politics of Change: A Jamaican Testament*

Michener, James A., *Caribbean*

Moyers, Bill, *A World of Ideas*

Nettleford, Rex M., *Caribbean Cultural Identity: The Case of Jamaica*

Obama, Barack, *Dreams From My Father*

Ibid, *The Audacity of Hope*

Senior, Olive, *A – Z of Jamaica Heritage*

Sherlock, Philip M. & Hazel Bennett, *The Story of the Jamaican People*

Tutu, Desmond, *No Future Without Forgiveness*

West, Michael O., *The Rise of an African Middle Class: Colonial Zimbabwe*

Williams, Eric, *Capitalism and Slavery*